PANZER ACES III

The Stackpole Military History Series

**THE AMERICAN
CIVIL WAR**
Cavalry Raids of the Civil War
Ghost, Thunderbolt, and
*   Wizard*
Pickett's Charge
Witness to Gettysburg

WORLD WAR I
Doughboy War

WORLD WAR II
After D-Day
Armor Battles of the
*   Waffen-SS, 1943–45*
Armoured Guardsmen
Army of the West
Australian Commandos
The B-24 in China
Backwater War
The Battle of Sicily
Battle of the Bulge, Vol. 1
Battle of the Bulge, Vol. 2
Beyond the Beachhead
Beyond Stalingrad
Blitzkrieg Unleashed
Blossoming Silk against
*   the Rising Sun*
Bodenplatte
The Brandenburger
*   Commandos*
The Brigade
Bringing the Thunder
The Canadian Army and the
*   Normandy Campaign*
Coast Watching in
*   World War II*
Colossal Cracks
Condor
A Dangerous Assignment
D-Day Bombers
D-Day Deception
D-Day to Berlin
Destination Normandy
Dive Bomber!
A Drop Too Many
Eagles of the Third Reich
The Early Battles of
*   Eighth Army*
Eastern Front Combat
Exit Rommel
Fist from the Sky
Flying American Combat
*   Aircraft of World War II*

For Europe
Forging the Thunderbolt
For the Homeland
Fortress France
The German Defeat in the East,
*   1944–45*
German Order of Battle, Vol. 1
German Order of Battle, Vol. 2
German Order of Battle, Vol. 3
The Germans in Normandy
Germany's Panzer Arm in
*   World War II*
GI Ingenuity
Goodwood
The Great Ships
Grenadiers
Hitler's Nemesis
Infantry Aces
In the Fire of the Eastern Front
Iron Arm
Iron Knights
Kampfgruppe Peiper at the
*   Battle of the Bulge*
The Key to the Bulge
Knight's Cross Panzers
Kursk
Luftwaffe Aces
Luftwaffe Fighter Ace
Luftwaffe Fighter-Bombers
*   over Britain*
Massacre at Tobruk
Mechanized Juggernaut or
*   Military Anachronism?*
Messerschmitts over Sicily
Michael Wittmann, Vol. 1
Michael Wittmann, Vol. 2
Mountain Warriors
The Nazi Rocketeers
No Holding Back
On the Canal
Operation Mercury
Packs On!
Panzer Aces
Panzer Aces II
Panzer Aces III
Panzer Commanders of the
*   Western Front*
Panzergrenadier Aces
Panzer Gunner
The Panzer Legions
Panzers in Normandy
Panzers in Winter
The Path to Blitzkrieg
Penalty Strike

Red Road from Stalingrad
Red Star under the Baltic
Retreat to the Reich
Rommel's Desert Commanders
Rommel's Desert War
Rommel's Lieutenants
The Savage Sky
Ship-Busters
The Siegfried Line
A Soldier in the Cockpit
Soviet Blitzkrieg
Stalin's Keys to Victory
Surviving Bataan and Beyond
T-34 in Action
Tank Tactics
Tigers in the Mud
Triumphant Fox
The 12th SS, Vol. 1
The 12th SS, Vol. 2
Twilight of the Gods
Typhoon Attack
The War against Rommel's
*   Supply Lines*
War in the Aegean
Wolfpack Warriors
Zhukov at the Oder

**THE COLD WAR /
VIETNAM**
Cyclops in the Jungle
Expendable Warriors
Flying American Combat
*   Aircraft: The Cold War*
Here There Are Tigers
Land with No Sun
MiGs over North Vietnam
Phantom Reflections
Street without Joy
Through the Valley

**WARS OF AFRICA AND
THE MIDDLE EAST**
Never-Ending Conflict
The Rhodesian War

**GENERAL MILITARY
HISTORY**
Carriers in Combat
Cavalry from Hoof to Track
Desert Battles
Guerrilla Warfare
Ranger Dawn
Sieges

PANZER ACES III

German Tank Commanders in Combat in World War II

Franz Kurowski

STACKPOLE
BOOKS

Published in 2010 by
STACKPOLE BOOKS
5067 Ritter Road
Mechanicsburg, PA 17055
www.stackpolebooks.com

Cover design by Tracy Patterson

Printed in the United States of America

10 9 8 7 6 5 4 3 2 I

ISBN 978-0-8117-0654-4

The Library of Congress has cataloged the first volume as follows:

Kurowski, Franz.
     Panzer aces : German tank commanders of World War II / Franz Kurowski ; translated by David Johnston.— 1st ed.
        p. cm.
Originally published: New York : Ballantine Books, 2002.
Includes index.
ISBN 0-8117-3173-1
1. World War, 1939–1945—Tank warfare. 2. World War, 1939–1945—Germany. 3. Tanks (Military science)—History. 4. Tank warfare—History. 5. Soldiers—Germany—Biography. I. Title: German tank commanders in World War II. II. Title.
D793.K86 2004
940.54'21'092243—dc22
                                        2004005895
ISBN 978-0-8117-3173-7

Contents

Ernst Barkmann after receiving the Knight's Cross to the Iron Cross.

CHAPTER 1

SS-Oberscharführer Ernst Barkmann

HELL ON WHEELS

Early on the morning of 4 February 1943, the tank commanders of the 2nd Company of *SS-Panzer-Abteilung "Das Reich"* were assembled in front of *SS-Obersturmführer* Lorenz[1], who had just come back from the battalion headquarters. Among the commanders was *SS-Rottenführer* Ernst Barkmann. The tall man from Schleswig-Holstein was in a padded cotton winter uniform. He had a wide scarf wrapped around his head and ears.

The company commander announced the mission: "Comrades, the company will attack advanced enemy forces as part of the battalion. We will attack Olchowatka and take the village. Following that, we will advance on the next village. Tank 221[2] will cover the left flank of the company; the remaining tanks will deploy in the usual wedge. Let's go!"

Barkmann hurried over to his 221, a *Panzer III* with a 5-centimeter main gun. He hopped aboard and disappeared into the commander's hatch, visible only from his belt on up. He checked his intercom system with the crew and then announced: "We're moving on Olchowatka, through the fold in the ground!"

The tanks moved out. The tanks reached the defile, entered it and continued to advance. They then turned out in the vicinity of the village, where tanks from neighboring elements were already receiving antitank-gun fire as they moved on the locality from the front. A Soviet heavy machine gun—a Maxim—opened fire on Barkmann's tank. Barkmann's gunner took it out with a single round.

The tanks headed towards the village at full speed.

"Watch out . . . Molotov cocktails!" The gas-filled bottles shattered on the front slope of the tank, with liquid fire seemingly splashing everywhere.

Popping out of his hatch, the loader attempted to wipe away shards of glass and burning liquid with an old jacket. Small-arms fire forced him back inside time and again. All of a sudden, Barkmann identified an antitank gun

---

1. Translator's Note: *Hauptmann* = Captain. For the reader unfamiliar with German ranks, a rank table is presented at the back of the book.

2. Translator's Note: 221 = 2nd Company, 2nd Platoon, 1st vehicle. The other tanks were numbered analogously.

1

at the side of a house, when it fired at another tank. By then, Barkmann's vehicle had closed to within 30 meters. The frantic Soviet crew attempted to manhandle the gun around to engage the rapidly approaching German tank. Barkmann could see the muzzle of the gun swinging towards him; they were still 10 meters away.

He ordered his driver to roll over the gun. The engine roared. At the very instant that his tank hit the gun and forced the barrel downward, the Soviets fired. The round bored into the soft earth under the tank. But that did not mean the danger was over. The German tanks could hear the constant crack of antitank rifles firing at them. Although the rounds could not penetrate the main armor of the tanks, a skillful gunner could fire into vision ports and open hatches, wreaking havoc.

The tanks of the battalion started to enter the village. The sounds of roaring engines were mixed with the reports of main guns firing. The enemy pulled back; the company commander ordered his tanks to set up an all-round defense in the village. Many tanks had suffered battle damage and were no longer operational. Only three tanks—including Barkmann's 221—reported they were still combat capable.

The company commander ordered the three operational tanks to return to the line of departure and fetch fuel and recovery vehicles.

Although they were engaged by the enemy, all three vehicles reached the line of departure without serious incident. The vehicle received fuel canisters. Before they took off, an experienced *SS-Oberscharführer* was placed in charge of Barkmann's tank. The *SS-Rottenführer* became the gunner. Barkmann was annoyed, but he was professional enough not to say anything about it.

Under the cover of darkness, the tanks headed forward to their comrades in the village. They had to move through deep snow, and a snowstorm started up, reducing visibility to barely 20 meters. The new tank commander lost sight of the other two tanks, and 221 soon bottomed out in a snowdrift in enemy territory. The men tried everything, but they could not get 221 unstuck. At first light, the tank commander and the loader headed back to the friendly lines on foot to get help. Barkmann and two others remained on board.

As it became lighter, several obsolescent Soviet fighter-bombers—*Ratas*—bombed and strafed the stricken vehicle, but they were unable to effect substantial damage. It was not until Soviet infantry started to attack across the snow-covered plains that it became more dangerous. Barkmann had both machine guns open fire, causing the Soviet ground effort to bog down. A few minutes later, the Soviet infantry received reinforcements, including antitank guns drawn by horses. Barkmann took charge: "We'll engage. We're not abandoning the vehicle!" He had the radio operator attempt contact with the battalion to ask for help.

The tank-versus-antitank gun engagement started. In short order, three antitank guns were eliminated.

The radio operator suddenly called out, clearly elated: "*Rottenführer,* I have contact. Help is approaching!"

"It's about time!" the former gunner, now functioning as the loader, exclaimed. "We only have 10 rounds left!"

Barkmann identified a fourth Soviet antitank gun. He made his round count; he scored a direct hit. The antitank gun and its basic load of ammunition flew into the air.

The loader announced that he saw the prime movers approaching. Right then, a Soviet antitank gun, had remained unidentified up to that point because it was concealed by a haystack, opened fire and hit the lead prime mover, which came to a stop. The 7.62-centimeter antitank gun then attempted to engage 221.

Barkmann's tank was knocked out in February 1943. He is seen here after having made his way back to friendly lines.

Barkmann aimed for the haystack and fired. Bright flames and thick smoke started to rise skyward. The smoke offered the Soviets enough additional concealment that they were able to manhandle their gun into another position, whereupon they took 221 under fire again. After four rounds, they hit the rear deck and the engine compartment caught fire. A bright flash of flame shot into the fighting compartment.

"Bail out!" Barkmann shouted as he popped open his hatch and jumped out to the ground.

Machine-gun and small-arms fire whipped towards the three men as they crawled through the snow and sought cover behind a snowdrift. The Soviet ground forces started to press towards them, and the three men pulled back several hundred meters. Finally, after what seemed like an eternity to the men, other tanks from the 5th Company started to arrive and take the pressure off of them. The battalion commander, *SS-Sturmbannführer Reichsherr* Albin von Reitzenstein, had sent them forward.

"We need to get our tank, *Hauptsturmführer!*" Barkmann implored the commander of the 5th Company.

Ernst Barkmann in his *Panther* at Lubuti in August 1943.

"Fine! We'll see what we can do!"

The 5th Company moved rapidly towards the stricken tank. Two tanks were knocked out along the way; 221, which was slowly burning out, could no longer be recovered.

A few days later—14 February 1943—Kharkov was evacuated by the Germans. Barkmann and other tankers who no longer had tanks were employed as infantry in guarding the remaining operational vehicles. Barkmann participated in the retaking of Kharkov—considered one of the masterstrokes of the *SS* in World War II. He was promoted to *SS-Unterscharführer* on 1 September 1943. Later on, following the ultimately unsuccessful fighting to eliminate the Soviet salient at Kursk, Barkmann's battalion was retrained on the *Panther*. It was in that vehicle that he would later take his place in the annals of tank warfare.

✠

Ernst Barkmann was born on 25 August 1919, the son of a farmer, in the village of Kisdorf in Schleswig-Holstein in northern Germany. Following basic schooling, he started working on his father's farm around Easter of 1935. Following the war, he would inherit the estate and carry on in his father's profession.

On 1 April 1939, he volunteered for the *SS-Verfügungstruppe*, the precursor of the *Waffen-SS*. By doing so, he fulfilled his military obligation as a draft-age youth. He received his basic training in Hamburg (Langenhorn). He was eventually assigned to the 3rd Battalion of *SS-Standarte Germania.*[3]

During the campaign in Poland, he was wounded while serving as a machine gunner in the 9th Company of the regiment. He was also badly wounded again in the Soviet Union during the fighting for the Dnjepr crossings at Dnjepropetrowsk (23 July 1941).

After convalescing, Barkmann was assigned as an instructor for Germanic volunteers in Holland. In the spring of 1942, he volunteered to become a tanker and was assigned to the tank battalion of *Division "Reich."* He and other tankers of the division were trained at the training area at Wildflecken and Fallingbostel.

He went to the Soviet Union for the second time with the division as a tanker. After the fighting for Kharkov and Kursk, he returned to France for training on the *Panther* and the reconstitution of the division. When the Allies invaded Normandy on 6 June 1944, the division was in southern France in anticipation of potential Allied landings there. The division was soon expedited to the Channel coast for commitment against that Allies.

✠

On 7 July, the Americans had crossed the Vire-Taute Canal with their 30th Infantry and 9th Infantry Divisions, advancing as far as Le Désert. To exploit the success, the U.S. 3rd Armored Division advanced across the fields northwest of St. Lô. *SS-Brigadeführer* Lammerding, the division commander, received orders from the *7. Armee* to conduct a counterattack.

The lead German elements advanced against the Americans north of San Sebastian–Sainteny on 8 July. The *4./SS-Panzer-Regiment 2*—Barkmann's company—was in the lead. Barkmann, a platoon leader, engaged a Sherman tank for the first time. Used to the wide expanse of the Soviet Union, he had to accustom himself to the difficult close-in fighting associated with the *bocage* country of Normandy, with its many hedgerows and broken terrain. Large-scale tank fighting was a thing of the past. At most, a single company could be employed at any given time. The tank commanders were often left on their own; in addition, they often had to fight without an infantry escort.

After knocking out a Sherman, Barkmann and the rest of the tanks of the company bogged down in the murderous artillery fire of the Allies. Ernst Barkmann dismounted his tank to crawl underneath, where wounded

---

3. Translator's Note: A *Standarte* was a regimental equivalent. *"Germania"* would later serve with distinction in both *SS-Division "Reich"* and *SS-Division "Wiking."*

infantrymen had been placed to escape the artillery fire. He helped dress their wounds.

On the next day, he participated in the second counterattack. In the area around Périers, the U.S. attack started to bog down. That signaled a round of daily engagements, in which the Germans and Americans slugged it out, while the latter desperately tried to find a gap in the German defenses. On 12 July, Barkmann's crew succeeded in knocking out two Shermans and immobilizing a third. He then pulled back to an ambush position in the hedgerows with the other tanks of the company.

"Wilke, fix the cover in front!" Barkmann ordered, when he saw that the foliage used as camouflage did not completely cover the front slope of the tank. The radio operator dismounted and rearranged the branches.

"The Yanks can come now, *Unterscharführer*!"

"We'll see!" was the laconic response.

The men waited. It was early in the morning of 13 July 1944. The sun had just risen over the horizon.

"It's going to be another hot day," the gunner, Poggendorff, chimed in.

"In more ways than one!" Barkmann responded.

He raised his binoculars and looked in the direction from which the enemy tanks had to approach. He noticed some movement behind a hedgerow.

"Turret: 11 o'clock! Load AP! 400!"

"Identified!" Poggendorff called out after traversing the turret and searching the terrain. A long tube started to poke through the vegetation, followed by the unmistakable superstructure of a Sherman.

"Six Yanks!" the driver, Heidorn, piped in, counting as the tanks exited the vegetation.

Barkmann issued his fire command and the first round was sent screaming down range. The round slammed into the first tank's hull, and the tank shuddered and came to a stop. Smoke started to exit the commander's hatch.

The other tanks stopped; one of them started to fire. The second round left the long barrel of the *Panther* and screamed towards the enemy. It ripped off one of the tank's tracks. Five meters next to the *Panther*, a main-gun round slammed into the hedgerow and ripped open a hole as big as a man.

The loader and the gunner worked with well-practiced moves. The immobilized enemy tank received a second hit, one which blew its turret right off of its race. The four remaining Shermans also started to fire, even with their machine guns. The automatic fire rattled against the front slope of the German tank. By then, Barkmann's gunner had hit and eliminated a third Sherman, which had exposed its flank while attempting to turn. The remaining three tanks quickly backed up into the protective concealment of the underbrush in a swell in the ground.

Another 10 minutes passed with no activity to the front. Just then, a grenadier came running up. "The Yanks have broken through behind you!" he exclaimed. "Be careful, they have antitank guns with them."

The *Panther* started to move out. It reached a patch of woods and moved through it. A short while later, Barkmann spotted the lead American elements.

"HE . . . 400! . . . Fire!"

The crown of a pine tree came crashing down when the round exploded in the midst of its branches. The second round slammed into the middle of a group of wildly moving men, forcing them to the ground. The tank's hull machine gun started firing. Serviced by the radio operator, the machine gun cut a wide berth through the vegetation.

"Ernst, they're pulling back!"

The enemy started to pull back in a panic. Barkmann's tank followed. Suddenly, there was a flash in front of the tank. An antitank-gun round hissed past the turret.

"Engage the AT!"

The first round from the tank went too high. The gunner corrected his sight picture and eliminated the antitank-gun threat with the second round.

There was a crash off to the right. Another antitank gun had joined in. Its round hit the front of the turret below the gunner's optics. Flames shot out from the vehicle.

"Bail out!"

The radio operator, driver and loader were able to bail out, but the gunner remained unconscious in the tank. Barkmann waited in vain for the gunner to emerge. When he realized something was wrong, he raced back to the tank, pulling the unconscious man through the tank commander's hatch.

When the tank did not receive any more fire, Barkmann ordered his crew to put out the fire on the tank. They succeeded in putting out the flames and getting the vehicle running again, bringing it back to the maintenance facility.

The next day, while waiting for his vehicle to finish being repaired, he received orders to take his platoon and hack free four tanks that had been encircled.

The company commander's orders were brief: "Barkmann, you know the way. Get the four tanks back. I'm giving you one of the reserve tanks, since yours is not yet ready."

When Barkmann boarded the other tank, which had just been repaired, he noticed the blood on the turret walls from his predecessor in the tank. The previous tank commander had suffered a common fate: a round to the head from being exposed outside of the protective armor of the vehicle.

Barkmann and the two other crews were able to make their way through to the encircled tanks without incident. The damaged tanks pulled back, and Barkmann received orders to take their place. Shortly thereafter, the Americans attacked again in an effort to force a breakthrough to the south. Barkmann's *Panther* knocked out three Shermans. Towards noon, the tank regiment commander, *SS-Obersturmbannführer* Christian Tychsen, appeared at Barkmann's location.

"Hello, Barkmann! How are things looking?" he greeted his subordinate.

"Hello, *Obersturmbannführer*! Turned back an enemy attack; three kills."

Tychsen, a tall, slim man, was a highly decorated soldier, who had earned the respect of his men in addition to both the Knight's Cross and the Oak Leaves, stood on the rear deck of Barkmann's tank. Tychsen was a battle-hardened veteran, who would later fall in the Normandy fighting, ambushed by an American patrol.

"We're going to move forward, Barkmann. Up front, in the house 800 meters ahead, the enemy is holding wounded from the division. We're going to get them back."

The three *Panthers* moved out. They reached the house and freed the wounded Germans from the American forces, which pulled back at the sight of the advancing tanks.

During the fighting the next day, Barkmann's tank was hit by an artillery shell, which damaged his running gear. It was only with great difficulty that the vehicle could be brought back to the repair facilities. When the crew reached the maintenance facility, *Panther* 424 had finally been repaired and was released back to its crew. Barkmann and the men switched vehicles.

The tank regiment was moved to the area around St. Anbin on 25 July. The front in that sector lacked cohesiveness, and the tanks of the regiment helped plug the gaps, supported by a handful of grenadiers. When the U.S. VII Corps then showed signs of breaking through in the area around Marigny in the direction of Avranches on that same day, the tank regiment was moved again in order to close a gap that had come about in the sector of the *Panzer-Lehr-Division*. After two days of carpet bombing by the Allies, the *Panzer-Lehr-Division* had lost combat effectiveness.

Despite the enemy's aerial activities, the move in general was made without incident. After leaving the former positions, however, 424 fell out due to carburetor problems. The maintenance contact team attempted to repair the vehicle on the spot. In order to finish more quickly, certain safety precautions were ignored—a step that would prove to have dire consequences when a group of four fighter-bombers attacked. The first rounds hammered into the open engine compartment. The coolant line and the oil cooler were shot up. The engine caught fire, but the fire could be extinguished. The maintenance personnel then had to work the entire night. The enemy had advanced to the rear of the tank by then. But the hard work paid off. At first light, 424 was fully mobile again and started to make its way to the new positions of the company. The *Spieß*[4], *SS-Hauptscharführer* Heinze, and the company maintenance sergeant, *Schirrmeister* Corth, mounted the tank to get to the new area of operations more quickly. They reached the area around Le Lorey, not far from the main road from Coutances to St. Lô. At the outskirts of the village along the curvy road, the tank ran into infantry and trains personnel.

"What's going on?" *Schirrmeister* Corth asked.

"Yank tanks advancing right on Coutances!" one of the senior noncommissioned officers called out, not breaking stride as he headed towards the rear.

"It must be a joke!" Barkmann replied, drily. "The Yanks can't be there yet!"

"Our tanks are there," Heinze chimed in. "But let's be careful anyway. Corth, you and I will screen to the front."

The two men dismounted and moved about 150 meters in front of the tank.

In the distance, Barkmann could make out the sound of fighting and aircraft through the din of his own engine's noise. The two men on the ground disappeared around a corner. A short while later, Barkmann heard submachine-gun and small-arms fire, with the first sergeant and the maintenance sergeant reappearing. The *Spieß* had been wounded in the upper arm and shoulder.

"What's going on?"

"We made it to the main road, where there were Yanks. They called out for us to surrender, waving Red Cross flags. When we started to run back, they fired at us. There were American tanks rolling along the road to Coutances. Behind them is a long column of vehicles."

"Stay with the *Hauptscharführer*, Corth! We're going up to the crossroads."

"Be careful, Barkmann!" Corth said, unnecessarily.

---

4. Translator's Note: Soldier slang for the company first sergeant. A *Spieß* is a pike, in military terms, and a skewer in more civilian usage. Either way, it seems to be an appropriate term for the chief enlisted "motivator" of a company.

Barkmann ordered his crew to prepare for combat. The loader reported the machine gun and main gun ready. The *Panther* moved out slowly. Fortunately, there was a wall on both sides of the street, which was covered with vegetation and offered concealment. The tank reached the crossroads and positioned itself next to a tall oak.

Barkmann kept his crew apprised of what was going on: "Tanks approaching from the left . . . 200 meters to the main road . . . we'll take out the first two tanks."

Poggendorff took up the first Sherman in his sights. The turret of the tank was knocked off of its race with the first round. The gunner started traversing in the direction of his next target. The second round left the barrel and scored another direct hit, with the second Sherman going up in flames. That blocked the crossroads for the tanks that were following. They turned back. Then the vehicles that had already passed the crossroads started coming back as well.

Barkmann told his gunner to fire at will, and round after round was soon barking out of the main gun. The coaxial machine gun fired several long bursts as well. Fuel and ammunition vehicles blew apart. Personnel carriers, jeeps and trucks were blown to bits. In the minutes that followed, the crossroads took on the appearance of a smoking, blazing military junk yard.

Barkmann suddenly saw two Shermans, which were approaching from off to the left. They had left the main road and attempted to approach Barkmann cross-country. Barkmann issued his fire command: "AT . . . 11 o'clock . . . fire!"

The tank-versus-tank engagement started. After the second round, the first enemy tank was ablaze. The second Sherman was able to hit the *Panther* twice, before it also started to burn when it was hit in the engine compartment with a well-placed round.

The smell of gunpowder mixed with the thick oily smoke that spread over the crossroads. Covered by the haze, other enemy vehicles made their way back from the direction of Coutances. Whenever the haze cleared a little, Barkmann re-engaged and created even more gaps in the long procession of enemy vehicles.

The fighting had lasted an hour before the Americans were able to bring up more tanks in an effort to knock out the solitary German holding up the advance to Coutances. Before they could make their appearance, however, fighter-bombers came howling in above the *Panther*. Their bombs fell to the earth, creating large craters. One of the bombs detonated about 5 meters from the tank, jerking it violently to the side. The bomb that followed toppled the oak tree next to the *Panther*. The shrapnel from the bombs pelted the walls of the vehicle. The tank heaved and shuddered.

Barkmann refused to give up, however. Whenever he saw a vehicle through the oily haze, he had his gunner fire. The fighter-bombers continued their assault. Armor-piercing rounds pelted the tank; bombs continued to fall, but none of the 50-pounders was a direct hit.

In the course of the assault from the air, the U.S. tanks started approaching from the flank. Once within range, they opened fire. Two rounds grazed the *Panther*. The turret and the long main gun traversed in the direction of the new threat. Two rounds were fired in quick succession, both direct hits. Thick smoke rising behind the vegetation told Barkmann all he needed to know—two more enemy tanks had been knocked out.

But the enemy also started to hit. One round grazed the hull. Another round dislodged one of the tracks from the drive sprocket. The ventilator in the fighting compartment ceased to function. The loader threw up from the fumes. The tank had literally become a "hell on wheels." The main-gun ammunition also started to run low.

Barkmann thought to himself: Should I surrender? But he did not have to follow that train of thought for long, since events soon overcame any deliberations.

Heidorn, the driver, had placed the sledge hammer, which was usually stowed on the outside of the vehicle, behind him in the driver's compartment so as not to risk the chance of losing it in battle. When the vehicle was hit, the sledge hammer dislodged from the place Heidorn had stowed it and hit him in the back, causing terrific pain. The pain and the heightened nerves from the fighting had him reach for the driver's hatch to open it. He discovered that it had become jammed as the result of battle damage. Fearing the worst—that he might be caught trapped inside the vehicle—he ripped off his headphones and started to turn the vehicle.

Barkmann could not see directly what was happening, but sensed it anyway. He called out to the radio operator: "Wilke, calm him down! He's turning us sideways. He needs to go back to facing the enemy!"

Wilke knew what was at stake, but before he could effectively intervene, rounds were slamming into the side of the vehicle.

Barkmann tried to restore calm: "Calm down! Pull back!"

By then, the driver had regained his composure. Pulling back with a dislodged track and a damaged drive sprocket required immense concentration. While trying to move, they also had to continue to engage the advancing enemy. One of the Shermans that had come closest was knocked out. The tank pulled back to safety and the spot where it had started its adventure. Heinze and Corth were still waiting and greeted the stricken vehicle with raised hands.

Corth was the first to speak when he climbed aboard: "You knocked out nine of their tanks and set another one on fire. I saw it all!"

Moving at a snail's pace, the tank made it back to a farmer's house in the small village of Neufbourg. Once there, they freed the imprisoned radio operator and driver by means of tanker's bars. It was because of them that Barkmann had not abandoned the tank, leaving the two crewmen to almost certain death. *SS-Hauptscharführer* Heinze was evacuated to the rear because of his wounds.

As a result of Barkmann's actions at the crossroads, the American advance was held up long enough that many formations that would have been written off were able to escape the attempted American encirclement. Barkmann himself was able to make it to Coutances later that day, picking up two immobilized *Panthers* on the way and towing them along as well. Enemy tanks had already entered the town, however. When three of them attempted to block his path, Barkmann knocked them out, aided by the ammunition he was able to take aboard from the two stricken tanks. One of the towed tanks was destroyed by an antitank gun and had to be abandoned. While continuing his attempt to get out of the town, he was attacked by fighter-bombers again but they were unable to inflict any serious damage. Another two tanks were encountered and knocked out. That brought the "kills" attributed to Barkmann's crew to 15 over the course of the two days.

The Seine was crossed on a military bridge. Moving through the next town and its narrow streets, many of the houses were hit by the large vehicles, causing walls to come tumbling down with a crash. At the end of the village, Barkmann's tanks were greeted by the local villages, who offered them flowers and wine, thinking they were the lead American tanks. When the two vehicles moved out of the village, they were attacked by fighter-bombers again. Kreller, the loader, was slightly wounded. Barkmann was also wounded by shrapnel to his left calf. That afternoon, they reached Granville on the Atlantic coast, where both men were treated.

On 30 July, the Americans were outside of the city. *Panther 424* broke through an encirclement for the third time, once again with another tank in tow. During the night, he moved unnoticed with an American convoy in the direction of Avranches. During the morning of 1 August, the towed tank had to be blown up. Barkmann's tank was also lost a short while later, when its ammunition went up. The crew had to make its way back to German lines on foot, finally reaching the company on 5 August.

Once there, they linked up with other crews that had had to make it back to the German lines on foot. Corth had reached the company earlier and had already informed the company commander of Barkmann's accomplishments.

He was submitted for the Knight's Cross to the Iron Cross, which he received on 5 September 1944 (with the award document being dated 27 August).

Barkmann had been promoted to *SS-Oberscharführer* by the time of the Ardennes offensive. On Christmas Eve 1944, he was part of the lead group of the 4th Company as it was employed against the villages of Manhay and Grandmenil. The regimental commander, *SS-Obersturmbannführer* Enseling, another Knight's Cross recipient, ordered that the advance be continued west after reaching the villages. The tanks were to continue on to Erezée in order to link up with a *Volksgrenadier* regiment[5] attacking there.

The company moved out at 2200 hours. *SS-Hauptscharführer* Franz Frauscher, a platoon leader and friend of Barkmann's, was in the lead. Barkmann moved behind the company commander. He was serving as the company headquarters section leader and reserve platoon leader. When the main road was reached, Frauscher's platoon started to receive fire; one tank started to burn.

SS-Hauptsturmführer Pohl ordered Barkmann forward to reconnoiter.

Barkmann's tank rolled and reached the road. It was a crystal-clear night—the heavens were full of stars—and the glittery snow on the ground allowed good visibility. Barkmann saw what he thought was Frauscher's halted tank. He looked off to the side of the road and determined that the open terrain was negotiable.

"Cross the road as quickly as you can!" he ordered his driver.

Moving as rapidly as it could, the tank reached the far side of the road without incident and took up position in a patch of woods. A short while later, determining the coast was probably clear, Barkmann had his tank move out towards the main road and through the woods.

Suddenly, Barkmann saw a silhouette off to the right. The tank commander had his upper torso out of the hatch. In the darkness, Barkmann thought it must be Frauscher. He ordered his driver to approach the vehicle. When they were side by side, Barkmann told his driver to kill the engine.

"What's going on, Franz?"

The man in the other turret disappeared in a flash into his tank and slammed his hatch shut. Barkmann suddenly realized what had happened. He yelled over the intercom: "Gunner, the tank next to us is enemy. Knock it out!"

The *Panther's* turret started to traverse, but the long main gun ran into the other tank's turret. The gunner cried out: "Can't . . . I'm hitting his turret."

5. Translator's Note: "People's Grenadier." The *Volksgrenadier* formations were formations consisting largely of males who were normally otherwise exempt from call-up by reasons of age or infirmity and led by cadres of experienced noncommissioned and commissioned officers. Despite this less-than-military mix, many of the formations acquitted themselves very well in this last-ditch measure.

"Driver, pull back 10 feet . . . move out!"

From the shortest distance imaginable, the gunner then fired into the rear deck of the neighboring tank. Soon, flames were glowing from the engine compartment. Barkmann then ordered his tank to move on; Frauscher had to be out there somewhere in front of them.

At that point, two enemy tanks started rolling out of a cut in the woods towards Barkmann's *Panther*. The lead tank was set ablaze with the first round. The other tank disappeared into the woods. Barkmann moved out again in order to establish contact with Frauscher.

The woods started to thin out. To the front was a large open area flanked by woods on all sides. The road made several turns across the open terrain. Barkmann could make out nine enemy tanks that were in position. Their main guns were trained on the road. Instinctively, the new driver, Grundmaier, halted when he also saw the enemy tanks in his vision port.

Barkmann ordered him to continue moving with the same speed. The *Panther* passed through the U.S. position without being engaged. The Americans must have thought the tank was one of their own. When the German crew had almost passed the group, the U.S. crews started bolting out of their vehicles and heading for the woods. They must have been warned by radio that something was afoot and the Germans were in their lines.

"Are we going to knock them out, *Oberscharführer*?" the driver asked.

"We can't afford to lose any time. The ones behind us can take care of them. We need to exploit the enemy's confusion and continue advancing."

The next patch of woods was reached. American infantry was marching along the road, getting out of the way of the tank with a curse. The *Panther* continued moving at high speed. Not a round was fired. Apparently, those men also thought the tank was one of their own.

Suddenly, there were houses on both sides of the road. Barkmann's *Panther* had reached enemy-occupied Manhay. The tank rolled past a headquarters, reaching a crossroads. The road to the left led to Erezée. He didn't turn; at that point, he just wanted to get out of the village. He continued straight ahead in the direction of Liége. But, by doing so, Barkmann inadvertently went from the frying pan and into the fire. He ran into the lead elements of a tank column. All of them were Shermans, in groups of nine, apparently in company formations. Parked in between were staff cars with officers in them. The tank crews stood around their vehicles, chattering and smoking. It was a completely crazy situation. Barkmann estimated he moved past at least 10 companies. Little did he know at the time that it was the forward elements of a combat command from the U.S. 2nd Armored Division, which had been brought forward to interdict the German advance.

All of a sudden, the loader pulled his tank commander down into the fighting compartment and turned up his collar. He pointed to the Knight's Cross dangling at Barkmann's Adam's apple. "It shows up too much in the moonlight, *Oberscharführer!*" Barkmann thanked the old hand for noticing.

The loader busied himself laying out belts of ammunition for the coaxial machine gun. Hand grenades were placed within easy reach. The gunner practically became one with his optics, searching the area in front of him, all the while keeping his hand on the traversing controls. The men wanted to be ready for any eventuality. The radio operator attempted to establish contact with the company, but all of his efforts proved to be in vain. The distance had become too great for the shorter-range radio in the tank. The *Panther* pressed past even more enemy march serials. Suddenly, the driver announced on the intercom: "A vehicle is approaching us!"

Barkmann peered out of his hatch. He saw that it was a jeep in which an officer was standing. He tried to get the vehicle to stop by using a signal flag.

"Run over it," Barkmann commanded.

Just as the vehicle started to pick up speed, the jeep driver stopped and put his vehicle in reverse. Despite his evasive maneuver, the distance between the two quickly narrowed. Soon there was a terrific crashing sound as the tank's right track grabbed the jeep. There was a horrific noise and then the *Panther* was over and past the wheeled vehicle, reduced to flattened piece of sheet metal and steel. Barkmann saw the officer and driver spring out of the doomed vehicle in the nick of time.

In the effort to reorient himself after the crash, the driver then careened into a Sherman. Barkmann held on for dear life in order not to be thrown from the hatch. The *Panther's* engine died. With its right-front drive sprocket jammed into the running gear of the Sherman, the German tank was temporarily stuck. The Americans started yelling orders.

"Back up . . . back up!" Barkmann yelled to the panic-stricken driver. Finally, he succeeded in starting the engine again. With a terrible rasping sound, the tanks disengaged. The driver then put the tank in gear, and the *Panther* picked up speed, passing the American combat vehicles. Soon, there was nothing but trains vehicles—ammo trucks, fuel trucks, field ambulances and recovery vehicles. Then there was open ground.

The Americans were coming to life. Turrets traversed. Engines roared as they were hastily started. They began firing in the general direction of Barkmann's escape route, but the rounds all fell wide of their mark. After about 800 meters, Barkmann had the tank halt. He looked down into the fighting compartment, only to see grinning faces. "Done good, once again!" It was the only thing he could think to say.

Soon, however, things turned serious again. Vehicles started pouring out of the village to pursue the solitary invader. Barkmann had the main gun orient to 6 o'clock. The lead vehicles, apparently half-tracks with infantry, were set alight with a few rounds. Then Barkmann started approaching his pursuers. Moving, halting, firing, moving again. He halted two more times to fire. In the course of his evasive maneuvering, the *Panther* had drifted too far to the northwest. Barkmann corrected course and moved to the left and into a cut in the woods.

Using the back roads and trails, he eventually got back to the main road. At first light, he reached Grandmenil, where his battalion had set up all-round defenses. His "hussar's ride" into enemy territory had turned out well; nothing the imagination could conjure up could surpass what he had actually done!

As it turned out, Barkmann had passed Frauscher's platoon. Frauscher, following behind, soon encountered the nine tanks that Barkmann had passed through. Although they had been manned again, Frauscher's platoon succeeded in knocking them out. Despite that, Frauscher himself had to change vehicles two times that night, when his own tank was shot out from under him. For his part in the fighting, he received the Knight's Cross to the Iron Cross on 31 December 1944.

On Christmas Day, Frauscher and Barkmann conducted screening operations north of Manhay together. Towards noon, enemy forces felt their way against the village. Both of the tanks each knocked out an enemy tank. The enemy turned back.

When the enemy tanks attacked again in the afternoon, Barkmann was wounded by shrapnel to the head behind his left ear. He collapsed, unconscious. The crew evacuated him to Manhay. During the night of 25/26 December, he woke up in a main clearing station; on his chest was an evacuation tag for movement to the military reserve hospital in Cologne. Barkmann pulled back the dressing that had been placed on his head and removed the shrapnel embedded in his outer skull by hand. The throbbing headache that plagued him disappeared immediately.

He left behind the evacuation tag on his stretcher when he mounted a messenger's motorcycle and rode back to the regiment, where he reported back to duty to *SS-Obersturmbannführer* Enseling. His regimental commander sent the plucky noncommissioned officer to the trains to recover from his wounds. Barkmann was able to take his crew along, where they all enjoyed a few days of rest. On 18 January, Barkmann was again wounded in the head by shrapnel. He remained lucky, even managing to remain with his crew. At the end of that month, the division was moved to Hungary

In March, Barkmann and his crew were again engaged in combat. *SS-Sturmbannführer* Kesten, a Knight's Cross to the Iron Cross recipient (12 November 1943), was entrusted with command of what remained of the regiment's tanks, which were consolidated into a battalion. *SS-Untersturmführer* Knoche led the 4th Company. The company attacked as part of the division between Lakes Valence and Balaton in a series of ill-fated efforts first to free the besieged city of Budapest and later to secure Hungarian oil for the *Reich*. In the course of the fighting, Barkmann again distinguished himself, knocking out four T-34's on one day in the vicinity of Heinrich Major. His battalion was encircled on 18 March. It was able to break out and was subsequently ordered to the area around Raab. In the process of attempting to rail load for the transport to Raab, the remaining nine tanks of Barkmann's company found that the Soviets had already bypassed the rail station. The company lost its contact with the division, so it reported for service to the local army commander.

In a night fight with Josef Stalin tanks, the 4th Company lost three tanks. With its six remaining combat vehicles, the company finally linked up with the tank regiment of the *1. SS-Panzer-Division "Leibstandarte SS Adolf Hitler."* *SS-Standartenführer* Peiper, the regimental commander, attempted to take the tanks and give them to his own tankless crews. In that effort, he was mistaken; the men of *SS-Panzer-Regiment "Das Reich"* refused to relinquish their vehicles.

From that point forward, the men of the 4th Company screened the rearward movements of the German forces along with Peiper's tanks. They were often written off for dead, but they somehow managed to fight their way out and rejoin their countrymen. In one instance, the company knocked out nine T-34's that were attacking.

Finally, the 4th Company made it back to its parent regiment, where the regimental commander personally briefed the men on their new defensive positions around Eszterhazy. At the beginning of April, they fought at Pandorf, to the south of Vienna. The number of tanks kept dwindling during the subsequent fighting in and around the Austrian capital.

On 12 April 1945, Barkmann was on the Brigitte Bridge in Vienna on his way back to the regimental command post with three *Panthers* when his tank was knocked out by an *Unteroffizier* with a *Panzerfaust*.[6] The panicked

---

6. Translator's Note: The *Panzerfaust* was a one-shot, shoulder-fired antitank rocket with a hollow-charge warhead. It was the precursor to the world-famous RPG-7, which the Soviets reverse-engineered from the German design. It had an effective range of only about 100 meters, but could destroy any armored vehicle in existence at the time thanks to its hollow-charge warhead.

noncommissioned officer had mistaken his tank for one of the Soviets. The round entered the turret and minute shards of shrapnel peppered Barkmann's lower body, his upper thigh area and his lower left arm. Barkmann's new loader was blinded in both eyes. The radio operator also suffered a number of shrapnel wounds. After evacuating the wounded and getting a new radio operator and loader, Barkmann continued on to the regimental command post with his tank. Barkmann was reduced to directing the driver through shouted commands to the loader or gunner, who passed them on, since the intercom had been destroyed in the *Panzerfaust* blast.

The next night, his tank bottomed out in a shell crater and could not be recovered. It was then destroyed with a *Panzerfaust*.

At the Florisdorfer Bridge, Barkmann and his crew were employed as infantry. *SS-Standartenführer* Rudolf Lehmann, the new division commander, summoned the seasoned tank commander to him: "Barkmann, do you think you can make it across the bridge?"

"Of course, *Standartenführer!*"

"Here's what I want: Tell *Hauptsturmführer* Boska to attack and relieve the bridgehead with all of the *Panthers* of his company." (Boska, a Knight's Cross recipient, was the commander of the 6th Company.)

Barkmann took his entire crew with him. One of them would surely get through! The men ran from one span to the next, always followed by enemy fire. All of them reached the far shore. Shortly thereafter, Boska moved out to relieve the bridgehead with his five operational *Panthers*. He served as the tank commander of the second tank, but it was knocked out while crossing the bridge. Boska sought cover behind his knocked-out tank; the rest of his crew had been killed. Boska himself was wounded. In that crisis situation, the maintenance sergeant of the 6th Company raced across the bridge in a motorcycle, picked up the badly wounded company commander and placed him in the sidecar, and then returned—followed by bursts of machine-gun fire but unscathed—to the far side.

In the vicinity of St. Pölten, northwest of Vienna, Barkmann and *SS-Untersturmführer* Knoche both received new *Panthers*. They linked up with the 6th Company and fought with it. They headed to the west along the Danube, crossing it at Krems. The 6th Company was loaded on trains there to participate in the relief effort directed towards Prague. The war ended as these and other elements were being sped throughout what remained of the *Reich* in desperate measures to try to stave off the inevitable.

Together with his long-time gunner, Poggendorff, Barkmann snuck through the American lines in the Bavarian Woods. Later on, he played a few tricks on British forces to make his way through their lines in an effort to make his way to northern Germany and home. After a journey of 1,000 kilometers, he finally reached Schleswig-Holstein.

✠

Ernst Barkmann passed away peacefully at his family farm in Kisdorf on 27 June 2009.

Leutnant Hans Bunzel after receipt of his Knight's Cross to the Iron Cross.

CHAPTER 2

Oberleutnant Hans Bunzel

UNPARALLELED TANK COMMANDER

"*Panzer maaaarsch!*"

Hauptmann Gerhard Tebbe, standing in the open hatch of his commander's vehicle, thrust his hand three times into the air. The steel giants of *Panzer-Abteilung 116* of the *16. Infanterie-Division (mot.)* started to move out. It was still dark. Stars lit up the sky, which appeared to have been wiped clean by a biting wind from the east.

The tracks of the tanks gave off crunching sounds. Vegetation was crushed underneath them. The sheets of ice on the ground broke like glass. The riflemen from *Panzergrenadier-Regiment 60 (mot.)*, who had mounted the tanks, cursed up a storm whenever they inclined steeply one way or another, when crossing ditches and depressions in the ground, and they had to hold on for dear life in order to keep from being thrown off.

The tanks of Bunzel's platoon were on the left flank of this steel assault wedge. *Oberfeldwebel* Hans Bunzel was an experienced soldier, who had been a tanker since the very beginning in 1934. He had started with *Panzer-Regiment 1* of the *1. Panzer-Division*.

All of a sudden, it occurred to Bunzel that he had been on an operation at this exact spot nearly a year earlier. He had to focus back to the present, however, when he heard the voice of his company commander coming in over the radio: "CO to Bunzel: Watch out! 11 o'clock! Distance 1,000 meters; enemy strongpoint!"

Bunzel's gunner called out a few seconds later that he had identified the target. He started to lay his gun in the general direction. The *Panzer III* halted to fire. The main gun fired soon thereafter. A short lance of flame spat out of the muzzle of the main gun, and the first round was racing on its way towards the enemy.

The round penetrated the cover that had been placed in front of the Maxim machine-gun position and caused a pile of ammunition to catch on fire. The engagement had started. The early-morning hours of 15 January 1943 were filled with the rattling of enemy machine guns and the crash of main guns firing from the tanks. All along the frontage of the attacking wedge of tanks there was antitank-gun fire. Rounds smacked into the ground and tore loose clumps of earth that had been frozen hard.

"Gittermann: Go around to the right . . . Leonhardt: Look out! Enemy AT in front of you!"

Orders and warnings, tips and reports buzzed back and forth and were received by the commanders of the individual companies. The tanks alternated in taking firing halts. Identified enemy antitank guns were eliminated, and the tanks continued to roll forward in platoon-size elements in order to reach their objective: the high ground to the rear of the enemy dug in there.

Hauptmann Tebbe directed the actions of the battalion; he had assumed acting command of it at Jaschkul on 28 October 1942. He had the companies advance in three assault wedges, so as to split up the enemy's fire. All three of the assault groups penetrated the enemy's positions.

"T-34 . . . 12 o'clock . . . 1,000!" *Feldwebel* Göcke from the *4./Panzer-Abteilung 116* reported. Göcke's gunner had identified the target. The tank halted. After taking a few seconds to get a final lay on the target, the report of the main gun could be heard. The round screamed out of the barrel and raced towards the enemy. A garish light lit up the area of impact, signifying a hit. The enemy had not been knocked out, however, not by a long shot! A muzzle flash could be seen from the long barrel of the T-34, and its round hammered into the ground not 10 meters away from Göcke's tank. Göcke's loader had already slammed another round in the breech. The second round raced towards the enemy. The empty shell casing hit the deflector with a loud bang and danced its way into the empty-casing bag. There was another hit on the far end. But it was not until the third round that the enemy tank went up in flames.

"Keep moving! Don't get held up!" the acting battalion commander ordered.

The companies rolled forward, boxed their way through the enemy positions, collapsed trenches and fired at the enemy antitank guns, which had immobilized one of the German tanks. First three, then four of the feared 7.62-centimeter antitank guns were eliminated.

Suddenly, two T-34's appeared from out of a patch of woods on the lower portion of the slope. They moved rapidly against the 3rd Company and opened fire with their long-barreled main guns. Hans Bunzel observed a vehicle of the 3rd Platoon knock out one of the T-34's immediately. The second one then turned around and escaped despite the hail of rounds that were then sent his way.

One after the other, the three tank assault groups reached the high ground. They reorganized and then headed into the village of Spornyi, firing all the way. Machine-gun fire raced towards them from out of windows and behind the remnants of walls. Antitank rifles joined in the fray, speeding their deadly rounds towards the advancing German tanks.

"Load HE!"

The high-explosive rounds hammered into the pockets of resistance that had been identified. One by one, they were silenced. *Oberfeldwebel* Bunzel observed the muzzle flashes through the bulletproof glass of his vision port, muzzle flashes that revealed the location of the enemy. He talked his gunner into the targets, which he then acquired in his sights. The targets were silenced through the practiced hand of the gunner.

"Move forward!" Bunzel, a platoon leader, ordered his driver.

The driver let out the clutch and the tank gave a jerk. The antitank round, which was intended for Bunzel and his crew, landed behind the rear deck in a depression, causing the dislodged snow to form a cloud as big as a house. Bunzel then saw his acting company commander, *Oberleutnant* Kühne, eliminate the antitank gun with a single round. All of the tanks continued to move forward.

It began to snow. The icy-cold wind from the east blew veils of snow against the vision slots of the drivers. But by then, Spornyi had been taken and there were no more operations anticipated. The crews were to be allowed to rest. But things turned out differently. *Hauptmann* Tebbe called the company commanders and platoon leaders together.

"Bunzel, you're familiar with the Manytsch dam from last year. Right now, it's the last crossing for the division on the way to Bataisk and Rostow. You'll take the lead in the direction of the dam. Move as fast as you can and get there before the Russians blow it sky high!"

Hans Bunzel knew what was at stake. He also knew that he had to beat the enemy to the punch. He had to prevent the dam from being blown up, as it had been the previous year.

"Everyone, follow me!" He ordered the tanks of his platoon, after he had briefed the tank commanders.

They moved out. Whenever they were taken under fire from the flanks, they felt an almost uncontrollable urge to stop to fire and eliminate the enemy. But their objective was not this enemy. Instead, it was the dam and the sluice gates of Kuma and Manytsch. It was imperative to get there and secure them!

Hill 29.6 appeared in front of Bunzel. The gates were between it and Manytsch. He had an uneasy feeling as they covered the last 200 meters to the hill. Had the enemy prepared the dam and the gates for demolition this time as well? Would both of them fly into the air as soon as they showed themselves on the hill?

They then reached the top of the small hill. Looking all around him, the *Oberfeldwebel* saw the antitank-gun belt that was rusting away from after the advance of the previous year.

The new enemy was not idle and started firing from the left and the right. Small-arms rounds and antitank-rifle rounds were smacking away against the sideskirts of the tanks.

"Everybody follow me and move like hell over the dam!"

They stepped on their gas pedals and the tanks rattled over the dam, firing like mad to the right and the left. The dam could go up in the air at any minute. Of course, if that happened, Bunzel and his men would go up with it. Nothing happened, however, and the tanks reached the off ramp at the far end of the dam.

"Disperse! . . . Establish a bridgehead! . . . All-round defense!" Bunzel issued his orders in quick succession and pulled the farthest forward with his tank. His other tanks formed a half circle to his right and left around the far end. They had done it; they had formed a bridgehead that they would be able to hold until the mechanized infantry could be brought forward.

Hans Bunzel radioed his report to the battalion commander: "Manytsch dam crossed; bridgehead established!"

The counterorder from the battalion arrived a little bit later: "Remain where you are and hold it!"

The four tanks of Bunzel's platoon then engaged the combat-engineer squads and assault groups that were trying to approach the dam and do the work that should have already been done.

Some of Bunzel's more experienced tankers had already dismounted and cut all the visible detonation lines.

Despite this, the men in the steel boxes breathed a sigh of relief when the mechanized infantry of the *III./Panzer-Grenadier-Regiment 60* came rolling over the dam. *Oberleutnant* Klappich, the acting commander of the battalion, waved to Bunzel, as they were guided into position. Hans Bunzel could see the Knight's Cross that Klappich was wearing, a sure sign of an experienced veteran. Klappich had received the award on 31 July 1942.

Oberleutnant Klappich made a sweeping movement with his hands indicating a movement along the south bank of the Manytsch and then turning off to the west. A village was there that was occupied by the enemy: Ssamodurowka.

Bunzel nodded to his comrade. Bunzel had not received new orders, so he remained defending his bridgehead. The tension began to slacken off, however. The first cigarette he lit up had never tasted better. The light snow flurries became heavier and heavier. The last vehicles of the *Panzergrenadier* battalion disappeared in the haze and swirling of the flakes.

"I hope we'll see you again, *Herr Oberfeldwebel!*" one of the *Panzergrenadiere* shouted out.

"Klappich will bring you back . . . you can count on that!"

✠

The tankers of Bunzel's platoon continued to hold the bridgehead. They greeted the tanks of their battalion both enthusiastically and with relief, as they closed on their location. At the same time, *Oberleutnant* Klappich's battalion had approached the eastern outskirts of Ssamodurowka through a wall of snow that was becoming increasingly thicker.

They started to receive fire. The rattling of machine guns could be heard. The machine guns mounted on the *SPW's* returned the fire. The *SPW's* continued to pick up speed. When the lead company reached the village, the company commander had his men dismount. One platoon provided cover while the other two platoons continued to advance and clear out the initial buildings.

Soon it was man-to-man fighting that was raging in Ssamodurowka. The battalion was locked in mortal combat with the Soviet 2nd Mechanized Brigade.

Oberleutnant Klappich assaulted the middle of the village with the main body of his battalion. They reached the command post of the enemy and took the brigade chief-of-staff and some of the staff officers prisoner.

"Don't stop! The enemy's weak and we have to eject him completely!"

That was typical Klappich. Systematically, the buildings and open areas were cleared. Soon, the grenadiers were at the western end of the village. That had done it. The officer's men started to establish positions in Ssamodurowka. Some valuable documents were found in the brigade headquarters, which revealed the enemy's intentions.

According to these orders, the formations of the Soviet 2nd Guards Army had been directed to hold the bridgeheads at Ssamodurowka and Manytschkaya until all of the corps of the field army had closed up. It had been intended to launch an attack from this area on Bataisk on 23 January.

It was clear to Günther Klappich that Ssamodurowka was one of the pivotal points on the front and that he had to hold this village with all the means at his disposal in order to thwart the Soviet leadership's intentions.

✠

Generalmajor Graf Gerhard von Schwerin, the commander of the *16. Infanterie-Division (mot.),* had been covering the approximately 300-kilometer-wide gap between the *1. Panzer-Armee* and the *4. Panzer-Armee* for months. As a result, he had protected both field armies from being encircled by the Soviet 28th Army. Around 10 January 1943, he received orders to pull his division back to Rostow. His first objective was the Manytsch and its crossing point, which was being held by the *LVII. Panzer-Korps* under *General der Panzertruppen* Kirchner.

A Manytsch bridgehead was being formed by the corps east of Proletarskaja. Among the forces in the large bridgehead were the *23. Panzer-Division*, the *17. Panzer-Division*, *SS-Panzer-Grenadier-Division "Wiking"* and *schwere Panzer-Abteilung 503*. Everything went well until 12 January 1943. Then, however, Soviet fast forces broke through in the direction of Proletarskaja, Salsk and Spornyi.

Generalmajor von Schwerin's division was outflanked. In addition, the Soviets were within reach of achieving their goals: first splitting up *Heeresgruppe A*, then blocking the withdrawal route of the *1. Panzer-Armee* to Rostow and, finally, cutting off and destroying the *17. Armee*, which was pulling back from the Kuban bridgehead.

In this phase of the campaign, fortune smiled on von Schwerin's division by providing it with the operations order of the Soviet 28th Army. Not only were the axes of attack marked on the maps, but also the orders to the individual corps were laid out. It was intended for one of these corps—the V Guards Mechanized Corps—to attack Spornyi with additional attached formations.

When *Generalmajor* von Schwerin received these documents, he had the *46. Infanterie-Division (mot.)*, which was attached to his command, move back as rapidly as it could to Spornyi. But when the lead elements of this division reached the town, the enemy was already there and Soviet fast forces were already rolling on towards Bataisk to the south/southeast of Rostow.

This meant that the *16. Infanterie-Division (mot.)* had been bypassed. By late in the evening of 14 January the motorized formations of the division had worked their way through the heavy snow up to the Soviet positions. *Generalmajor* von Schwerin issued orders to attack the next morning.

The events of this day were portrayed in the opening section of this chapter. It can be seen from it that two soldiers of the division created the prerequisites for the further actions of the division and, indeed, its survival:

- *Oberfeldwebel* Hans Bunzel, who took the decisive crossing point over the Manytsch at Spornyi, and
- *Oberleutnant* Günther Klappich, who took a decisive bridgehead of the enemy—Ssamodurowka—in a fight and then sat there like a thorn in the side of the Soviet forces.

It was from here that the door to Bataisk remained open for German forces. A handful of tanks and a battalion of grenadiers had tipped the scales.

✠

For his actions, Hans Bunzel was submitted for the Knight's Cross, which he received on 10 February 1943.

Oberleutnant Günther Klappich, who had already received the Knight's Cross, was recommended for the Oak Leaves, which he posthumously received on 8 June 1943 as the 254th member of the German Armed Forces. He was also promoted posthumously to *Hauptmann*. He had been killed in action on 22 January 1943.

✠

Hans Bunzel was born on 29 April 1915 in Hagnau (Silesia). On 1 April 1933, he joined the *1./Kraftfahr-Abteilung 4* in Dresden. He was not quite 18 at the time. At the beginning of 1934, Bunzel's company was transferred to Leipzig. One other company of the battalion, the *3./Kraftfahr-Abteilung 4*, was also stationed there. The other two companies of the battalions were moved to Magdeburg. Over the next few months, Hans Bunzel received driver's training and received his first two classes of driver's licenses. On 26 June 1934, he was transferred to Ohrdruf, the home of the newly formed Motorization Training Command. He was assigned to its 8th Company.

It was intended to form a regiment each of the newly formed tank arm in Ohrdruf and Zossen. Training was to be conducted in both locations on the few tanks that were available.

As a *Gefreiter*, Bunzel received the highest class of license for wheeled vehicles on 15 October 1934. Five months later, he received his license for tracked vehicles. He then became a tank driver. On 1 July 1934, he became an *Unteroffizier*. Three months after that, he was transferred to the *7./Panzer-Regiment 1* of the just-forming *1. Panzer-Division*. The Motorization Training Command provided the cadre for these newly forming tank formations. Hans Bunzel was an active participant in the formation of the German Army's first armored division.

By 1936, Bunzel had driven every type of vehicle that was in the division's inventory at the time. He also had every type of driver's license and instructor's certificate that the army offered. He served as a driver, a driver instructor and then as the section leader of a maintenance section. He remained in the latter capacity after the start of the Second World War and until the campaign in Russia.

He worked industriously as a maintenance section leader and was even presented the Iron Cross, Second Class, for his performance under fire while recovering an immobilized *Panzer III* near Belfort during the French campaign.

Shortly before the start of the campaign in Russia, Bunzel became a tank commander and a section leader after *Unteroffizier* Farmetzky took over Bunzel's former maintenance section. Bunzel became a section leader in the 2nd Platoon of the *6./Panzer-Regiment 1*. His company commander was *Oberleutnant* Darius.

Feldwebel Bunzel participated in the first tank engagement of the division in Russia at Rossienie. *Panzer-Regiment 1* was employed in a counterattack early on 25 June 1941 against a large Soviet armored attack five kilometers outside of Vosiliskis. The Soviets had attacked the *II./Schützen-Regiment 113* of *Major* von Kittel with KV-I's and KV-II's, overrun its positions and then collapsed the trenches. Bunzel advanced against these steel giants in his *Panzer III*. A dramatic firefight developed, and Bunzel saw how the rounds from his main gun would not penetrate the frontal armor of these enemy tanks at all. The Russian tanks simply rolled past them.

"Turn around!" *Oberleutnant* Darius radioed his crews. They turned around and followed the enemy's tanks. They finally caught up with them, and Bunzel found himself getting closer and closer to the lead KV-I. When his tank was only five meters away from the colossus and his gunner could count every rivet on the enemy tank through his sights, Bunzel issued the order to fire. The first round raced from the main gun. It penetrated the rear; seconds later, flames from the fuel tank shot up.

"That one's finished!" Bunzel exclaimed. "Let's go and approach the next one!"

Once again, they closed up to a KV-I. After firing two rounds, they succeeded in knocking out this heavy tank as well. A round hit Bunzel's tank on the turret, but it ricocheted skywards. To both the right and the left, Bunzel's comrades also engaged the enemy at short distance. In all, they succeeded in knocking out 18 of the heavy KV-I's. *Feldwebel* Bunzel ended the day with a total "kill" score of three.

Feldwebel Bunzel was submitted for the Iron Cross, First Class, which was presented to him on 21 July 1941. He had demonstrated both circumspection and, at the same time, decisiveness as a tank commander in this engagement.

The advance of the *1. Panzer-Division* in the direction of Leningrad continued. Hans Bunzel participated in all of the fighting of his regiment.

He was there when his company approached the Dudenhof Heights on 11 September 1941 and reached the key terrain at Hill 167. It was at this point that *Oberleutnant* Darius transmitted the radio message that those who are still alive still remember: "I see Leningrad and the sea!"

The area that was reached on this day was held for the next 10 days. A series of heavy tanks were once again knocked out—this time at Rechkolowo and Mal. Kabosi. The platoon was attached to the *I./Schützen-Regiment 113* at the time. Under the command of *Leutnant* Stoves, the platoon leader, 12 KV-I's and T-34's were knocked out. Two German tanks were lost, and *Leutnant* Stoves was badly wounded. In the end, only Bunzel's tank was operational from the platoon. Together with *Hauptmann* von Berckefeldt and the company headquarters section, *Feldwebel* Bunzel advanced on Mal. Kabosi, which had been occupied by the enemy. The tanks were accompanied by *Leutnant* Katzmann of the *3./Schützen-Regiment 113*, who rallied his men to accompany the attack. Bunzel was able to clear a path into the village by fire. In an engagement with an antitank gun, Bunzel was hit in the throat by shrapnel. Had it penetrated a few centimeters farther back, it would have been all over for the young tank commander.

Two days later, in the supplement to the German Armed Forces Daily Report, *Hauptmann* von Berckefeldt, *Leutnant* Stoves and the tanks of *Feldwebel* Bunzel, *Feldwebel* Guhlich and *Unteroffizier* Oerlein (who was killed in the fighting) were mentioned by name. Hans Bunzel was already in the field hospital when this occurred. While he was there, the stocky Silesian received both the Tank Assault Badge in Silver and the Wound Badge in Black.

In the middle of October, during the assault on Kalinin, Bunzel's tank was knocked out for the third time. For the first time, Bunzel lost a crewmember from his original crew. It was his driver, Richard Große—known to his friends as "Rigo"—who was mortally wounded.

At the beginning of December, *Feldwebel* Bunzel returned to his regiment and his company from convalescent leave. He was greeted there by *Leutnant* Stoves, who had recovered from his severe wounds shortly before. At the time, the regiment was in the Klin area, in the center of the Russian Front.

✠

"Bunzel, we'll be continuing the attack on Jamuga tomorrow!" Stoves said this to the tank commander on the evening of 8 December 1941. "We're supposed to support Krieg's [*SPW*] battalion in its attack on Jamuga from out of the woods north of Klin."

On the next day, the tanks moved into the woods around 1100 hours. They continued through the woods and were outside of Jamuga at 1330 hours. But the bridge was blown up, so that the tanks could only advance to just south of Jamuga. They were supported in this effort by an attached company of tanks from *Panzer-Regiment 25* under *Oberleutnant* Horst Fortun.

The tanks literally slid forward over the iced-over roads that were flanked on both sides by dense woods.

Hans Bunzel was the lead tank. A short while later they received fire. Bunzel heard the crack as an enemy round hammered into the front slope of his tank. The tank then received another hit and was immobilized. *Leutnant* Stoves's tank received several hits. A third tank was immobilized with final drive damage. The attack began to waver. The last two tanks could not be brought over the deep tank ditch. The attack was called off and the tanks pulled back.

During the next few days, Bunzel was involved in increasingly difficult defensive fighting against an enemy who was constantly attacking. He participated in relief attacks in the direction of Woronino and succeeded in knocking out a few enemy tanks.

A short while later, Division Order 81 was published. According to it, the *1. Panzer-Division* was to hold Klin while a general withdrawal was initiated.

The division held until the morning of 15 December 1941. The division was to fight its way back. It needed to reach the new defensive positions along the Lama and Jausa.

The withdrawal started. On 18 January 1942, the recently promoted *Oberfeldwebel* Bunzel participated in an attack on Borodino as a platoon leader. The objective was to open up the rail line from Szytschewka to Rshew. The attack was led by *Oberleutnant* Poehl, the commander of the *7./Panzer-Regiment 1*, who had assembled his tank and a few others for the assault. Among the tank commanders participating besides *Oberfeldwebel* Bunzel were *Oberfeldwebel* Kühne, *Oberfeldwebel* Röder, *Feldwebel* Strippel (who would later receive both the Knight's Cross and the Oak Leaves), *Feldwebel* Schäfer, *Feldwebel* Hafner and *Oberfunkmeister* Adam. Using skillful fire and movement, the few tanks succeeded in ejecting the enemy.

Because there were so few tanks left, many of the crews were employed as infantry for this assault. One of the officers who led the dismounted tankers was *Leutnant* Kühne, who would later be Bunzel's company commander. In addition to the tankers, there were *Panzerjäger* without antitank guns, signals personnel and trains personnel. All were forced to be committed due to the desperate situation. Eventually, Sucharewka, which had been contested for many days, was won back.

During the snowstorms of January and February, these few soldiers held the strongpoint south of Rshew. The fighting was bitter in what would later be known as the "Winter Battle for Szytschewka." It was here that Hans Bunzel learned the school of hard knocks for tankers, where he had to fight again and again against numerically superior groups of the enemy. At the end of March, *Panzer-Regiment 1* was pulled out of the line to be reconstituted.

During the time of its reconstitution, *Panzer-Regiment 1* had to give up a battalion equivalent to the *16. Infanterie-Division (mot.)*. As a result of personnel levies throughout the regiment, but primarily from personnel of the *I./Panzer-Regiment 1*, three companies were formed. *Oberfeldwebel* Bunzel went to the *3./ Panzer-Regiment 1*, which was commanded by *Hauptmann* Stölting.

Before the battalion departed, however, Hans Bunzel was shot through the throat. While Bunzel was hospitalized, his battalion was sent south to the *16. Infanterie-Division (mot.)* under the acting command of *Hauptmann* Feldtkeller, where it was redesignated as *Panzer-Abteilung 116*.

✠

Oberfeldwebel Bunzel was back with his battalion when the *16. Infanterie-Division (mot.)* advanced in the summer of 1942 as part of the German summer offensive. On 2 July 1942, Stary-Oskol was taken. He was a platoon leader in the *3./Panzer-Abteilung 116* when Woronesch was taken and the fighting was continued during the pursuit of the enemy over the Don and Donez Rivers. When the fighting centered on Manytsch, the border between Europe and Asia, Bunzel was again at the very front with his platoon. He has provided us with a firsthand account of his experiences during this round of fighting:

In the early light of morning, the tank battalion prepared to attack the Manytsch Dam. We advanced in an inverted wedge with the 3rd Company on the right and my platoon the farthest to the right.

During the first part of the attack, we received heavy artillery fire as well as fire from "Stalin organs." The attack was focused on Hill 29.6, which was about 2 to 3 thousand meters from the dam. In the process, the battalion encountered a strong antitank-gun belt that was established on the ridgeline.

Because the terrain was completely without cover, we asked the friendly artillery to take out the antitank-gun belt. At the same time, I received orders from my company commander, *Hauptmann* Stölting, to go around the high ground to the right and prevent the destruction of the dam. Two dug-in antitank riflemen, who had engaged me during the attack, were eliminated. I went around the high ground to the right, moved along the left edge of Spornyi and then reached the dam in a single move.

I could see that the dam also had a small hoist for boats. I advanced as far as the gates with my tank and then dismounted. My tank moved behind a building, which apparently was an administrative building, and provided me with cover.

I saw several demolition charges on the gates that were interconnected with cable. While my gunner engaged Russian infantry on the dam, I cut everything that I could identify as a cable.

While I was still working at doing this, the enemy started the charges. At a distance of about 100 meters from me, the dam flew up into the air. I was able to do one thing, however: The gates were intact. A little later on they could be used as a bridge after the dam had been repaired. We would also use this bridge/dam crossing one year later.

Despite the objective accounting, it is clear how *Oberfeldwebel* Bunzel risked his life in order to keep the crossing point intact. On 10 August, Hans Bunzel was wounded again. On 23 August, he received the Wound Badge in Silver.

On 28 October 1942, *Hauptmann* Gerhard Tebbe assumed acting command of the battalion from *Major* von der Schulenburg, who had taken ill. On 17 November 1942, *Generalmajor Graf* von Schwerin became the new division commander.

The fighting continued and, on 20 November 1942, Hans Bunzel was again wounded, this time by a piece of shrapnel in the upper thigh. Hans Bunzel was with the division when it was farther east than any other formation of the German Army on the Eastern Front. The *Windhund-Division*—so-called because of its insignia, a greyhound—was in the area around Elista at the time, where it had advanced as far as the Caspian Sea and on the southern mouth of the Volga.

In the huge expanse of the steppes, the division experienced firsthand the immeasurable vastness of the Soviet Union. It was all on its own. It was thanks to the aggressive yet circumspect leadership of the division commander, *Graf* von Schwerin, who knew how to lead in just such an isolated situation, that the division was later able to escape from its exposed position when the Soviets attacked with the 2nd Guards Army, which consisted of a rifle corps, three mechanized corps and a tank corps.

In contravention of a *Führer* order, *Generalmajor* von Schwerin ordered his division to pull back to a blocking position along the Manytsch. This was the situation at the outset of this chapter, a situation that grew increasingly critical in the middle of January 1943. By moving back to these positions, however, the division was able to strike at the last moment and thwart the Soviet attempt to surround the *LVII. Panzer-Korps.*

During the night of 15/16 January 1943, *Oberleutnant* Leonhardt had reached Nowopawlowskij with his *4./Panzer-Abteilung 116.* Only the lead platoon of *Oberfeldwebel* Schreiber was able to actually penetrate into the village. All of the other tanks had fallen out on their way there. *Oberleutnant* Leonhardt worked feverishly to get them all operational again.

When the main body of *Panzer-Abteilung 116* rolled towards the command post of *Panzergrenadier-Regiment 156* in Lenin during the morning, the Russian attack on Nowopawlowskij had already started. *Oberfeldwebel* Schreiber's calls for help reached the battalion commander, and *Hauptmann* Tebbe did everything in his power to get the immobilized tanks back up to the front. But all of that was to no avail; it would have taken too long to get there. The four tanks of the *Oberfeldwebel* were all by themselves in the village and were being attacked by a pack of Russian tanks. One of the tanks was lost. The remaining three then received instructions to break out and pull back in the direction of Lenin. *Hauptmann* Tebbe got everything he could lay his hands on ready to launch an immediate counterattack. Nowopawlowskij was retaken in the counterattack that ensued. The enemy pulled back to Manytschkaja.

The preparations for another attack were made in Lenin. *Hauptmann* Tebbe's tanks had been reinforced by the *Panzer III* platoon of *schwere Panzer-Abteilung 503.* The tanks were armed with the short-barreled, 7.5-centimeter main gun and reported to *Oberfeldwebel* Burgiß.

When the news was received during the morning of 17 January 1943 that *Hauptmann* Karl and his *Panzergrenadiere* in Nowopawlowskij were ejected from the village once again, *Hauptmann* Tebbe committed his 2nd Company under *Leutnant* Gittermann and the *Panzer III* platoon of *Oberfeldwebel* Burgiß. Even while they were blasting the enemy out of the village and reestablishing themselves there, Soviet tank attacks were starting up again against the village, this time from the rear. Ssamodurowka, which was still being held by *Oberleutnant* Klappich and his men, was likewise being attacked by the Soviets. It was clear to the Soviet commanders that these localities could not be allowed to remain in German hands. No matter what they attempted, however, *Oberleutnant* Klappich and his men remained firm.

A short while later, the division issued orders that the bridgehead was to be reduced and that the tank battalion was to cover the withdrawal of the grenadiers. At this point, the enemy launched an attack that proved exceedingly dangerous.

Soviet armored formations advanced into the middle of the withdrawal movements on their way towards Tschekanow. *Oberleutnant* Kühne, the commander of the 3rd Company at the time, was the first one to see the attacking enemy. The warning that he radioed to his comrades was also received by Hans Bunzel.

Hans Bunzel issued his first fire command. His gunner acquired the target and knocked the track off of a T-34 with his first round. After a few dozen rounds were fired at the enemy, they disappeared without a trace.

On the morning of 19 January 1943, all of *Panzer-Abteilung 116* and elements of *Panzergrenadier-Regiment 60 (mot.)* moved out against Ssamodurowka, which *Oberleutnant* Klappich had been forced to abandon. The *3./Panzer-Abteilung 116* was on the right; the *2./Panzer-Abteilung 116* on the left. Strong snow squalls whipped into the faces of the tank commanders who were standing in their cupolas. It was cold and dreary. But—and every tank commander knew this—it was imperative to eject the enemy from Ssamodurowka again.

Oberfeldwebel Bunzel, who was moving at the head of his platoon, attempted to gaze through the blowing snow. When he saw the first muzzle flashes from enemy antitank guns ahead, he dropped down into the turret.

"Stand by to engage!"

"Both weapons up and ready to fire!" the loader reported. All of a sudden, the muzzle flashes could be seen from tanks and antitank guns firing across a breadth of two kilometers. Rounds hurled over to the German tanks. They smashed into the ground and whipped up fountains of snow that were mixed with steel.

The company commander issued orders: "Advance by platoon! One platoon always providing cover!"

The tanks rattled forward as fast as they could. They crashed through vegetation that seemed to shatter like glass due to the icy cold. The tank crews replied to the enemy with round after round. Enemy rounds smacked into steel hulls and penetrated them, leaving fighting vehicles as burning torches on the battlefield.

An antitank-gun position appeared in front of Bunzel's tank. The gunner took quick aim, depressed the firing button and the round hit right in the middle of the position.

"Pull forward 30 meters and stop!" Bunzel ordered.

The tank rolled forward and the crew saw a T-34. Its turret was traversing towards them with its long trunk of a main gun. But before it could traverse completely, the round from Bunzel's tank hit the T-34 right between the turret and the hull, dislodging the turret from its race.

"Keep on going, through them . . . through them!"

Bunzel knew what he had to do. The vehicles of his platoon followed him. They rolled forward against the wall of fire that was spewing against them. Whenever they halted and fired, one more antitank gun or tank was silenced.

Tanks fought against tanks; tanks against antitank guns!

Gittermann and Bunzel both knocked out several enemy tanks. When it was all over, 6 T-34's and several antitank guns, as well as a number of antitank rifles, were captured. For the second time, Ssamodurowka had been torn out of the hands of the enemy.

Then Gerhard Tebbe—affectionately referred to by his men as *Panzer Tebbe*—found out that there was only a single ammo truck and a single fuel truck immediately available. That precluded a continuation of the attack. A half hour later, a congratulatory radio message was sent from the division concerning the successful recapture of the village.

It was not until the morning of 20 January 1943 that another ammo truck made it forward to Tebbe and his men. The tankers, who had to pull security during the night under barbarously cold conditions, breathed a sigh of relief. The relief was to be short lived.

The battalion commander soon called his company commanders and platoon leaders to a meeting. Tebbe told them that the Russians were positioning themselves to attack Ssamodurowka; tanks noises could be heard. There was no doubt that the enemy would attack shortly. The men received their instructions and returned to their units.

The Russians soon attacked. Their main effort was directed against the sectors manned by *Leutnant* Gittermann's and *Oberfeldwebel* Bunzel's men. The leaders told their crews to allow the Russians to approach.

Practically shaking with excitement, the loaders and the gunners waited nervously at their stations, while their tank commanders searched the terrain. Bunzel gave his order to fire at 0535 hours. The muzzle flashes shot out of the main guns of his four tanks almost simultaneously. The rounds hammered into the approaching T-34's. Flames leapt out of the hatches as they were thrown open; Red Army tankers bailed out. The attack had been thwarted . . . for the time being. Another fuel truck appeared an hour later, but it was too late by then to consider pursuing the scattered enemy.

Once the tanks were refueled, *Hauptmann* Tebbe moved out in the direction of Pustoschkin and Reshnikow. Both localities were taken. At 1400 hours, Tebbe decided to also advance on Manytschkaja. This attack had to be broken off in the face of extremely heavy defensive fire from the enemy, which especially affected the grenadiers who were following the tanks.

During the morning of 21 January, the battalion moved out again to attack Manytschkaja. This village, which is located at the confluence of the Manytsch and the Don, had been transformed by the Soviets into a heavily defended fortress in the meantime. Many T-34's were dug in up to their turrets. In addition to his tanks, *Generalmajor* von Schwerin had also committed all of *Panzergrenadier-Regiment 156* for this attack.

The tanks approached the village from the south and the southeast, closely followed by the grenadiers. The buildings along the southern edge of the village could be seen, when the tanks encountered a large tank ditch. *Leutnant* Gittermann submitted a situation report. A few seconds later, his tanks received devastating fire from antitank guns, antitank rifles and dug-in tanks.

Hauptmann Tebbe moved along the edge of the tank ditch, closely followed by *Leutnant* Gittermann. They wanted to find a "ford" through the ditch. Finally, Tebbe found a spot that had been flattened out through impacting artillery rounds. He rolled through the tank ditch. Gittermann followed right behind him. Both of the tanks then rolled into Manytschkaja, all guns blazing. Tebbe's tank received a direct hit there and was immobilized. The battalion commander and his crew had to dismount. As they were in the process of helping the wounded driver out, they heard a crashing sound. Gittermann's tank had also been hit.

They raced back towards their own forces, followed by fire from the Russians. They finally reached the forward outposts of the battalion.

"We can't get through the way we've been doing it!" Tebbe said later at the division command post. "We first have to silence the Russians' heavy weapons."

Early in the morning of 22 January 1943, the long-promised reinforcements for this sector arrived. The first element was the *III./Panzer-Regiment 15* of *Generalleutnant* Balck's *11. Panzer-Division.* The latter division had been sent via priority movement from the northern part of the Eastern Front. It was intended for the two divisions to eliminate the Soviet bridgehead at Manytschkaja.

Oberst Graf Schimmelmann, the commander of *Panzer-Regiment 15*, led the combined armored forces of the two divisions. A wild engagement ensued at the end of which *Graf* Schimmelmann sent the following radio message to his division headquarters: "Manytschkaja firmly in our hands. The enemy has been blown to bits!"

While *Panzer-Regiment 15* was carrying out this fight, *Panzer-Abteilung 116* led the secondary attack against Ussmann. The *1./Panzer-Abteilung 116* under *Oberleutnant* Schmidtchen advanced into Ussmann. Schmidtchen's vehicle received a direct hit from an antitank gun; he was killed instantly. The second tank into the village was also lost. Once again, it was not possible to achieve a breakthrough.

At this point, the tanks of the *3./Panzer-Abteilung 116* arrived. At the head of the pack in his "ride" was *Oberfeldwebel* Bunzel. Bunzel cleared a path by fire into the village. Then the entire company engaged the enemy. A tank from Bunzel's company was on fire in the middle of the village, but enemy tanks were also knocked out. Antitank guns were engaged and destroyed after they had succeeded in knocking out two more German tanks.

Hauptmann Wolff's grenadiers then arrived. They had mounted up on the tanks of Lechler's platoon. It was the grenadiers who turned the tide. They were able to move through the village and take out the last remaining pockets of resistance. By doing so, they successfully completed the mission of the division.

General Rotmistrow, the commanding general of the V Guards Mechanized Corps, reported the following to Colonel General Malinowski, the commander-in-chief of the 2nd Guards Army: "Based on the current situation and the high casualties sustained, out forces can no longer conduct active operations."

The V Guards Mechanized Corps had only 2,200 soldiers and seven tanks available to it. All of the brigade commanders had fallen in this battle of attrition for the bridgehead.

In the weeks that followed, *Hauptmann* Tebbe's tanks participated in the seesaw fighting. *Oberleutnant* Kühne and *Oberfeldwebel* Bunzel were bulwarks of the battalion in the fighting. *Panzer-Abteilung 116* lost tanks to enemy fire and mines. Its struggle in this sector was to keep open the gates to Rostow, through which the entire *1. Panzer-Armee* had to pass.

Hans Bunzel and his platoon continued to fight at Ssamodurowka and the group of hills at Ssidorkin, which were occupied by the enemy. It would lead us too far astray if all of the separate engagements of Hans Bunzel were described in detail.

✠

With an effective date of 1 February 1943, Hans Bunzel was promoted to *Leutnant* on 30 Apri 1943. On 27 March 1943, he was transferred to the battalion staff as a liaison officer. Staff work did not agree with this front-line soldier, and he quickly requested he be returned to his "home," the 3rd Company. By this time, everyone in the battalion knew who Hans Bunzel was. His name was inextricably linked with an irrepressible aggressiveness.

Hans Bunzel is awarded the Knight's Cross to the Iron Cross in the field in early 1943.

Leutnant Bunzel participated in hard defensive fighting along the Mius in the summer of 1943 and in that round of bitter fighting associated with Isjum and Slawjansk. It was the "old hands" who kept the battalion afloat and taught the younger replacements how to survive in combat.

It was during this round of fighting that the taciturn *Leutnant* from the Iser Mountain Range of Silesia knocked out no fewer than 10 tanks on one day between breakfast and noon. This was on 3 August 1943, when the Soviets attacked near Isjum with large forces. A pack of Soviet tanks broke into the positions of the division's grenadiers. *Leutnant* Bunzel and *Stabsfeldwebel* Schulze were on the scene immediately.

Heinrich Schulze, who was in the lead, knocked out the first 2 T-34's. But there were still 16 T-34's remaining that had been identified. Round after round headed down range towards the enemy from the two tanks. The enemy responded in kind against the two *Panzer IV's*.

Bunzel radioed to his friend: "Heinrich, let's pull back to the depression . . . we'll be safer there!"

"I'm on the way, Hans!"

They pulled back. When they reached the depression, they discovered that the clouds of dust and dirt churned up by the impacting rounds of the enemy obscured their vision.

"Damn, this won't work!" Schulze exclaimed.

"Then back into the last position!" Bunzel replied, even though he knew that the enemy must have gotten even closer in the meantime. He was counting on the surprise that this would bring to the enemy.

They rolled forward again. When the veils of dust and dirt had cleared, both Bunzel and Schulze saw the massed enemy tanks in front of them.

Stop . . . aim . . . fire . . . fire . . . fire! Within minutes, *Stabsfeldwebel* Schulze had knocked out 4 T-34's. Hans Bunzel maneuvered off to the side. His first round from the long-barreled *Panzer IV's* main gun proved deadly for the targeted T-34. He then took out a second one. Once again, he had to change positions. The entire engagement lasted only eight minutes. The last remaining T-34 moved out of a depression and showed his flank to Bunzel. From a distance of approximately 10 meters, Bunzel's gunner blew the turret clean off the enemy tank.

The outflanking maneuver that the Soviets had intended had been thwarted. *Stabsfeldwebel* Schulze had knocked out 10 tanks; Bunzel was credited with 6. This raised Bunzel's "kills" to a total of 25. In all, some 86 enemy tanks were knocked out by *Panzer-Abteilung 116* in the Isjum and Slawjansk areas. Hans Bunzel continued to fight with the battalion during the next few months with varying degrees of success. He was wounded once again, but he remained with his men.

In June 1943, the *16. Infanterie-Division (mot.)* was re-designated as the *16. Panzergrenadier-Division*. In 1944, the division was converted into an armored division and re-designated as the *116. Panzer-Division*. In May of that year, the former *Panzer-Abteilung 116* was sent to Grafenwöhr for new-equipment training on the *Panther*. *Panzer-Abteilung 116* was redesignated as the *I./Panzer-Regiment 16*. From there, the battalion was attached to *Panzer-Brigade 111*, where it was sent into the area of Lothringen as part of the *5. Panzer-Armee* and committed in the area of Dieuze. In the middle of October, the battalion was sent back to Grafenwöhr after having transferred its remaining *Panthers* to *Panzer-Regiment 15* of the *11. Panzer-Division*. From there, it rejoined the division in the area of Mönchengladbach at the end of November. Gerhard Tebbe, promoted to *Major* in the meantime, became the commander of the *Panther* battalion. The commander of the *Panzer IV* battalion, the *II./Panzer-Regiment 16*, was *Major* August *Graf* von Brühl, another very experienced armor commander. Von Brühl had been awarded the Knight's Cross on 3 November 1942 while serving as a *Hauptmann* and the commander of the *8./Panzer-Regiment 2*.

Graf von der Schulenburg bids farewell to some of his officers. From left to right: von der Schulenburg, Bunzel and *Hauptmann* Gerhard Tebbe.

At the beginning of the Ardennes offensive on 16 December 1944, the *116. Panzer-Division* advanced west from its assembly area around Prüm (in the Eifel Mountains). On the very next day, Hans Bunzel was knocked out for the 14th time, after he had advanced four kilometers with his company. He had engaged two tanks and two antitank guns, knocking out two of the guns and one of the tanks. The second tank got him, however.

As a result of this engagement, Hans Bunzel was wounded for the seventh time and lost his left eye. Despite the division's initial success, it was unable to reach its objective, the Our River along the border.

Hans Bunzel returned to his regiment from a military hospital on 16 February 1945. He had received the Wound Badge in Gold and was promoted to *Oberleutnant* on 20 March 1945, with an effective date of rank of 8 February 1945. He experienced the end of the war with his division in the western part of Germany. He was fortunate in being able to rejoin his family soon after the war ended.

✠

Hans Bunzel passed away on 12 November 1995 in Neukirchen (Heilug Bluth).

Generalleutnant Bayerlein, the commander of the most fully equipped armored division of the German Army, the *Panzer-Lehr-Division*, with two regimental commanders, *Oberst* Scholze and *Oberst* Gutmann. Bayerlein had been Rommel's chief-of-staff in North Africa. This image was taken in Normandy in 1944.

Oberleutnant Otto Carius wears a prewar summer-style field uniform after award of the Oak Leaves to the Knight's Cross to the Iron Cross. He was the youngest Oak Leaves recipient in the German Panzer Forces. Note that the postwar censor has erased the swastikas on the insignia and awards.

CHAPTER 3

Oberleutnant Otto Carius

**THE YOUNGEST OAK LEAVES RECIPIENT OF THE
GERMAN PANZER FORCES**

"Carius, I want you to screen out front with your tank."

Major Willy Jähde, the commander of *schwere Panzer-Abteilung 502 (Tiger)*, smiled when he issued the orders to the young, slender officer who had just reported to him. The narrow face and high forehead of the lieutenant had a thoughtful character to them, but Jähde knew that Carius could be tough as nails and that he could depend on him.

"Do you think the Russians have come through the marshes again, *Herr Major?*"

"There's no doubt. Our supply columns were engaged an hour ago. You need to move ahead by yourself. The rest of the company will follow shortly."

Leutnant Carius left the command post in Tschernowo and, a short while later, *Unteroffizier* Köstler, the driver of the tank, engaged the clutch. The *Tiger* moved out slowly.

Carius observed through his binoculars. The road in front of the tank climbed off to the right and disappeared behind a rise 2,000 meters ahead of him.

"The rest of the battalion is supposed to join us from there," Carius informed the gunner, *Unteroffizier* Clajus, a somewhat older tanker, who had joined the army while still a long-time "professional" student.

There was a sudden jolt in the tank. A noticeable clank told them that something was not right with the tracks. Carius had his crew dismount to check out the running gear.

The radio operator manned his station and Carius remained in the commander's hatch to observe, while the rest of the crew dismounted to see what was wrong. Köstler, as the driver, was in charge of fixing any running-gear problems.

Clajus called up from the ground: "There's our tanks, *Herr Leutnant!*" He pointed to the right, where the lead tanks appeared on the road on the rise.

"There's infantry mounted on them!" Carius countered, observing though his field glasses. Not two seconds later, he knew exactly what he was seeing, and it wasn't tanks from the battalion: "Ivan! Mount up!"

The men disappeared into their hatches in a flash. The Soviets appeared to take no notice of the single tank located off the side of the road. They continued their movement.

Carius was about to issue a fire command when Clajus fired. The round struck the T-34, which was barely 60 meters away, right between the turret and the hull. It turned off, smoking, into the ditch and remained there, motionless. The infantry that had been riding along jumped off and scattered to the four winds.

The 11 enemy tanks that followed started to panic. One drove into another. Several turned off. One of the T-34s directly approached the *Tiger*; that was a fatal mistake.

In quick succession, the rounds left the barrel of the deadly 8.8-centimeter main gun. The gunner and loader worked like machines: calculated, sure and in a steady rhythm. The turret would traverse first to the right, then to the left, seeking new victims for the main gun. Within the next three minutes, there were an additional four smoking hulks on the battlefield. The T-34's were no match for the *Tiger*, especially taken by surprise at point-blank range.

Of the 12 enemy tanks, only two escaped. Ten remained behind on the road, smoking and burning testimony to the awesome *Tiger* and its equally awesome main gun.

The enemy advance came to a standstill in that sector. It was not until the evening that Carius's tank was summoned back. The company had not been sent forward; there was no need for it there. Carius informed his crew that they would be moving out to conduct operations at Schelkunicha. The battalion commander had radioed instructions to him. The *Flak* that had arrived in the area would assume the screening mission.

The mission at Schelkunicha proved uneventful, and Carius was ordered back to the crossroads of his previous action two days later. When he returned, he was joined there by *Feldwebel* Dittmar's *Tiger* from the 3rd Company, as well as the 8.8-centimeter *Flak* already in position.

The Soviets arrived around noon. The two *Tigers* were near the road, when the Soviets arrived from the direction of Vitebsk. The Germans had buttoned up in anticipation of the fireworks. The Soviets approached from the southern high ground, where their main line of resistance was located, and moved north in the direction of Newel.

Carius issued orders to fire when ready.

Both of the tanks fired almost simultaneously. The first T-34 was hit and immobilized. A second one was hit by a round from the *Flak* and blew up. It took only five minutes for the engagement; at its end, there were five knocked-out and burning enemy tanks on the road.

Carius then decided to reconnoiter in the direction of the Soviet lines. Both of the tanks headed south. At the foot of the high ground, they encountered Soviet infantry, which engaged them with antitank rifles. Inside the tanks the rounds cracked against the hull as they sought vulnerable spots in the armor. If they struck the regular armor, there was no danger, of course, but a well-aimed round to a vision port could wreak havoc. Carius was able to determine that the Soviets had succeeded in bringing strong reinforcements forward through the marshland.

When it started to turn dusk, the two tanks returned to their former positions. Carius received orders by radio to take the village behind the high ground the next morning. He was supposed to be reinforced to do that. That night, two more *Tigers* came forward, as well as three self-propelled 2-centimeter quad *Flak*.

Just before first light, the small *Kampfgruppe* rolled out. It had received word that the infantry regiment, which was to follow it into the village and clear it out, was approaching.

The *Tigers* and the quad *Flak* rumbled through the darkness. Exposed in his hatch, Carius observed the terrain in front of him thorough his binoculars. Up to that point, not a round had been fired.

Köstler said the enemy must mistake them for one of their own. At that point, Carius decided to conduct a reconnaissance by fire: "Halt . . . open fire on the village! Do not fire left of the road!"

Rounds sped towards the village and slammed into the houses from the four main guns and the 12 combined 2-centimeter barrels of the *Flak*. Not replying, Soviet infantry tried to escape to the south. Finally, a Maxim machine gun opened up with a long burst.

In the excitement, one of the quad *Flak* fired to the left of the road. The wind coming from the east then blew the smoke from the fires and explosions across the line of sight of the attacking vehicles.

Carius had no choice left at that point: "Into the village!"

The four tanks rumbled forward and overran three antitank guns, before the enemy was able to get off a single round.

A few days later, the Soviets made preparations to retake the small village of Ssergeizewo. During the night of 14/15 November, they moved out with four tanks and infantry. All four of the enemy tanks were knocked out, thanks to the alert German defenses. The enemy broke off his attack.

On 23 November 1943, Carius was awarded the Iron Cross, First Class, for his role in the recent successful operations.

✠

Carius discussing operations with some of his tankers: *Unteroffizier* Kramer; *Feldwebel* Kerscher; *Stabsgefreiter* Hennig; *Obergefreiter* Lönneker and *Gefreiter* Wagner. Carius is seen wearing his non-regulation field cap, which he considered his lucky talisman.

During an advance on a Soviet strongpoint in December 1943, Carius's *Tiger* got stuck in a tank ditch, unable to budge. *Oberfeldwebel* Zwetti, a member of Carius's platoon, rolled forward to render assistance. Under a hail of mortar fire, the two tanks attached tow cables. While hooking up the cables, Carius was struck by shrapnel to the temple. Had it gone another centimeter, it would have been all over for the plucky tank commander.

"Pull the shrapnel out!" he told *Unteroffizier* Kramer, his new gunner. (Clajus had received a student deferment to return to school.) When Kramer pulled out the piece of metal, the wound started bleeding heavily. Zwetti applied a field dressing. Once that was done, the recovery operation commenced, and Carius's *Tiger* was pulled back to the German lines and out of danger.

At first light the next day, the two *Tigers* were able to cross the ditch on a bridge erected by the engineers during the night. They were then able to advance as far as the Soviet positions. The two antitank guns that were covering the mine obstacles were taken out by Zwetti. The Soviets started to engage the *Tigers* with more than a dozen antitank rifles. The rounds smacked against the steel walls of the tanks. In short order, none of the vision ports were intact.[1]

1. Editor's Note: All tanks carried several spare armored glass vision blocks for such an eventuality.

Carius ordered the tanks to engage the earthen wall ahead of them. He had a hunch there was something lurking there.

Both of the tanks opened fire on the designated target. Clumps of earth shot skywards after the impact of the high-explosive rounds. The Soviets countered with hand grenades. For some reason, no friendly infantry came forward. The cat-and-mouse game continued for several hours. All of a sudden, Zwetti radioed his platoon leader: "Oil or water under your vehicle!"

Carius had Köstler start up the engine. Carius's worst fears were soon realized. The engine temperature climbed to 110 degrees (230 Fahrenheit). The radiator had started to leak as a result of the antitank rifle and mortar fire. The tanks had no choice but to pull back. Both of them made it through the open terrain that was infested with mines and reached the hastily constructed engineer bridge. It sagged in the middle under the weight of the tanks, but both made it through. Soon both of the tanks were back to comparative safety in the marshland. Not all operations ended successfully, but through a combination of skill and luck, Carius's platoon suffered remarkably few casualties.

On 15 December, he received the Wound Badge in Silver. That was followed the next day by a successful attack along the Vitebsk-Newel road, which resulted in the destruction of several Soviet tanks. When Soviet fighter-bombers started to close in soon thereafter, Kramer traversed the turret in their direction, elevated the main gun, took hasty aim and fired. Amazingly enough, one of the fighter-bombers was hit in the wing, crashing a short distance behind the tank.

✠

Otto Carius was born on 27 May 1922 in Zweibrücken, the son of a school principal.[2] He attended college preparatory school there and received his diploma in March 1940. On 25 May 1940, he received his draft notice and was sent to *Infanterie-Ersatz-Bataillon 104* in Posen, where he celebrated his 18th birthday. He had originally requested assignment to the antitank branch, but was detailed as an infantryman, since there was no need for additional personnel at the time. When he was eventually assigned to Darmstadt, closer to his home, he had a stroke of luck. One day, his company commander asked for volunteers to become tankers. Carius was among the first to raise his hand.

2. Translator's Note: Carius' memoirs, *Tigers in the Mud*, are available through Stack-pole Books for the reader inclined to learn more about this highly decorated and successful officer.

He was sent to *Panzer-Ersatz-Abteilung 7* in Vaihingen (near Stuttgart), where he was once again relegated to the status of a recruit. His tank commander for initial training was *Unteroffizier* Dehler, and Carius was detailed as his loader. The battalion was equipped with captured Czech tanks, the Skoda medium tank armed with a 3.7-centimeter main gun, which the Germans re-designated as the *Panzer 38(t)*. Carius underwent tank gunnery at the main German gunnery range at Putlos in northern Germany. Carius was assigned to the 1st Company of *Panzer-Regiment 21*, the tank regiment of the newly formed *20. Panzer-Division*. The division was moved to the Ohrdruf Training Area shortly before the start of the campaign in the East.

At the start of the offensive on the morning of 22 June 1941, the tank forces of the *20. Panzer-Division* were arrayed in the woods southwest of Kalwarya. That same evening, they reached the city of Olita and its airfield, some 120 kilometers beyond the frontier.

That evening, Soviet fighter-bombers attacked the German positions. Everyone dove for cover. *Unteroffizier* Dehler could be heard cursing, when he discovered *Gefreiter* Carius had landed on his evening meal. The next day, Carius found himself busy loading the main gun; things had turned hot in the armored fighting around Olita. A crossing was then forced over the Njemen. The advance continued on Vilna, which was entered on 24 June.

Operations then continued in the direction of Minsk. On 8 July, Dehler's tank was in the lead. It crossed the Düna at Ulla on a pontoon bridge. Once on the far side of the river, it was engaged by Soviet forces arrayed along a wood line. As the tank approached the woods, there was a hard blow to its armor. A metallic crash, the cry of a comrade—that was all that Carius heard. The crew bailed out. As Carius crawled along a roadside ditch, he determined he was bleeding in the face. A couple of teeth were loose; three or four shards of steel were embedded in his skin. A Soviet 4.7-centimeter antitank gun round had entered the tank through the radio operator's position. The radio operator lost his left arm, and Carius had to have the damaged teeth removed at the main clearing station.

He hitchhiked his way back to his company the next day, which he reached outside of Vitebsk. A series of tough engagements followed, which were climaxed by the twin battles of Jelnja and Smolensk. On 1 August 1941, Carius was promoted to *Unteroffizier*.

Three days later, he received marching orders to Erlangen, the home of *Panzer-Ersatz- und Ausbildungs-Abteilung 25*. It was there that he was awarded his Armored Assault Badge in Silver. After undergoing driver's testing, he was detailed to an officer-candidate school in Wünsdorf (Berlin).

Although promoted to *Feldwebel*, he was informed on 1 February 1942 that he had not met "the standards of the class," along with two other comrades.

His section leader consoled him by saying he was sure he would achieve those goals at the front. Carius's section leader was *Major* Ernest Philipp, an experienced armor officer and a man whom the officer candidates revered, who had been awarded the Knight's Cross to the Iron Cross on 28 November for his actions in France as part of *Panzer-Regiment 1* of the *1. Panzer-Division.*

Once he returned to his regiment, he found it in winter fighting positions in the vicinity of Gshatsk. The regiment had lost almost all of its vehicles. Only one company still had tanks. When new tanks were received and the 10th Company was back at full strength, Carius was assigned to that company as a platoon leader. The defensive operations around Gshatsk and east of Viasma continued until the end of June. The division was then moved to Ssytschewka. Carius was reassigned to the regiment's headquarters company, where he became the regimental combat engineer platoon leader, learning more combat skills. Finally, on 14 November 1942, he was promoted to *Leutnant der Reserve.*

When his platoon was clearing mines in front of the lines one day, it received machine-gun and automatic weapons fire from the Soviet lines. Carius received a grazing wound to the hand. He remained with his soldiers. A short while later, he was transferred back to his old 1st Company. His former tank commander, August Dehler, had also become a platoon leader in the meantime.

In January 1943, Carius was scheduled to take home leave before a leave prohibition was levied. One day before his departure, Dehler was guiding a tank out of an icy dugout. While the tank was backing out up the incline, Dehler slipped on the ice and slid into the left track. Despite the cries of the crew and the driver stopping as soon as he could, the tank's track had advanced as far as Dehler's upper thigh. He was killed immediately. Carius had lost his best friend at the front.

While on home leave, Carius received orders transferring him to *Panzer-Ersatz-Abteilung 500* in Paderborn. He discovered that combat-experienced officers were being sent there to be trained on a new type of tank, the *Tiger.* The chief instructor was *Hauptmann* von Lüttichau.

Carius was assigned to the 2nd Training Company. After a short period of training in the Bretagne, his battalion, the newly formed *schwere Panzer-Abteilung 502*, was hastily dispatched on the feast of Corpus Christi to Gatschina on the Eastern Front. When the third battle of Lake Ladoga started, the battalion *Tigers* were rail-loaded again on 21 July and dispatched to Sniigri, a small rail station in the vicinity of Mga.

The 3rd Company was committed into action right from the railhead. By the time the 2nd Company had detrained, *Hauptmann* Oehme and *Leutnant* Grünewald of the 3rd Company had already been killed. Fighter-bombers fired on everything that moved, and the 2nd Company moved out into the witch's cauldron.

In the subsequent fighting at Ssinjawino, along the Masurian Route and at "Bunker" Village, important positions were retaken. During the defensive fighting in the area around Newel that was described at the beginning of this section, Carius distinguished himself.

When the *Tigers* of the battalion reached Gatschina, the train station was already receiving heavy Soviet artillery fire. The 1st Company, which had already been employed there, had sustained heavy casualties. It had been surrounded by the Soviets on a road. *Major* Jähde had wanted to wait to employ his battalion as a whole, but he had been given no other choice.

After the war, Carius told the author: "*Major* Jähde was the best commander we ever had in the 502nd. He was always an example to us on a personal level, because he also gave all for his men. He was always with us in critical situations. That's the way he was, and that's the way we will always remember him."

Gatschina was abandoned. Forces of *Heeresgruppe Nord* started to pull back long the Gatschina-Wolossowo-Narwa road. The *Tigers* formed the rear guard. When the Soviets surrounded the command post of a division in the vicinity of the transportation hub of Wolossowo, Carius immediately headed in that direction, punched a hole through the encircling forces and freed the headquarters. The division commander was the last one out, riding on Carius's tank.

Following that, Carius was entrusted with holding a blocking position at Opolje, along with an infantry battalion, until the withdrawal could be continued. His four *Tigers* were positioned along the southern edge of a patch of woods, while the infantry were located behind them. During the night, the infantry pulled back, leaving Carius and his *Tigers* all by themselves. Despite that, Carius held his ground and also knocked out two antitank guns. The situation became increasingly critical, however, and he waited anxiously for the order to withdraw to come from the battalion.

Towards morning, *Feldwebel* Wesely reported that his cooling system was leaking. A half hour later, the same misfortune visited another tank. When the order to withdraw finally came, the two stricken tanks had to be towed.

When it turned first light, the men saw a *Kübelwagen*[3] approaching them. It was *Major* Jähde, who could not bear the thought of remaining in the rear while he had tank crews exposed to the threat of being left behind.

---

3. Translator's Note: The *Kübelwagen* was the German equivalent of the jeep and, like the jeep, performed a variety of roles. There was also an amphibious version, known as the *Schwimmwagen*.

✠

In the Narwa sector, the *III. (germanisches) SS-Panzer-Korps* was entrusted with holding the bridgehead against increasingly stronger Soviet attacks. Carius was detailed to support one of the divisions, the *11. SS-Panzergrenadier-Division "Nordland."* He made his way to the headquarters to report to the division commander, *SS-Brigadeführer und Generalmajor der SS* Fritz von Scholz.[4] A converted bus served as the division's main command post. It was located not far from the main line of resistance along the river. In fact, it was as close to the front lines as the regimental command posts.

The commanding officer greeted the company-grade officer with a toast to a good working relationship. Following the *Schnaps,* the general briefed Carius on the situation: "I have established new bridgehead positions. Your mission is to assist the men up front to get to the best positions, which then need to be improved and held. Since the Russians in my division sector are only weak advance guard elements at present, it should not be all too difficult to hold them back and allow my men the time needed to improve their positions."

Carius knew the commander's intent and headed out to execute it. He set up his tank east of Narwa. South of the city, the front ran along the far side of the river up to the city limits, where it jumped across and ran west of the river until it emptied in the Baltic.

The tanks on the east side of the river line were threatened when the Soviets started to fire on the last remaining intact bridge capable of supporting the tanks. If the bridge spans were to be destroyed, the tanks would be caught in a trap. Carius briefed the general on the changed situation and requested permission to withdraw his platoon to the west side, which was granted.

Just as Carius was conducting his new mission, he ran into a staff car on the west bank of the river, which had a field-army command pennant on it. Getting out of the vehicle was the commander-in-chief, *Generalfeldmarschall* Model. Carius reported to him and briefed him on what he was doing. When he finished, it seemed as if the skies had opened up on him. He was given no chance to reply. He quickly mounted his tank and moved back to the east side of the river, the words of the field marshal still reverberating in his ears: "I am holding you personally responsible that no Russian tank breaks through!

---

4. Author's Note: Von Scholz , a former Austro-Hungarian artillery officer in World War I, transferred into the *SS-VT* from the Austrian *SS Legion* in 1934. He was a highly competent and decorated soldier. He was awarded the Swords to the Oak Leaves to the Knight's Cross of the Iron Cross posthumously on 8 August 1944. He was the 85th member of the German armed forces to be so honored. He was killed in the fighting along the Narwa sector on 28 July.

None of your tanks can be eliminated by enemy action! We need every single gun here!"

Carius's tanks soon knocked out four enemy antitank guns. The *SS* division was soon in its new positions, and the army tanks were withdrawn for use elsewhere.

✠

Carius rode in the staff car to Lembitu. He had been told to assume acting command from the company commander, who had taken ill.

The company commander was there with two tanks. The commander of the second tank was *Feldwebel* Albert Kerscher, one of the best tank commanders of the battalion.[5] The Soviets had established themselves south of the railway embankment at Lembitu, and the signs were growing ever more apparent that they intended to attack shortly. Up through 15 March 1944, there was a deceptive calm. On that day, Carius's tank was hit by a mortar round, causing battle damage to its running gear and rendering it immobile. Kerscher's tank had to tow it to the rear for repairs. The next day, two additional tanks were sent forward to replace the gap left by the departure of Carius.

Carius was able to effectively use the repair time to rest and recuperate. He was suffering from pleuropneumonia and frequent visits to a sauna helped. A day later, the company maintenance sergeant, *Oberfeldwebel* Delzeit, was finished with Carius's tank. Since the two replacement tanks were having mechanical problems in the meantime, Carius needed to return up front as soon as possible. The next day, Carius arrived back at his old position. Since it was quiet, he decided to get some sleep. That thought was soon rudely interrupted by Soviet barrage fire. The entire sector of the *61. Infanterie-Division* was under heavy fire from guns of all calibers. When the fires started shifting farther to the rear a half hour later, the crews were finally able to climb back aboard their vehicles and more forward.

As they moved forward, they soon encountered infantry soldiers without weapons. Vehicles streamed past the tanks to the rear. Another group of about 30 soldiers approached. Carius dismounted and ran over to them. He discovered that the Soviets had already started their attack and were rapidly approaching the road. Three strongpoints had already been abandoned.

Carius headed out as rapidly as he could to his designated strongpoint, closely followed by Kerscher. As he closed in, he saw a few tanks out in the open, followed by infantry. Carius ordered Kerscher to maneuver to the

---

5. Author's Note: He would later receive the Knight's Cross to the Iron Cross on 23 October 1944.

left. He had counted six enemy tanks approaching the embankment by that point.

While the *Feldwebel* moved to block the enemy force, Carius swung towards the five enemy antitank guns positioned along the railway embankment. They were threatening the flanks of the *Tigers* and, at the moment, their most dangerous opponent. He had already started to receive fire from them. He could hear a crash in his running gear. Then he could see the muzzle flashes of the guns.

Carius succeeded in putting all five guns out of commission. He had received several hits, but the rounds ricocheted off the thick armor of the heavy tank. While his gunner, *Unteroffizier* Kramer, was engaging the last antitank gun, Carius happened to look to his left. He saw a T-34 that had turned around and was heading for Kerscher.

Carius radioed: "Albert! There's a T-34 behind you!"

Kerscher had his vehicle turn around. The turret also started to traverse, and the first round from the long barrel of the main gun was a direct hit. The tank rolled into a shell crater, smoking, and did not come out.

The five remaining T-34's joined the fray. Carius's gunner worked quickly and methodically. His feet on the traversing pedals never had a chance to rest. The turret traversed right when he pressed forward; to the left when he pressed back with his heels. When it was all over, there were an additional five burning hulks on the battlefield.

The critical situation was not over, however. Between Lembitu and the place in the woods where the railway embankment disappeared, there was not a single German soldier to be seen. It was not until the afternoon that a machine gun on the right flank of the *Feldherrnhalle* Division started to fire again. The tanks were left to their own devices. It was thanks to Carius and the other tank that the Soviets had been prevented from breaking through into the rear of the *III. (germanisches) SS-Panzer-Korps* and the army elements in the Narwa bridgehead.

In the afternoon, the Soviets attacked for a second time. They advanced across the railway embankment again. The two *Tigers* knocked out five T-34's and a KV-I.

Carius reported to the battalion an hour and a half later that the Soviets were preparing for another attack from behind the embankment. Ten minutes later, a third *Tiger* was sent forward to their position as reinforcement to the tiny force. The Soviets moved out for the third time against the Germans with a battalion-sized force that included tank support. It took the loss of 3 T-34's before the Soviets called off their efforts.

Two hours before midnight, the three *Tigers* moved to the rear to resupply with rations, fuel and ammunition. Each *Tiger* needed 100 main-gun rounds and 200 liters of fuel. The company first sergeant, *Hauptfeldwebel* Sepp Rieger, passed on news from the company. Whenever an enemy tank was knocked out, he provided the men with a bottle of *Schnaps*.

Towards midnight, the tanks returned to their positions around the shot-up farmstead. Carius continued on to the location of the orphanage, the regimental command post of the infantry. He discussed counterattack options with the commander there. At 0500 hours, the three *Tigers* positioned themselves between Lembitu and Tirtsu to attack. An enemy-occupied ruin was retaken and two T-34's knocked out. At that point, the enemy started to return fire with heavy salvoes of artillery and mortars. The squad of grenadiers behind Carius's tank suffered two dead and two badly wounded. The men were evacuated; the attack on the second set of ruins had to be broken off, since there seemed to be no prospect of taking it.

When the Soviets then launched an immediate counterattack on the strongpoint and the farmstead, they lost 2 T-34's and one T-60 from the fires of the *Tigers*.

Despite their heavy losses, the Soviets did not give up their efforts to take the Narwa bridgehead. On 19 March 1944, they attacked again after an intense artillery preparation. Six T-34's and one T-60 were knocked out in front of Carius's positions. Despite that, they succeeded in entering the German main line of resistance. Before the German infantry could form up to launch their own immediate counterattack, Carius received a call for assistance. The infantry in a small patch of woods, where four Soviet assault guns and two T-34's had advanced and gone into position, were being engaged. The infantry was fearful of being overrun. Carius did not wait for orders: "Kerscher, follow me!"

The two tanks moved as quickly as they could in the direction of the Soviet positions. They started to receive main-gun rounds, which raced above their turrets. Maneuvering evasively, they reached a good firing position. The crews—well-oiled teams—fired rapidly and eliminated all of the enemy's assault guns and tanks in the advanced position. The infantry breathed a sigh of relief, a giant weight lifted from their shoulders. The two *Tigers* had saved them.

The young officer then turned his attention to the enemy's machine-gun positions and his infantry. In continuing to attack, Carius and Kerscher knocked out two more armored vehicles and temporarily brought relief to the sector. A day later, Kerscher eliminated 2 T-34's at Point 33.7. All of the Soviets attacks were turned back.

The next day, Gruber's tank bottomed out on a shell crater. During the effort to recover him, a 15-centimeter artillery round with delayed-action fuse hit the driver's hatch of Carius's vehicle. The radio operator was badly wounded in both arms, and his left lower leg was torn off.

In the period between 17 and 22 March, Carius's three tanks knocked out 38 Soviet tanks, 4 assault guns and 17 artillery pieces. His company received a by-name mention in the Armed Forces Daily Report of 21 March. Carius, who was largely responsible for the company's success, was submitted for the Knight's Cross to the Iron Cross.

✠

At the end of March, the tanks were withdrawn from the sector of the *61. Infanterie-Division.* They were held back for an operation designed to reduce the Soviet salients into the German lines referred to as the east and west "sacks." The commander of the *ad hoc* force was *Oberst* Strachwitz, a dashing and highly decorated armor commander, who had previously commanded the tank regiment of *Panzergrenadier-Division "Großdeutschland,"* the army's premier armored division. The battalion assembled in Sillimä, where it alternately rested and trained for the upcoming operation.

Carius enjoyed the respite enormously. He was able to listen to music, and he won the companionship of the company mascot, a German shepherd named Hasso. The dog accompanied the sprightly officer everywhere. At night, he would sleep at Carius's feet.

The first operation, which resulted in the recapture of the west "sack," did not see any participation by Carius's tanks. The *Tigers* were too heavy for the sector of the attack; *Panzer IV's* from the *Großdeutschland* and *Feldherrnhalle* formations were used. Strachwitz summoned Carius for the discussions on the taking of the east "sack," however.

Carius's platoon assaulted in the first wave on 6 April. The lead tank was commanded by *Feldwebel* Kerscher. Carius followed him, with Gruber and then Zwetti bringing up the rear. The German artillery preparation started 15 minutes before the tanks moved out. Heavy weapons of all calibers in the front lines participated. Farther to the rear, a *Nebelwerfer* regiment fired in support, first using flame-oil rockets, followed by high explosive.

Huge flames arose from the enemy's positions and singed the upper branches of the trees. When the 28-centimeter howitzers started up, the tanks moved out and headed under the shifting barrage towards the railway embankment.

On the far side of the railway crossing, the tanks turned and rolled along the embankment. Seven antitank guns were knocked out. All of a sudden, Carius's *Tiger* was struck from behind. Gruber's tank was hit in the running

The impressive view as a *Tiger* moves forward.

gear, immobilizing him. Gruber's tank was struck again by a Soviet antitank gun that was skillfully positioned in the woods. The round penetrated Gruber's turret, wounding him and his loader. Zwetti was able to take out the enemy antitank gun. He then recovered the stricken vehicle and pulled it to safety in the rear.

Despite the misfortune, the attack objective was reached and the east "sack" eliminated.

On 15 April, Carius was again summoned to an orders conference with *Oberst* Strachwitz. The next operation was to eliminate what remained of the Soviet bridgehead on the German side of the Narwa. While the Count was discussing his plan, his adjutant entered the briefing room. "What do you need?" Strachwitz asked impatiently.

The officer came to attention. *"Herr Graf,* it was announced in the news that the *Führer* had awarded *Herr Graf* [6] the Diamonds to the Knight's Cross. May I be the first to congratulate you?"

The Count dismissed him. He stated the radio was not official channels and that he no longer wished to be disturbed.

✠

Early on 19 April, the attack took its intermediate objective, a marshy ditch, whereupon Strachwitz halted his force. Strachwitz announced the attack would be continued the following day. During the night, combat engineers leveled the ditch so that the *Tigers* could cross.

When the *Nebelwerfer* regiment opened fire in support on the morning of 20 April, its rounds landed too short and hit the German positions. Terrible detonations shook the earth. Tank hatches popped open due to the

---

6. Translator's Note: It was standard German practice to address superior officers in the third person.

tremendous concussive effect. In desperation, Carius radioed for the firing to stop. But the preparation continued for the full five minutes that had been planned. The nearby infantry battalion was decimated. Almost all of its men were wounded, killed or otherwise incapacitated.

Carius then crossed the ditch with his *Tigers*, so as to cover the evacuation of the wounded. At the same time, he received orders from the Count to continue the advance on Point 312. The Count assured him that a new battalion of infantry would be brought forward.

Just as Carius wanted to light up a cigarette and bent over so his gunner could give him a light, a terrific blow was felt against the tank. The tank commander's cupola was sheared off. Carius felt the stabbing pain of white-hot shrapnel against his temples and face. Blood flowed across his chin, but he was not seriously wounded. Had he not bent forward at that instant, he would have been decapitated.

A short while later, the offending Soviet assault gun was identified. When Kramer, who had come forward with his *Tiger* in the meantime, fired, his gunner hit it with his first round. Unfortunately, there was a second assault gun, which then opened fired against Carius as well. Its round struck between the hull and the turret. Carius ordered his crew to bail out.

A few seconds later, Carius and his crew were outside and climbing aboard another *Tiger*. Carius ordered his tanks to pull back to the tank ditch. One of his tanks went up in flames from another direct hit; its crew was unwounded, but it had to be pushed off the road and into the marshland.

The third Strachwitz operation ended with the loss of all four of the lead tanks of the operation. The ground was unsuited for tanks, and the Soviets knew exactly where the Germans would attack. Although Strachwitz failed in his third attempt, his overall operations significantly delayed Soviet offensive intentions in the area and bought the Germans considerable breathing room.

✠

At the end of April, the company received orders to move to Pleskau. The battalion had received a new commander, *Major* Schwaner, and Carius met him for the first time. On 4 May, Carius was awarded the Knight's Cross for the decisive role he had played in the operations in the Narwa bridgehead. He was then granted convalescent leave for four weeks, since he was suffering from asthma. But he was only home for five days when he was summoned back to the front.

Once there, he was immediately committed to combat operations again. In his first attack, he lost all of his *Tigers*, with the exception of his own. During the night, two of the tanks could be recovered, but the *Tiger* of *Feldwebel* Wessely had to be abandoned, since a Soviet patrol had taken it. Despite the loss of the vehicles, the main line of resistance was retaken.

On 15 July, Carius and his platoon were sent to the sector of the *270. Infanterie-Division*, to which they had been attached in support. He was ordered to screen in the vicinity of Maruga. A few days later, fighting erupted that Carius would remember for the rest of his life.

During the night of 19/20 July, reports filtered in that the Soviets had attacked in the sector of the infantry division and broken through. It was reported that they were advancing on the Dünaburg-Rossitten road with some 90 to 100 tanks. Carius, who had been designated an acting company commander, moved out with his operational tanks. Around 1100 hours, they reached the railway bridge over the Düna. Two *Tigers* joined the six Carius already had. Carius's 2nd Company then resupplied at the battalion logistics point in the cemetery west of the road about five kilometers northeast of Dünaburg. *Oberleutnant* Bölter's 1st Company was already moving out.[7]

"Take your time, Otto!" Bölter called out to his friend in jest. "By the time you come, we'll have taken care of everything!"

By noon, Carius's vehicles had been resupplied and were headed on the road east towards Polozk. The hot summer son bore down relentlessly on the steel boxes, practically roasting the men inside. All of a sudden, Carius heard the sound of fighting to the north.

"Kerscher, did you hear that?" Carius radioed.

"Firing, *Herr Leutnant* . . . main guns!"

"Let's get in the *Kübelwagen* and check it out."

Together with Kerscher, Carius headed off in the direction of the sound of the fighting. What he saw had him soon gasping for breath. He saw nothing but headless flight along the Dünaburg-Rossitten road to the southwest. Trucks, staff cars and motorcycles were intertwined. All of the vehicles packed to the rafters. Nobody stopped anywhere. Finally, they caught up with a *Feldwebel* who was wheezing as he made his way through the roadside ditch. He reported that the Soviets had broken through and had entered the village in front of them.

The tankers then moved in the direction of the village. They encountered an officer from an assault gun brigade there. His brigade was positioned north of Krivani. In the attempt to break out to the south, the brigade had

---

7. Author's Note: Bölter (19 February 1915–16 September 1987) was another highly successful tank commander, platoon leader and, ultimately, company commander within the ranks of *schwere Panzer-Abteilung 502*. Like Carius, he was also destined to receive the Oak Leaves to the Knight's Cross of the Iron Cross (581st recipient on 10 September 1944).

lost seven guns. The officer had been sent to try to get some someone to hack the formation out.

"Get back to your unit," Carius told the other officer. "We'll get you out within the next two hours!"

Carius then had his company move up to the village. On the high ground outside of Krivani, he discussed his plan with his platoon leaders and commanders. He wanted two tanks to move into the village at full speed, surprising the Soviets. He did not to give them any chance to fire. *Leutnant* Nienstedt was to bring the remaining six tanks forward, but only as far as a reverse-slope position, where they were to await further orders. Carius said: "Nienstedt, it's your first operation with us. One thing is paramount: Everything will work if you'll only wait. The first two tanks will be Kerscher and I. Everything clear?"

Radio communications were checked one more time and then the engines fired up. Both of the *Tigers* rumbled off. They came into observation range of the Soviets, but not a shot was fired. Carius moved as far as the center of the village. Kerscher followed close behind. Everything took place in a matter of seconds. When Kerscher saw that two T-34's were swinging their turrets in the direction of Carius, he fired. The single round went though both tanks, knocking them out. In the meantime, Carius had continued on to the end of the village, where he encountered the newly introduced heavy Soviet tank, the Josef Stalin. Carius directed his gunner to fire at the closest tank, which was broadside to them along a barn.

The huge vehicle started burning after the second round. With its 12.2-centimeter main gun and muzzle brake, it resembled the German *Königstiger*. Other tanks were engaged. Most of the crews, surprised by the sudden appearance of the Germans, simply abandoned their vehicles. At that point, Carius ordered his tank to move out to engage the soft-skinned vehicles.

The ammunition vehicles soon went up with ear-deafening roars. Other trucks were set alight or peppered with machine-gun fire. The sounds of battle reverberated in the men's ears.

"Nienstedt, come over the rise!"

Only two enemy tanks succeeded in escaping. The company assembled in the village, with three tanks screening from the outskirts to the east. The motorcycle and sidecar of the brigade commander of the assault gun brigade came racing up. Carius had opened the path for the assault guns, as he had promised. In the meantime, the knocked-out tanks were counted: 17 Stalins and 5 T-34's. The Soviet tanks were from the elite "Josef Stalin" 1st Tank Brigade. The brigade had formed the iron fist of the Soviet assault force. The

Soviets that followed were still unaware of the fate that had befallen their brethren.

Carius had six of his tanks set up in a swell in the ground that allowed them to control the approach road. He climbed aboard *Feldwebel* Kerscher's tank, which was positioned a bit off to the side, since he left his own tank behind as part of the covering force. Where it was positioned, it did not need a tank commander in order to effectively engage. The road could be clearly observed for a distance of about three kilometers.

The men then awaited the arrival of the Soviet main body. Carius picked up clouds of smoke and dust through his binoculars, and told his men to stand by to engage the approaching force. The Soviet tanks neared the village. The main guns were locked in the travel position, and infantry road on the back decks, seemingly unconcerned. Moving with the tanks were the trains. The entire force looked like it was on parade. Carius waited until the Soviets approached and entered the killing zone.

"Fire!"

What followed next was a horrific spectacle. Carius dismounted in order to be able to see and direct fires better. He called out his commands through the ground intercom system, and the orders were relayed by radio to the other tanks. Round after round was fired. Fuel trucks went up in gigantic fireballs; tanks were immobilized, knocked out and destroyed; ammunition trucks blew up in horrific fireworks displays. The *Tigers* gradually stopped firing. The Soviet column was a sea of flames.

Then it was all over. Occasionally, a turret would be lifted off of its race by exploding ammunition, some landing several meters from the hull. Carius counted 28 knocked-out, burning and smoldering tank hulks. The scene among the Soviets was complete chaos.

Carius went back to the battalion command post, which was located near the command post of the *270. Infanterie-Division. Major* Schwaner congratulated Carius on his decisive success, which had cost the enemy 49 tanks that day. The "Josef Stalin" brigade had been wiped out in its first combat operation. The elimination of the Soviet lead elements was of critical importance, not only for the *270. Infanterie-Division*, but also for all of the other formations north and northeast of Dünaburg. Without the decisive actions of Carius's company, it could have been a disaster for the Germans, resulting in heavy casualties.

✠

On 24 July, *Leutnant* Carius headed along a field path from Dünaburg to the northwest in a motorcycle with a sidecar. He wanted to reconnoiter from some high ground. There was a farmstead in front of the men. Carius was looking at his map, when Lokey, his driver, called out: "Russians in the farm!"

They started to receive fire.

Carius ordered Lokey to turn around. In the effort, Lokey stalled the Zündapp 700-series motorcycle.

The men jumped out. Lokey was able to reach the roadside ditch safely in the hail of Soviet fire. A round shattered Carius's upper thigh, however.

The men then tried to crawl back towards the German lines. Carius's strength soon left him.

"Take off and get *Leutnant* Eichhorn, Lokey!"

"I'm staying here, *Herr Leutnant!*"

Lokey could not be ordered otherwise. They continued to crawl back. The Soviets fired whenever they exposed themselves. They were also rapidly closing in on the two. Finally, they reached the roadside ditch.

They fired from a distance and Lokey received a grazing wound to his upper left arm and another four rounds in his back. The men remained motionless. The Soviet firing stopped, and everyone suddenly heard the sound of tanks. The Soviets continued to approach. The two tankers were staring death in the face. Carius turned to face the Soviets three meters away. The officer in the middle shouted: "*Ruki werch!*—Hands up!"

The two soldiers with the officer trained their submachine guns on Carius. Then, Germans tanks rounded the corner, causing the Soviet soldiers to disappear in a flash. The Soviet officer remained and raised his pistol. At the same moment, Carius turned to face the advancing German tanks. As a result of that movement, the one round of the three fired did not mortally wound Carius when it struck. It passed through his throat next to the spinal column without hitting the artery. The other two rounds missed.

The *Tigers* got nearer. *Leutnant* Eichhorn was in the first vehicle. He continued moving up the road to provide cover. *Oberfeldwebel* Göring stopped next to the wounded men. Carius suddenly felt safe as *Stabsgefreiter* Marwitz, Göring's loader, sprung out of the tank and landed next to the two wounded men in the ditch. Using his suspenders, Marwitz applied a tourniquet.

Oberleutnant Wolf, the leader of the battalion's scout platoon, evacuated Carius and Lokey. Wolf held the head of the badly wounded company commander in his lap. He did not think that his comrade would reach the hospital alive. But Carius, ever tough, survived the trip. The next day, *Major* Schwaner appeared at the main clearing station. The battalion adjutant informed Carius that he had been recommended for the Oak Leaves to the Knight's Cross. Two days later, Carius was evacuated to Reval. He was then shipped out to Swinemünde and then taken by hospital train to Linden an der Ems.

On 27 July 1944, Carius read in the newspaper that he was the 535th member of the German Armed Forces to be honored with the Oak Leaves. On 5 August, he was promoted to *Oberleutnant der Reserve*. On 11 September 1944 Carius was made a regular *Oberleutnant* with seniority back to 1 August 1944. Based on his requests, *Feldwebel* Kerscher and *Unteroffizier* Kramer were awarded the Knight's Cross to the Iron Cross; *Oberfeldwebel* Göring was awarded the German Cross in Gold.

In the middle of September, Carius made his first efforts to walk. He soon received the third level of the Tank Assault Badge for having participated in 75 or more separate armored engagements. The hospital commander also presented him with the Wound Badge in Gold.

But that was not the end of the war for the plucky officer. From 2 January to 11 February 1945, he was at the *Tiger* Replacement Battalion in Paderborn. At the end of a course of instruction, he assumed command of a *Jagdtiger* company in *schwere Jagdpanzer-Abteilung 512.*[8] *Hauptmann* Scherff was the battalion commander. Carius was committed with his 10 *Jagdtiger* tank destroyers in the fighting in the Ruhr Pocket. On 21 April, Carius received the fourth and highest level of the Tank Assault Badge, signifying 100 or more separate armored engagements. Carius went into captivity in the vicinity of Iserlohn, but he was soon released.

✠

From 1947 to 1949, Carius got his start in pharmacy as an apprentice. After additional testing, he served in Freiburg (Breisgau) in a pharmacy until 1952. In 1956, he was fully licensed and opened a pharmacy in Herschweiler-Pettersheim, which he dubbed the *Tiger* Pharmacy. Although officially retired, Carius continues to direct the activities of his pharmacy to this day and delight in the numerous inquiries he receives from history buffs around the world, who never seem to tire of his exploits as a tank commander.

---

8. Translator's Note: The *Jagdtiger* was the tank destroyer version of the *Tiger*. It was outfitted with a 12.8-centimeter main gun in a fixed superstructure and a gun mantel that allowed limited traverse.

The diminutive Carius in the commander's hatch of his *Tiger*.

The formidable, but somewhat ponderous, *Jagdtiger*.

Major Hans-Detloff von Cossel as a Knight's Cross to the Iron Cross recipient.

CHAPTER 4

Major Hans-Detloff von Cossel

BLACK HUSSARS IN THE LEAD

"The 1st Battalion takes the lead, the 2nd follows close behind!"

Oberstleutnant Eberbach had reached the bridge the engineers had constructed over the Marne with his *Panzer-Regiment 35.* The regiment started to cross the river. The *4. Panzer-Division* had been ordered to pursue the withdrawing enemy. The enemy was to be hounded without respite until he surrendered.

The first light tanks that crossed almost got stuck in the marshy terrain on the far bank. As a precautionary measure, the motorcycles had been loaded on the rear decks of the tanks; otherwise, they would not have been able to make it through. The thunder of cannon in the distance told the tankers where the French had to be. The division continued its advance. It had already defeated the enemy at Merdrop in its first large-scale armored engagement (see the chapter on Eberbach). It had also forced a crossing over the enemy positions along the Dyle that were part of the Weygand Line.

At the head of the column of the 6th Company was its commander, *Oberleutnant* von Cossel. Von Cossel stood in the commander's hatch and intently observed the terrain to his front, where the 1st Battalion was halting. A glance at his watch told him it was 0800 hours. Orders soon reached them from the battalion commander, *Hauptmann Freiherr* von Jungenfeld, that the 2nd Battalion was also to halt. It was to resupply after the strenuous night march.

Von Cossel's tanks went into a tactical halt. The tankers dismounted, stretched and took it easy while awaiting the resupply vehicles. After a short while, the fuel trucks arrived, and the men started to refuel, one 20-liter fuel can at a time. After half an hour, they were finished and ready to continue the march. Von Cossel was summoned to the battalion commander's location.

"Cossel," the battalion commander started, "I'm giving you and the 6th a special mission. Advancing rapidly, you have to cover the left flank of the division. Can you handle that?"

"Of course, *Herr Hauptmann!*" The blue eyes on the narrow face of the officer were beaming. Von Cossel, who had entered the army as a horse cavalryman, thought it a perfect mission.

"Move as far as Montmirail, past the division, and then head left, until you reach this village," the commander said, pointing to a spot on the map.

Three minutes later, the 6th Company raced ahead of the rest of the battalion, which had also started to move out. Von Cossel waved to his comrades as he passed. He saluted when he saw the vehicle of the regimental commander at the head of the column. *Oberstleutnant* Eberbach returned the salute.

When the 6th Company reached Montmirail, it was in front of the division. Before turning off to the left, von Cossel observed the terrain ahead of him through his binoculars. The enemy could not be seen and, yet, he had to be out there, not too far in front.

They continued on and approached the village that von Jungenfeld had designated as their objective.

"Something just doesn't seem right, Beckmann," the *Oberleutnant* said to one of his company officers, as he set his binoculars aside. "I think there's something going on on the other side of the village."

"We should stay here and not allow ourselves to become engaged, *Herr Oberleutnant!*" *Leutnant* Beckmann replied with a mischievous grin on his face. He could read his commander well and anticipated his next order.

"We need to check it out. How are radio comms with the regiment or division?"

"We're no longer getting through, *Herr Oberleutnant*. The radio signal is too weak."

"Very well, then! We'll move through the village."

The company commander ordered his men to get ready for battle when they had approached to within 800 meters of the village. The tank commanders slammed their hatches shut. The loaders and gunners made their final checks. The vehicle weapons swung in the direction of the village.

They were 400 meters from the outskirts of the village, when they suddenly started to receive machine-gun fire. Then the tankers started receiving artillery fire, with the first shells rushing over and exploding near the tanks.

"Deploy and advance!"

Von Cossel steered straight for the middle of the village in his command tank. The rounds from his 3.7-centimter main gun on his *Panzer III* slammed into buildings in the locality. All of a sudden, a French armored car appeared, trying to make an escape. The vehicle next to von Cossel opened fire. Its second round hit the armored car. Flames shot out of its rear deck. The vehicle careered to the right and slammed into the wall of a house. The remnants of the wall still standing began to shower down on the stricken vehicle.

The tanks continued moving into and through the village. Wherever the enemy had established himself and tried to engage the Germans, he was eliminated by well-aimed tank fire. The 6th Company rattled through the streets of the village. The buildings were cleared by the combat engineers, who had mounted up as part of the small screening force.

Von Cossel ordered his men to continue the advance to the high ground on the far side of the village. From there, he believed he would be in a good position to successfully execute the mission his battalion commander had given him.

Von Cossel moved with the lead tanks of his company to the high ground. Once up there, however, he could scarcely believe his eyes: About 600 meters in front of him in the depression was a road crossing their axis of advance and—as far as his eyes could see—there was nothing but enemy vehicular columns! Everything—horse-drawn and motorized vehicles—then seemed to turn at once towards the high ground the Germans were on. They wanted to take the hill, which they assumed was still unoccupied, and go into position in order to engage the enemy that they had not seen but had already heard from the previous fighting in the village. Von Cossel's loader called out: "Look . . . armored cars . . . tanks over to the right!"

Von Cossel coolly issued a fire command to his entire company, which had since closed on the high ground and assumed preliminary fighting positions.

"At my command . . . fire!"

Streams of lead and steel soon poured down on the unsuspecting enemy from all of the main guns and machine guns of the 6th Company. Main-gun rounds slammed into the approaching armored cars and brought them to a halt. Three vehicles quickly caught fire, thick, oily smoke rapidly rising skyward.

For someone who was not there, a description of the scene would border on the fantastic. Sheer chaos erupted, with soldiers and vehicles madly dashing about to escape the withering fires. Trucks sprouted huge fireballs when the ammunition they were carrying caught fire and exploded with a mighty roar. Two vehicles ran into each other at top speed when they attempted to get off the road as quickly as possible.

The machine guns and main guns of the 6th Company continued their deadly harvest. They simply had to traverse in one direction or the other. It was as though they were on a gunnery range.

Suddenly, one of the *Panzers* reported enemy tanks in the patch of woods off to the company's right. Von Cossel ordered Ussath's and Bergmann's tanks—the company's heavy section with two of the infrequently encountered *Panzer IV's* with a short 7.5-centimeter main gun—to engage the enemy armor. He told the "heavy" tanks to wait until the enemy had closed within 400 meters to engage.

As instructed, the two tanks waited until the enemy was about 400 meters distant before they opened fire. After the third round, the one enemy tank on the left was blazing like a torch. The crew bailed out. The second enemy tank turned around and moved at speed for the protective concealment of the woods from which it had come. It disappeared into relative safety.

Von Cossel ordered the company to improve its defensive positions and assume a wider interval between vehicles. He summoned Pikra, as *Oberleutnant* Krause, the leader of the combat engineers, was known.

"Lay mines down there on the road in front of us."

The engineers went to work. Von Cossel had accomplished his mission in a singular fashion.

✠

While the battles of attrition were waging on the Western Front in World War I, Detloff von Cossel was born on 1 July 1916 in German Southwest Africa. He and his twin sister were born in an internment camp, the offspring of Elizabeth and Detloff, a *Hauptmann* in the *Kaiser's* Colonial Forces. The young Detloff was deeply influenced by his father, who had lost everything in Southwest Africa during the war. It was only by dint of hard work and an unshakeable will that he succeeded in reestablishing himself in the Uckermark province of postwar Germany. As a youth, Detloff wanted to be a soldier. As soon as he turned 18 in 1934, he joined *Reiter-Regiment 6*. He was commissioned an officer on 1 April 1937. On 1 September 1938, when *Panzer-Regiment 35* was formed in Bamberg as the tank regiment of the *4. Panzer-Division*, von Cossel was there. It was there that the young officer became familiar with the "father" of the regiment, Heinrich Eberbach, who would serve as a continuous example to von Cossel over the course of three campaigns.

Just before the war started, von Cossel was promoted to *Oberleutnant* and given command of the 6th Company. He participated in the campaign in Poland, earning his baptism of fire. He was in the lead in the race to Warsaw. During the decisive fighting along the Bzura, he demonstrated élan and aggressiveness. His bravery was rewarded with both classes of the Iron Cross. He was also wounded for the first time.

Barely healed, he rolled with his company into France. Armentières was taken in a night attack. That was followed by the capture of the bridges over the Seine at Romilly and the advance on Dijon. At the time of the ceasefire, he was located along the Isère.

✠

The campaign in the Soviet Union signaled the decisive moment in the young officer's life. It was there that he advanced to the peak of his professional prowess.

The regiment reached the Stalin Line at Stary Bychow at the beginning of July 1941 by advancing through Baranowitschi. By then, von Cossel had been given command of the regiment's 1st Company. *Oberst* Eberbach, since promoted and given brigade command, had received the mission of advancing into the enemy lines, taking Stray Bychow and securing the bridges over the Dnjepr.

During the early-morning hours of 4 July, von Cossel moved out with his company. As a result of the bad roads, more and more tanks broke down or got stuck in the marshlands to either side. Von Cossel drove on the tanks that remained. Finally, after the tortuous advance, some houses surfaced in front of the men. Behind them was the silvery band of the Dnjepr.

"That must be Stray Bychow . . . we're attacking!"

The six tanks were greeted by fire. They replied with their main guns, mostly 5-centimeter tank cannon. Some of the wooden structures started to go up in flames.

Von Cossel guided his gunner into some targets: "Enemy AT on the road, just a finger to the right of the house!"

"Identified!" Two seconds later, the main gun reported, and one of the antitank guns fell silent. A few seconds later, however, the men in the tank also heard a dull crack near them.

One of the tank commanders reported: "Hit in the turret race . . . two wounded . . . tank non-operational, *Herr Oberleutnant!*"

"Holthusen, bail out and make your way back!"

Von Cossel's gunner knocked out the other antitank gun with his next few rounds.

Von Cossel ordered his tanks to advance to the river at full speed.

The five tanks rattled through a burning Stary Bychow. There were flames all around them. The enemy started firing artillery on the advancing tanks. Shells impacted all around them. The concussions seemed to swat the tanks back and forth. Von Cossel's tank reached the wooden bridge. A shell impacted into the bridge 10 meters ahead of him and tore out a section of the railing.

"Faster . . . faster . . . we need to get over as soon as possible!"

The first vehicle reached the far side of the river in the artillery fire, which was getting more intense by the minute. He sought cover by a slope. The next one then attempted to cross; it also made it over. It was then followed by the three remaining operational tanks. The remaining tanks had barely taken up concealed positions along the reverse slope, when three mighty detonations

Tankers of the *11. Panzer-Division* enjoy a break in the action.

shook the earth and raised the bridge off of its pilings. The span collapsed into the river.

"Man, that was close!" *Leutnant* Hintze exclaimed, after the smoke from the demolition had cleared. "Now we're here all by ourselves and cut off, *Herr Oberleutnant!*"

"Send a question to the regiment, Sparks: Should we continue to advance?"

The radio operator began to tap out the Morse code. He received a reply to wait. A minute later, the answer came through: "Continue to advance, Cossel. Mission important!"

When the tanks began to leave the protective blind they were in, they started to receive fires from dozens of Soviet field pieces positioned along the Stalin Line. Whenever the enemy could be identified, the tanks replied in kind. They eliminated bunkers, fighting positions and other field fortifications. With a thunderous crack, one of the five tanks flew into the air after a direct hit. Not a single man of the crew emerged from the steel coffin. Soon, there was a crack against the command tank as well. A round had hit the right side of the hull. Fortunately for the crew, it ricocheted skywards. A few seconds later, the next tank reported it had received a direct hit. While the tank commander ordered his crew to bail out, the third tank also received a hit, setting it ablaze.

Von Cossel instructed his driver to start evasive movements. It was also to no avail. In the middle of a turn, a round slammed into the superstructure. The driver, Zünkley, was killed immediately. Von Cossel was slightly wounded. Before he could issue another order, however, the tank was again struck by a mighty blow.

Von Cossel ordered his surviving crew to bail out.

The man jumped out of the stricken tank. They were pursued by bursts of machine-gun fire. They were able to take cover in an abandoned Soviet dugout, which they had only just overrun a few minutes previously. When they crawled inside, they found another four tankers of the company. That was all that remained of the company on that side of the river.

"Ivan's coming!" someone yelled out.

"What in the world . . . "

The *Feldwebel*, who had also bailed out with von Cossel, pointed in horror to two tankers who ran towards a group of Soviets with raised hands. When they reached the Soviet position, the Soviets started beating them with entrenching tools, killing them. Von Cossel ordered his men to take the small group of Soviets under fire. The tankers only had their small arms and a submachine gun. Nevertheless, the Soviets took cover and then disappeared.

When the firing ceased, von Cossel looked around in the cramped quarters. There were seven men there. Artillery started to be registered in their general area. Von Cossel attempted to calm the men's nerves by telling them they were receiving friendly artillery fire in support.

Silently, the officer expected hand grenades to be tossed into the dugout at any moment. But nothing of the sort happened. Von Cossel wondered to himself: had they pulled back under the artillery fire? Had they been ordered to return to their unit? What had happened? Even more ominously: What would happen to them?

A thunderous impact suddenly turned everything dark. Earth came cascading down on the men. The beams holding up the earthen ceiling of the bunker started to bend dangerously—but they held up under the pressure.

"We've been buried, *Herr Oberleutnant!*" One of the men cried out, horrified.

"Keep calm! . . . We'll get out of here! Now that we're buried, we don't have to worry about the Russian searching for us. We just have to wait for the regiment to arrive!"

The men held out in the covered dugout for 36 hours. Only a small opening kept on feeding air to the men. Even von Cossel's patience had an end, however. When he noticed they were about to spend their second night in the hole, he announced: "Let's go to work and dig our way out! We're not going to wait any longer!"

Using a bayonet and their hands, the men widened the air shaft that had been keeping them alive. Finally, at 0330 hours, the hole was large enough for them to slip through.

The night was illuminated by the moon. They crawled back in the direction of the river. Practically dehydrated, they took whatever moisture they could get from the blades of grass. All of a sudden, the Soviets got wind of the movement. Submachine-gun fire blazed away from the outposts. One of the men was hit and killed. The rest sprang up to run the rest of the way to the river, but two more men were killed in the effort. Rounds whizzed past the heads of the survivors, who dove into some vegetation along the riverbanks.

Von Cossel announced he was going to try to swim the river to get some help. The others said they would try to find some sort of watercraft to ferry them across. Von Cossel waded through the reeds. When he reappeared in the open, he was taken under fire by artillery. A machine gun also joined in. Diving into the water to escape being hit, he saw the silhouette of the destroyed bridge and headed for it, in the hopes it would provide some cover. Once there, the machine gun continued to churn up the water around him. Exhausted, he held on to a piling that still jutted out of the water. He was about to give up, when he heard the sound of something moving in the water. It was his four men. They had been able to find a small rowboat! The officer made his presence known, and the men pulled him aboard. Without further incident, they reached the German side of the river.

In their stocking feet, they ran cross country and into the street of Stary Bychow, which was still burning and smoldering. Fortunately, all Soviet resistance had evaporated in the village. A German outpost challenged them. They identified themselves and were taken to the regimental commander.

Oberst Eberbach was still asleep when his adjutant awakened him. Hearing the news, he jumped out of his field cot and raced to his headquarters. Von Cossel, upon seeing his commander, started to come to attention to render a report. But he did not get that far. Eberbach embraced the young officer, who had been reported missing for two days. To Eberbach, it was as if one of his own sons had come back form the dead.

"Hans!" Eberbach called out repeatedly. "Hans, I can't believe it's you!" He then turned his attention to the four other tankers, who had also made it back, shaking each ones hand individually.

"I guess I need to get the letter back that I had already written to your parents!" a happy Eberbach said. The men were brought clean clothes and offered a *Schnaps*. The men's wounds were tended to. Eberbach added: "The letter was 10 pages long!" A radio message was sent to the field post office. The men there rifled through the mail bags until the letter could be found.

Von Cossel was evacuated because of his wounds. He was flown to Warsaw, where he then boarded a train to Berlin. Once there, he was able to call his parents. He was allowed to convalesce in the military hospital in the Charlottenburg portion of Berlin. On 23 July, he flew back to the front and his regiment.

For his dashing assault on Stary Bychow, the crossing of the river and his assault on the Stalin Line, von Cossel received the Knight's Cross to the Iron Cross on 8 September 1941.

✠

Von Cossel took charge of his company again and participated in the advances of that summer. He helped take Tscherikow, Kritschew and Rosslawl in joint operations with *Generalleutnant* Model's *3. Panzer-Division*. In the fighting at Klimowitschi, von Cossel's company knocked out a large number of antitank guns and destroyed a number of field fortifications. As a result, he was inducted into the German Army Honor Roll on 19 August 1941. Four Soviet rifle divisions had not been able to withstand the combined might of *General der Panzertruppe* Geyr von Schweppenburg's *XXIV. Armee-Korps (mot.)*.

In the final fighting for the Kiev Pocket, von Cossel, who had been promoted to *Hauptmann* in the meantime, was badly wounded again. The doctors at the military hospital harbored reservations as to whether he would recover. But the energetic optimist and officer with the devil-may-care attitude pulled through. By February 1942, he was back with his division again, reassuming command of his old company.

During the positional warfare around Mzensk, the slender but tough officer with the combed-back blonde mane of hair was constantly in combat. The difficult fighting north of Orel in the summer of 1942 demanded the utmost of him and his subordinates, but there was not a single man in the company who would not have walked through fire for him. In one instance, von Cossel and his men were cut off for an entire week from their rearward lines of communications, but they were always able to turn back any Soviet effort to eliminate them and inflict heavy losses. The company lost many if its tanks, but none of the men gave up hope. Von Cossel constantly radioed back from his beleaguered position that he could still hold out, and hold out he did until a relief force personally led by *Generalmajor* Eberbach hacked him out of the encirclement.

At the beginning of November 1942, Eberbach entrusted von Cossel with command of the 1st Battalion of the regiment. When Eberbach was reassigned from the division on 26 November, he summoned von Cossel. As was so often the case, when the two were alone, he addressed him informally: "Hans, you're the last to bear the family name. I'm sending you back."

"But I want to remain with my battalion."

"You'll get it back when you're married and have a boy!"

"Please let me stay, *Herr General!*"

In the end, Eberbach's desires were not realized, and von Cossel remained at the front. Von Cossel was promoted to *Major* on 1 May 1943, and he participated in the bitter fighting around the city of Ssewsk at the end of March 1943. He advanced into the Soviet positions and started taking extremely heavy fire. Due to that murderous fire, the grenadiers were unable to follow the tanks. They started to seek cover. Noticing that, von Cossel halted his tank. He dismounted and ran through the hail of fire to the bogged-down infantry.

"Come on, get up!" he called out. "Form up behind the tanks to attack!"

The grenadiers jumped up, inspired by the example set by the slight officer. The attack succeeded.

For his actions in the attack, von Cossel was awarded the German Cross in Gold on 5 May 1943.

✠

At the start of the difficult fighting in the Orel Bend in the summer of 1943, von Cossel's battalion was ordered to conduct an immediate counterattack against several Soviet rifle divisions that had broken through.

Leading the way, von Cossel advanced deep into the Soviet attack wedge. He advanced far to the south. Left to his own devices, he held out for two days. He took an important piece of high ground and then, 24 hours later, advanced into the flanks of a Soviet armored spearhead. His battalion knocked out 20 enemy vehicles.

Eventually, however, the enemy forces proved too strong, and von Cossel's force was summoned back. During the delaying action, von Cossel conducted a mobile defense that constantly took the advancing Soviets by surprise.

✠

On 22 July 1943, the Soviets again attacked the thin German lines with strong forces. They penetrated and von Cossel's battalion was called out to conduct an immediate counterattack. The first engagements with the T-34's started. Two, then three of the Soviet tanks were engulfed in flames, when the battalion commander's tank was rocked by a direct hit. The basic load of ammunition went up; no one on the crew survived.

Fate had dealt a terrible blow to that exemplary and decent officer. On 23 July, he was buried at the military cemetery in Kromy, 40 kilometers south of Orel, with full military honors. *Generalleutnant* Dietrich von Saucken performed the eulogy at the gravesite. On 29 August 1943, he was posthumously awarded the Oak Leaves to the Knight's Cross of the Iron Cross, the 285th member of the German Armed Forces to be so honored.

Panthers advance during a training exercise.

Heinrich Eberbach as an *Oberst* and recipient of the Oak Leaves to the Knight's Cross to the Iron Cross.

CHAPTER 5

General der Panzertruppen Heinrich Eberbach

HONORARY TANKER OF THE U.S. 4TH ARMORED DIVISION
In the small, sleepy village of Notzingen, near Kirchheim unter Teck, a military band from the German Armed Forces played the March of the "Old Comrades" in front of the guest house *Hirsch* on 24 November 1965. Three men with the Knight's Cross around their necks stood at the entryway to the establishment. They were waiting for the guest of honor, who was turning 70 that day: the retired *General der Panzertruppen* Heinrich Eberbach.

Then he came out into the open. He was average in stature, with an expressive face that was marked from the fighting in two world wars.

Following remarks by the mayor, *Oberstleutnant* Wöhl, the commander of a tank battalion from Dornstadt, gave an address. His battalion maintained a traditions link with Eberbach's first tank regiment, *Panzer-Regiment 35*.[1] That was followed by very cordial remarks by the commander of the 3rd Battalion of the 35th Armored Battalion, Lieutenant Colonel Tilson. Tilson's battalion was located in the former German Army facilities in Bamberg, where Eberbach's *Panzer-Regiment 35* had likewise also been headquartered.

Appearing next to Eberbach was retired *Oberst* Hans Christern, who was the last commander during the war of the regiment Eberbach had formed. Christern was also decorated with the Knight's Cross to the Iron Cross, which he had been awarded when he had been a *Major* and commander of the *II./Panzer-Regiment 31* of the 5. *Panzer-Division*. Both of the men had known one another for more than 30 years. Another Knight's Cross recipient appearing with Eberbach was former *Major* Wollschläger, who had commanded a company under Eberbach and had received his award on 23 January 1942, after the self-sacrificing fighting of the winter of 1941/1942 on the Eastern Front.

The retired general had undergone three difficult operations the previous year, but on the occasion of his 70th birthday celebration, he seemed to be the commander of old. It was the Eberbach who had led the bold tank raids

---

1. Translator's Note: The reader is again reminded that the history of *Panzer-Regiment 35, Knight's Cross Panzers,* is also available through Stackpole.

at the head of his forces on battlefields of various theaters of war. It was the Eberbach whose tank or command vehicle had been shot out from under him more than a dozen times and subsequently found him leading his tanks into battle on foot. It was the Eberbach, who had been commissioned a *Leutnant* after only nine months of combat experience in the First World War. And it was the Eberbach who was always the comrade to those in need, such as the time when the Soviets committed masses of T-34's for the first time and the Germans had to fall back. Moving to the rear, Eberbach had his tank halt next to a burning engineer vehicle. Together with a noncommissioned officer[2] and the regimental surgeon, he had saved the life of a badly wounded combat engineer, all the while taking heavy Soviet fire.

He was the type of commander who was always the last one back whenever there was a withdrawal. He was the commander who never abandoned wounded on the battlefield. It was all those qualities and more that resulted in the cordial and heartfelt birthday celebration of that day, not only from soldiers, but also from his fellow citizens and from former enemies as well.

Eberbach, who had commanded the *4. Panzer-Division*, was named an honorary tanker of the U.S. 4th Armored Division. His former enemies from the invasion front recognized those qualities of integrity and rectitude in him as well.

✠

Heinrich Eberbach was born in Stuttgart on 24 November 1895. His father, a businessman, died when he was just six years old. His mother did not have an easy time of it with her five children, but her sunny disposition made those early years of the children considerably easier.

As a schoolboy, young Eberbach enjoyed exploring Stuttgart and the area around it. He was also the head "rascal" in a company of schoolboys that was tolerated with some impatience. At the end of July 1914, he was graduated from his college preparatory school. That same month, he entered the Wurttemberg *Infanterie-Regiment 180* in Tübingen as a noncommissioned officer candidate. He had decided to become a soldier.

On 15 August 1914, Eberbach moved to the field in the Vogese Mountains with his regiment. In September, the regiment was pulled out of the line there and dispatched to northern France. In the Calbrai-Thiepval sector, Eberbach experienced his first attacks with fixed bayonets. On 12 October, he received the Iron Cross, Second Class. Four days later, he was promoted to *Unteroffizier* and also wounded in the upper thigh by shell fragments.

---

2. Translator's Note: See the section on Bix in *Panzer Aces*.

His company commander at the time informed him that he had to be evacuated to the military hospital. But the tough soldier refused to go and remained with his unit. In January 1915, Eberbach became an officer candidate and, on 25 February, after only nine months of active service, he was commissioned a *Leutnant.* It had to be some sort of a record.

During the fighting in the summer of 1915, Eberbach demonstrated a unique ability to lead from the front and serve as an example to his soldiers. On 25 September, the French launched a large-scale offensive in the Champagne region. The Germans were able to turn back the first assault wave, but Eberbach's platoon soon lost contact with the friendly forces to its flanks. The enemy attacked again, and Eberbach and his men found themselves surrounded.

"We need to pull back, *Herr Leutnant!*" one of the men called out.

But Eberbach counted on an immediate counterattack on the part of his comrades. His holding out would be of incalculable value in aiding that effort. For eight hours, Eberbach's platoon fought with the courage of desperation. It started to run out of ammunition.

Eberbach realized that the immediate counterattack was not forthcoming. He ordered his men to fight their way back, and he took the lead at the head of his shrunken force. Eberbach ran with his men through the churned-up trenches towards the rear. All of a sudden, the enemy appeared in front of them. Eberbach felt a sharp blow to his left half of his face and was thrown to the ground. He lost consciousness. When he finally came to, he found himself and a few of his soldiers in French captivity. The French dressed his wounds and evacuated him.

Of course, the lot of a prisoner of war did not appeal to Eberbach. At the beginning of 1916, after having recovered somewhat, but horribly mauled and missing a good portion of his nose, he attempted to escape. He was caught and then made his way through assorted prisoner-of-war camps and punitive camps, where he was not treated with kid gloves. Eventually, he was repatriated to Switzerland in December 1916 during a prisoner exchange of badly wounded soldiers. On 10 May 1917, he was awarded the Wurttemberg Friedrich Order, Second Class, with Swords, while still in Switzerland. While there, he was operated on five times. He was given a prosthetic nose and had recovered to a middling degree.

On 26 August 1917, he was repatriated to Germany and was admitted to the military hospital in Tübingen, where he made the acquaintance of Anna Lempp, a nurse. She would become his future wife. On 4 October 1917, he was belatedly awarded the Iron Cross, First Class, for the fighting on 5 September 1915. That October, *Leutnant* Eberbach reported back for duty at the front.

In December 1917, he was assigned to the East Prussian *Infanterie-Regiment 146* and sent to Macedonia. In February 1918, he moved with his new regiment to Palestine. During the fighting in East Jordan, Eberbach again demonstrated his pluck. In April 1918, due to his knowledge of the Turkish language, which he had learned from Turkish prisoners in French prisoner-of-war camps, he was assigned to the Turkish 8th Army headquarters in Tulkerim.

After the collapse of the Turkish front in Palestine on 20 September 1918, Eberbach was entrusted with the command of a Turkish rearguard during the general withdrawal, a sign of the confidence he had earned from his Turkish brothers-in-arms.

At Tulkerim, Eberbach engaged the attacking English cavalry formations, holding them back and covering the general retreat. For the next five days, he fought it out with the British with his *ad hoc* formation, consisting of Turks, Austrians and Germans. Then, he was stricken with malaria and became a British prisoner-of-war.

While in the British military hospital in Cairo, he discovered that he had been promoted to *Oberleutnant* on 18 October 1918. After a short stay at the officer camp at Sidi Bishr (near Alexandria), he departed in November 1919 aboard a Turkish ship bound for Brunsbüttelkoog by way of Gibraltar and Southhampton. He was back home for Christmas 1919, where he became engaged to Anna Lempp.

In January 1920, Eberbach was taken into the garrisoned police of Württemberg at Eßlingen. On 1 May 1921 he married, later becoming the proud father of three sons. He was promoted to *Polizei-Hauptmann* on 1 March 1921. On 1 June 1933, after several changes of station, he was promoted to *Polizei-Major*. He was then detailed to the Directorate of Police within the *Reich* Ministry of the Interior, where he worked on plans for incorporating the garrisoned police of Germany into the Armed Forces. On 1 August 1935, Eberbach himself was transferred into the army.

After his assignment in Berlin, he was assigned to *Panzer-Abwehr-Abteilung 12* in Schwerin as its commander. In the fall of 1937, he was promoted to *Oberstleutnant*. He participated in the large-scale military maneuvers of 1937, which were attended by Mussolini, his Field Marshal Badoglio, British Field Marshal Sir Cyril Deverell, a military mission from Hungary and many others. Part of the maneuvers featured large-scale armor operations at division level, in which the founder of the *Panzertruppe*, Heinz Guderian, played a key role.

Although Eberbach had been an *Oberstleutnant* for only a year, he was selected to command *Panzer-Regiment 35*, which was forming in Bamberg. Eberbach crossed the Polish frontier on the morning of 1 September 1939 with his regiment and defeated the enemy at Mokra in its first engagement.

Eberbach then led the charge in the direction of Warsaw, entering its outskirts on the evening of 8 September.

When there was decisive fighting along the Bzura and a crisis developed for the *4. Panzer-Division*, it was Eberbach's men who tipped the scales in the Germans' favor.

For his actions in the campaign in Poland, Eberbach was awarded Iron Cross clasps, indicating he had been a recipient of both classes of the Iron Cross in both wars.

The most memorable armored engagements of the campaign in France for *Panzer-Regiment 35* were fought at Hannut-Merdorp and in the forced crossing of the Dyle Position. The regiment also took Armentières in the first night engagement of armored warfare.

At Péronne, the *4. Panzer-Division* advanced through the Weygand Line as far as Roye. After reorganizing, it moved out south of the Marne at Mortmirail and entered combat again. Eberbach's regiment got to the bridges over the Seine at Romilly in a single move. It took the bridge intact and the city fell by midnight. The division then continued south in a strenuous movement: It advanced through Dijon, on to Lyon and then as far as the Isère.

During the fighting at Sémur, Eberbach heard from lamenting women that their two children were stuck in a vehicle between the two lines. Eberbach personally headed there and fetched the children out of harm's way, despite placing his own life at risk. Despite his martial prowess, Eberbach could also demonstrate his compassionate side. When his opponents were defenseless, he did what he could to help them.

His first love, however, was that for the soldiers entrusted to his care, although he was not above being tough and demanding to the utmost, whenever the occasion demanded it. When one of his battalion commanders requested a break to perform urgently needed maintenance on the vehicles, he felt compelled to turn him down. It was imperative not to allow the fleeing enemy a chance to regroup. He said at the time: "If the only thing we have left is a field mess, then we'll attack with it without pause until the enemy is defeated!"

On 4 July 1940, Eberbach was awarded the Knight's Cross to the Iron Cross for his actions at Romilly. That was followed on 14 August by his promotion to *Oberst*.

At the start of the campaign in the Soviet Union, the *4. Panzer-Division* was under the command of *Generalmajor Freiherr* von Langermann und Erlenkamp, who had commanded the *29. Infanterie-Division (mot.)* in France. It was one of the five divisions of the *XXIV. Armee-Korps (mot.)* of *General der Panzertruppen Freiherr* von Geyr von Schweppenburg. In turn, the corps reported to *Generaloberst* Guderian's *Panzergruppe 2,* where it was assigned on the field army's right wing.

The division moved out from Koden on the day of the invasion and headed in the direction of the Brest-Kobryn road. It initially followed the *3. Panzer-Division.* After a call for assistance was received, Eberbach's regiment wheeled in the direction of Baranowitschi, taking the city by surprise.

Despite Eberbach's success, the division commander considered pressing court-martial charges, since Eberbach had handled the attack on his own initiative and deviated from the division's mission. With the taking of Stary Bychow, a bulwark of the Stalin Line, and the successful fighting around the bridges at Propoisk, Eberbach won back the good will of his commander.

On 2 July, Eberbach was named the commander of the *5. Panzer-Brigade,* a headquarters elements within the division. As a brigade commander, Eberbach was given increasingly large *Kampfgruppen* to command and control. The successes of the division continued to mount over the summer: Tscherikow, Kritschew and Rosslawl were some of the cities that fell to the formation.

After the fighting to eliminate enemy forces in the vicinity of Klimowitschi, where Eberbach's men again distinguished themselves, the corps—the *3. Panzer-Division,* the *4. Panzer-Division* and the *29. Infanterie-Division (mot.)*—turned south on 15 August. The corps was advancing on the Desna in an effort to cut off the enemy forces in front of the *2. Armee* and encircle them. The forces were then sent in the direction of Bachmatsch, which fell on 10 September. That signaled the final push for the closing of the ring around the Soviet forces around Kiev.

Saturday, 14 September, was when that happened. Just north of Lubni, the lead elements of *Generalleutnant* Model's *3. Panzer-Division* linked up with engineers from *Panzergruppe 1.* Eberbach's forces had taken Konotop as their part in the effort. After that, they were finally allowed to rest for six days.

On 30 September, orders were received to move out again. The forces headed towards the north this time, in the direction of Orel. The first objective was Essmanj. Just before reaching the objective, the brigade encountered Soviet armored forces and scattered them. Eberbach ordered his men to continue on in the direction of Ssewsk. The force then overran Soviet infantry forces. Eberbach did not have his men halt to mop up; that was something for the forces that followed.

The next day, the city of Ssewsk emerged in the morning twilight in front of the armored forces. Fighter-bombers and *Stukas* helped pave the way for the ground forces. Through his binoculars, Eberbach observed the havoc they wrought. When the *Luftwaffe* had finished, Eberbach ordered his tanks to move out and aim for the city.

Enemy antitank guns on both sides of the axis of advance of the brigade started to open fire. The brigade commander conducted the battle from the turret of his command tank. *Major* Lauchert, the commander of the *I./Panzer-Regiment 35*, was ordered to try to envelop the city. The maneuver worked and, a short while later, German tanks entered the city, advancing as far as "Windmill Hill."

"Attack objective reached, *Herr Oberst!*" *Major Freiherr* von Jungenfeldt, the commander of the brigade's advance guard, reported.

"The next objective is Dimitrowsk, Jungenfeldt. Continue as the advance guard. Report any stiffening resistance."

Major von Jungenfeldt took off in a cloud of dust. His vehicles started to pursue the enemy, while Eberbach's staff reassembled and reorganized the brigade for the follow-up.

Eberbach confers with Heinz Guderian.

Von Jungenfeldt did not have to wait long for enemy contact. He soon started receiving fires from the woods adjacent to his route of march. Von Jungenfeldt sent his report to the brigade headquarters.

"Keep going, Jungenfeldt! Don't concern yourself with them or what remains behind you to either flank!"

While the advance guard pressed ahead, *Generaloberst* Guderian arrived at "Windmill Hill" and discussed operations with Eberbach.

The commander-in-chief did not mince words: "I heard you needed to halt, Eberbach?"

"Halt, *Herr Generaloberst?*" Eberbach replied, surprised. "We're in our stride . . . you never stop then."

"And your fuel situation? According to the latest reports, you're out of fuel."

The dust-encrusted face of the *Oberst* started to smile. Soon, he could contain himself no longer, and he started to laugh: "Well, *Herr Generaloberst,* we're riding on the fuel that everyone from platoon leader on up keeps as an emergency reserve!"

Guderian started to laugh as well: "Fine, Eberbach. Keep going!"

✠

Eberbach kept going. His forces slammed into the middle of the Soviet 13th Army, enveloped them, reached Dimitrowsk and then proceeded on to Kromy. The force was a few kilometers outside of Orel when enemy fighter-bombers hit the columns. It did not faze the unflappable Eberbach. He ordered his force to keep moving.

No one knew whether they would have enough fuel. The tanks started to have to borrow fuel from the motorcycle battalion, which still had ample reserves. The men were crossing their fingers that they would have enough to cover the remaining 30 kilometers to the city.

At the bridge on the near side of the city, the Soviets had improved their field fortification with everything they had. Up to that point, *Panzer-Brigade Eberbach* had covered 180 kilometers in three days. The wall of fortifications was a new challenge, which the inventive Eberbach soon found a way to overcome.

Using two tank companies, he deceived the Soviet defenders by launching a feint. The main body was then committed in an envelopment movement. The edge of the city was reached by taking a bypass that the Soviets evidently did not think could be negotiated by an armored force. The Soviets started to commit their last reserves in a desperate gamble to save the city. Cadets at the city's military academy charged the German tanks in death-defying courage, but they were no match against the German steel. The Germans entered the city; the sound of fighting and explosions echoed throughout the night.

By the next day, Orel, a bulwark of the Soviet defenses in that sector, fell to the bold assault. Unbelievable amounts of supplies fell into German hands.

The advance continued east in the direction of Mzensk. In the subsequent fighting for that city, Eberbach's forces encountered a Soviet tank brigade that was equipped with T-34's and KV-I's. Not only did the Soviets have superior numbers, they also had superior tanks. The Germans had to pull back in the face of the enemy's superiority. In the middle of the retrograde movements, a powerful blow struck the command and control vehicle of the brigade commander.

"We're immobilized, *Herr Oberst!*"

"Bail out!"

They dismounted in the middle of the fighting. Lauchert's tank battalion started to pull back to avoid being cut off. The brigade commander and the brigade surgeon made their way back on foot. On their way, they encountered *Feldwebel* Bix, whose tank had also been shot out from under him. Bix had just pulled a wounded combat engineer from his vehicle before it blew up. The two officers and the noncommissioned officer then grabbed their wounded comrade and helped carry him to the rear.

Later on, *Oberfeldwebel* Bix stated that this commander's actions moved him deeply. Later on, he vowed never to leave a wounded man behind. He had personally seen how his commander was the last one back and had not left a wounded man in the lurch. Of course, it came as no surprise that the commander had reacted that way instinctively. In addition to being a commander, he often acted like a concerned father. He knew most of the men of the brigade. He knew what was going on with their families in the homeland. He was bereaved whenever death ripped a gap in the ranks. It was he who frequently personally held the eulogies at the gravesites of his fallen men.

Despite the setback, the men continued their advance the next day. Mzensk was finally taken in fog and a snowstorm. On 22 October, Eberbach was given an even larger force to command, when *Panzer-Regiment 6* (*3. Panzer-Division*) and *Panzer-Regiment 18* (*18. Panzer-Division*) were attached to him. He was directed to advance on Tula without regard for his flanks and take the city by surprise. The operation would turn out to be one of his greatest successes.

In a night attack conducted on 24/25 October, his forces advanced into the enemy's rear north of Mzensk and into Soviet armored formations. Bitter fighting ensued. Eberbach's men had run into a reinforced Soviet tank brigade. Thanks to skillful tactical employment, his tanks defeated the mass of Soviet armor. The night was filled with the sounds of mechanized fighting. In the end, some 20 to 30 enemy tanks were eliminated, the flaming wrecks burning and smoldering on the battlefield. The Soviets fought to the last round, but Tschern fell on the morning of 25 October. The Soviet tank brigade commander committed suicide when it became obvious he had been defeated.

Eberbach's forces were reinforced again, this time with additional elements from the divisional artillery, as well as one of the division's motorized regiments and all of *Infanterie-Regiment (mot.) "Großdeutschland,"* an elite mechanized formation. Guderian's orders were simple: "Full speed ahead and take Tula!"

The weather did not cooperate. After the snow, there was unexpected rainfall. The weather became almost as bitter an opponent as the Soviet forces. The only road heading north turned into an ocean of mud. Guderian himself accompanied the forces in their advance on Tula on 27 and 28 October.

When one of the battalions of the *Großdeutschland* regiment ran out of gas, its men mounted up on the back of Eberbach's tanks. He knew he dared not stop.

On 29 October, *Kampfgruppe Eberbach* was four kilometers outside of Tula. He recommended that the heavily defended city be taken in a night attack. His proposal was not accepted. The attack was shifted to 0530 hours on 30 October. Eberbach personally made his way forward to the positions of the riflemen of *Großdeutschland* to inform them to call off their efforts for the day, even though he was convinced they could have succeeded.

The next day, Eberbach was back up front for the attack. *Leutnant* von Oppeln briefed him on the terrain, where the Soviet outer defenses were located.

"The red brick building over there appears to be part of some military facilities. It's full of AT, mortars and snipers."

Eberbach thanked the young officer for his briefing. *Oberst* Hoernlein, the commander of *Großdeutschland*, approached, his familiar walking stick in his hand. "It must be time, Eberbach," was all he said. Both of the commanders observed the attack.

By the end of the day, the assault groups had only been able to cover 500 meters. The attack bogged down, and Eberbach's tanks were unable to crack the Soviet antitank defenses. Knocked-out and burning German tanks were mute testimony to that fact. The Soviets then launched an immediate counterattack, spearheaded by T-34's. The tank fighting did not end until it was dark. Once again, there were heavy losses. It proved impossible to crack the ring around Tula.

Efforts by the *Luftwaffe* also fell short. The Soviets had massed antiaircraft weaponry around the city, and it succeeded in shooting down numerous German aircraft.

The next day, *Kampfgruppe Eberbach* transitioned to the defense. When the enemy started attacking the *LIII. Armee-Korps* in the area of Teploje, Eberbach's forces were sent there to assist. With their help, the corps was able to stop the enemy by 13 November and throw him back in the direction of Jefremow.

That same day, the commanding general employed *Kampfgruppe Eberbach* in an attack towards Wenew. By then, Eberbach could only report 50 operational tanks. The authorized strength was closer to 300.

The onset of extremely cold weather also caused problems for the tankers. On 13 November, the temperature had sunk to -22 (-7.6 Fahrenheit). The gun optics fogged up and oil turned as thick as molasses. There were no winter uniforms or antifreeze.

Despite all that, Eberbach's men moved forward with confidence. Uslowaya was taken on 21 November. On 24 November. Eberbach's tanks entered Wenew. By the evening of the next day, they reached the area south of Kaschira, 60 kilometers south of Moscow, in a monumental effort. In temperatures ranging to a low of -40 (-40 Fahrenheit), the advance continued in the direction of the Tula-Serpuchow road. It was taken on 3 December.

For these operations, which were linked with unbelievable hardship, Eberbach was inducted into the Army Honor Roll on 8 December 1941. But the recognition was of little solace to him, since the general retreat had been ordered two days before. Due to a lack of fuel, almost all of the heavy equipment and weapons had to be blown up. On 31 December, the senior field-grade officer was awarded the Oak Leaves to the Knight's Cross of the Iron Cross, only the 42nd member of the German Armed Forces to be so honored up to that point. Nevertheless, the recognition did little for Eberbach to console the many losses his forces had suffered.

✠

When *Generalmajor* von Langermann und Erlenkamp was given corps command, *Oberst* Eberbach was designated as the acting commander of the division. On 1 March 1942, he was promoted to *Generalmajor* and designated as the official division commander. He took leave of the division for a short while in April, when he had to be admitted to the hospital for hemorrhaging kidneys. By the time the division had settled down to positional warfare in the vicinity of Mzensk, he was back at the helm.

On 26 November 1942, Eberbach—still a *Generalmajor*—was designated as the acting commanding general of the *XXXXVIII. Panzer-Korps*, which was fighting outside of Stalingrad. He thus left the command and control of the *2. Panzer-Armee*. On the occasion of his departure, the commander-in-chief, *Generaloberst* Rudolf Schmidt, wrote him the following:

Dear Eberbach!
On the occasion of your departure from the *2. Panzer-Armee*, I would like to thank you once again for what you meant to us as the commander of the formidable *4. Panzer-Division*. We cleared up many a critical situation with your brave forces. I always knew one thing: Wherever the *4. Panzer-Division* was committed, the enemy would be thrown back and the position held. Through your energy and operational artistry, you have taken the withered division of the previous winter and transformed it into one of the best divisions of the field army. Your sudden reassignment shows how much the *Führer*

values you, since you have been sent to an especially responsible command position in the hot spot of the fighting during a difficult time.

You can rest assured that neither the field army nor I will forget you and your influence within the *2. Panzer-Armee.*

In the highest regard, I remain

Yours truly

/signed/ R. Schmidt

Generaloberst and Commander-in-Chief

Two days later, Eberbach, who had been promoted to *Generalleutnant* on 18 December, was wounded in the chest by shell fragments when he personally tried to rally a Romanian armored division to attack. He was hospitalized until 1 February 1943. On 5 February, he was designated as the inspector general for the Armored Forces of the Replacement Army. It was there that he worked closely with *Generaloberst* Guderian, when the latter was recalled to active duty to fill the post of inspector general of the Armored Forces.

On 8 August 1943, Eberbach was promoted to *General der Panzertruppen.* In October of the same year, he was designated the commanding general of an armored corps that was involved in heavy fighting in the Shitomir area. One month later, he became the commander-in-chief of *Armeegruppe Nikopol.*[3] In December, he had to return to the hospital for hemorrhaging of the kidneys again. He remained there from 2 to 20 December, convalescing the bare minimum.

At the beginning of January, he returned to his former position as the inspector general for the Armored Forces of the Replacement Army, a position he held until 30 May 1944. In June, he was detailed to *Heeresgruppe Model* for a short period. On 6 July, he was designated as the commander-in-chief of *Panzergruppe West,* which was employed along the invasion front in France. Its sector was opposite the British 21st Army Group. Eberbach's forces enjoyed success against the British in the fighting around Caen. A large armor battle was fought from 18 to 20 July, when the British attacked with overwhelming numbers. Despite the British numerical superiority, the Germans fought them to a standstill and the Allied force suffered the loss of 569 armored vehicles.

---

3. Translator's Note: An *Armeegruppe* was an *ad hoc* formation that consisted of forces larger than a traditional field army but smaller than a field-army group. Generally, it was formed whenever a section of the front had been shattered and the remaining forces needed to be grouped under a unifying command. *Panzergruppe West,* which is referred to later on, was a similar organization, under which several mechanized formations were given a command and control headquarters.

When the situation around Mortain became stalemated, the German Armed Forces High Command gave Eberbach the command of several armored divisions, which were then referred to as *Panzergruppe Eberbach*. It was hoped that the general could restore the situation in the southern portion of the invasion front. But even Eberbach could not perform miracles in the face of the overwhelming Allied superiority. The divisions that had been committed to him were engaged in combat operations and could only be pulled out of the front lines to form an attack group with difficulty. Furthermore, German logistics had practically evaporated. Eberbach saw the hopelessness of the situation and continuously requested permission to pull back. When the orders arrived, it was already several days too late. Eberbach was able to mount a counterattack with the forces of the *II. SS-Panzer-Korps*, but its success was limited to enabling large German forces to escape the encirclement at Falaise.

On 16 August, Eberbach assumed command of the *7. Armee*. He attempted to reestablish a cohesive German front with the remnants of divisions that had broken out of the Falaise Pocket. On 31 August, he was captured by the British south of Amiens, thus ending the war for one of Germany's most gifted armor commanders.

✠

In December 1945, he was flown to Aurich to serve as a character witness for *Panzermeyer*, who was being court-martialed. On his return to the British Isles and the infamous District Cage in London, he suffered a general collapse. In the fall of 1947, he was transferred back to Germany and sent to the American camp at Neustadt in Hessia. He was released from captivity on 6 January 1948, whereupon he was admitted to a hospital, undergoing six months of treatment.

After he had convalesced, the former general was placed in charge of refugee affairs for Protestant charities in Ravensbrück. From 1950 to 1962, he was a director of the evangelical academy in Bad Boll, where he specialized in ministering to the military starting in 1956, the year the *Bundeswehr* was founded.

✠

Heinrich Eberbach passed away on 13 July 1992 in Notzingen, one of the last living general officers of World War II.

Hauptmann Gerhard Fischer after receipt of the Knight's Cross to the Iron Cross. Modern German censors have blocked out the swastikas on his awards, since their display, even in books, is legally questionable in Germany.

CHAPTER 6

Major Gerhard Fischer

TANK COMMANDER IN 200 ENGAGEMENTS

With the crossing of the Manytsch River in the early daylight hours of 1 August 1942, the lead elements of the *23. Panzer-Division* had reached the Asiatic portion of the Soviet Union. Two days later, the division took Radykowskoje. Dimitrijewskoje was bypassed to the east, and Besopassnoje was reached in a rapid advance. The lines of communication for *Generalmajor* Breith's *3. Panzer-Division* also extended to there. Large Soviet forces had been bypassed as a result of this rapid progress. In the combat areas, there was wild confusion. The German lines, which were only manned by a series of strongpoints, were constantly attacked by the Russians. This round of fighting climaxed early on 6 August 1942 when the Soviet 4th Rifle Division attempted to break through.

✠

"*Herr Leutnant, Herr Leutnant* . . . wake up, wake up!"

Drunk with sleep, *Leutnant* Fischer awake with a startle from the heap of hay he was on in Dimitrijewskoje.

"What's happening, Elsner?" he asked, when he recognized the noncommissioned officer from his platoon.

"Ivan's attacking from the west. He's already wiped out the light *Flak* section in Brilutschni. He's already in Swatschinzew, where's he's blocked the LOC[1] for both our division and the 3rd."

While Elsner was still reporting to him, Fischer had already jumped into his uniform, grabbed a submachine gun from where it was hanging and run out into the open. Orders were echoing through the darkness. German artillery was already opening fire from Dimitrijewskoje on the enemy, who had advanced to within 4 kilometers of the division's positions. The engines of the tanks of the *II./Panzer-Regiment 201* were already warming up.

"*Leutnant* Fischer and his light platoon will report directly to me!" *Hauptmann* Fechner, the acting battalion commander, ordered. His four companies were making their final preparations for launching the immediate counterattack to the southwest.

---

1. Translator's Note: Lines of communication.

"The motorcycle infantry will advance wide in the direction of Besopassnoje and block the way east to the advancing enemy. The 5th Company will advance west past Swatschinzew in the direction of Bilutschni. The 6th Company will remain behind it as the second wave."

✠

Despite the darkness, *Leutnant* Fischer saw *Oberleutnant* Krämer give orders to his 5th Company to move out. *Oberleutnant* Gran's 6th Company followed behind. The glowing exhaust stacks quickly disappeared in the darkness.

Hauptmann Fechner then moved out with his 8th Company. The two tanks of the light platoon followed. Fischer heard on the radio that the 5th Company had already made enemy contact. He conducted a radio check with *Feldwebel* Elsner, who was following him in the *Panzer II*. Suddenly, he heard a report that made his ears perk up. It was coming from the *5./Panzer-Regiment 201*: "Two Russian artillery groups are attempting to pull back to the northwest."

The acting battalion commander called Fischer: "Light Platoon: Get after them!"

Moving at full speed, the two tanks crossed the main supply route of the *3. Panzer-Division*. After moving 2 kilometers, the first Soviet trucks appeared in front of them. These were followed by motorized and horse-drawn artillery.

"Engage at will, Elsner! Move on them from the left!"

"Understood!" Elsner replied. He then pulled out to the left.

"In front of us . . . 500 . . . 12 o'clock . . . large truck!"

"Identified!" the gunner reported. He was already taking up a good sight picture.

The first round thundered downrange. The tracer element could be seen disappearing into the truck. It blew thunderously apart when its ammunition detonated.

"AT aiming at us, *Herr Leutnant!*" The driver called out, as soon as he discovered it.

A slight correction in the direction of march had the tank turn somewhat in the direction of the guns. The second round left the barrel. Once again, it was a direct hit. The antitank gun was destroyed. At this point, *Feldwebel* Elsner's tank also opened fire. Soviet infantry jumped up and ran towards both of the tanks with hand-held antitank weapons.

The tanks' machine guns kept their heads down. Then both of the tanks moved into the enemy, firing with everything they had. The enemy started to flee. Burning trucks, exploding ammunition haulers and fuel vehicles engulfed in red flames that were on the side of the road turned the morning into an inferno. The sounds of the heavy weapons firing from the tanks as well as the rattling of machine guns could be heard over and over again.

At this point, both of the tanks were in the middle of the mass of Soviets. Throwing open their commander's hatches, both Fischer and Elsner tossed out hand grenades. The Soviets to the right and left stopped and started to surrender.

"Faster, Haumann!" the *Leutnant* egged his driver on.

They reached the first elements of the fleeing guns. The Soviet resistance stiffened once again, then everything quieted down. The artillery battalion surrendered to the two light tanks.

It was at this point that Gerhard Fischer figured out that he had advanced 7 kilometers to the west with his two vehicles.

The breakout attempt of the Soviet 4th Rifle Division had been bloodily repulsed. *Leutnant* Fischer returned to Dimitrijewskoje along with the rest of his battalion.

✠

On 7 August 1942, the advance into the Caucasus continued. Prochladnyj was reached on 26 August. On 2 September, Fischer's battalion was attached to *Generalleutnant* Recknagel's *111. Infanterie-Division.* It had the mission of crossing the Terek River south of Mosdok and expanding the bridgehead that had been established there.

The fighting for the high ground started on 6 September. Late in the afternoon of 7 September, a Soviet attack group composed of tanks and infantry assaulted the bridgehead from the east along the southern bank of the Terek. Fischer's battalion moved out so that it could advance into the left flank of the enemy by launching an immediate counterattack to the north.

Leutnant Fischer received orders to remain where he was, however, with his *Panzer III* and its short-barreled 5-centimeter main gun. He was to observe and be prepared to assist the infantry.

✠

"Something appears to be going on over there, *Herr Leutnant!*"

The gunner on the platoon leader's vehicle was indicating the row of vegetation that stretched out about 600 meters in front of the tank.

"Prepare to engage!" Fischer ordered. A few seconds later, four T-34's broke out of the vegetation, fired with everything they had and rolled towards the positions of the infantry battalion.

"The tanks are going to overrun our men!"

The infantry started to run back as the enemy tanks reached their positions, rolled up the trench lines and fired into the trenches along their line of movement.

"Aim for the lead tank . . . let's get a little closer, otherwise we won't penetrate . . . Right here . . . Fire!"

The flame from the muzzle moved like lightning through the vegetation. It revealed Fischer's position to one of the T-34's. It approached Fischer's vehicle rapidly, turret traversing. Before he could swing his main gun into position, however, Fischer's gunner had fired another round, which engulfed the T-34 in flames.

The T-34 came to a standstill barely 100 meters in front of Fischer's tank. Its crew attempted to bail out, but it was eliminated by the infantry.

"Let's get the next one!"

The round that followed was just a hair above the traversing turret of the T-34. The other two tanks were also turning and took up concealed positions behind the row of bushes. One of the rounds that was fired in their direction hit one of the steel monsters, but it ricocheted off.

As a result of his decisive actions in preventing the Soviet breakthrough in the infantry's sector, *Leutnant* Fischer received the German Cross in Gold on 28 November 1942.

✠

On 14 September, Fechner's battalion encountered a Russian tank hunter/killer battalion. *Leutnant* Fischer had to turn back hunter/killer teams armed with Molotov cocktails over and over again. The enemy was picked off with machine-gun and submachine-gun fire, before he could bring his deadly firebombs into striking distance. Several German tanks were set on fire, however, before many of the remaining crews dismounted and smoked out the enemy in his foxholes. *Leutnant* Fischer engaged the Russians in their holes with his main gun and machine guns.

On the following day, the entire battalion was engaged in fighting. Rounds from Russian antitank rifles penetrated the armor of *Leutnant* Fischer's tank, but they did not cause casualties or damage.

On 17 September, the Russian steppes experienced a gigantic massing of armor. The passage from Ernst Rebentisch in his divisional history of the *23. Panzer-Division, Zum Kaukasus und zu den Tauern*, best explains what happened:

Under the command of *Oberst* von Liebenstein, *Panzer-Regiment 6* and *Panzer-Regiment* 201 attacked together to clear the terrain in front of the German lines of the Russian formations that had been badly battered on the previous day.

The regiments moved out in a 6-kilometer-wide arc to the east and the south. The wall of dust extended widely into the steppes. The Russians defended with infantry and antitank guns. Once again, the widespread use of the antitank rifles was noticeable; the Russian snipers fired them even against the narrow vision slots of the tank cupolas. They were often successful, whenever a tank commander opened the vision port wider than absolutely necessary. *Leutnant* von Viereck was killed; *Leutnant* von Weise was badly wounded. Two German tanks, including the tank of the battalion surgeon of the *I./ Panzer-Regiment 201*, were lost.

✠

Gerhard Fischer was born on 4 December 1915 in Görlitz. After attending grade school in Marklissa (Silesia), he attended a four-year course in mechanical engineering. In 1934, he joined the military and was assigned to the Command for Instruction in Motorization at Zossen (near Berlin). Ever since he was a child, Gerhard Fischer was an enthusiastic gymnast and amateur athlete. With his entrance into the German Army, his interests in this regard were further advanced.

From his assignment at Zossen, Fischer was transferred to *Panzer-Regiment 5* (*3. Panzer-Division*), which was located at Bernau, also near Berlin. The regimental commander was *Oberst* Nehring, one of the leading lights of the fledgling *Panzertruppe*.

As a platoon leader in the 1st Company of the regiment, *Feldwebel* Fischer took part in the Polish campaign. His platoon was the lead element to storm across the bridge over the Braha on 1 September 1939, which was then captured. During the fighting in the Tuchel Heath from 2 to 5 September, Fischer and his platoon received a special mission. In an audacious attack, his platoon destroyed a series of Polish antitank guns. Following this, he conducted a reconnaissance-in-force against the Polish training area at Dolna-Gruppa.

For his successful efforts, *Feldwebel* Fischer was later awarded the Iron Cross, Second Class. Fischer and his platoon subsequently took part in the fighting for Zabinka Kobryn (14–16 September) and operations south of Wlodaw (17–19 September).

✠

In the campaign in the West, Fischer was still a platoon leader in the 1st Company. He participated in the armored fighting at Hannut, in which the Berlin-based *3. Panzer-Division* took on a Paris-based armored division. Fischer and his platoon helped contribute to the successful outcome of the battle for the Germans. He then participated in the breakthrough through the Dyle Position, the pursuit from the Dyle to the Charleroi Canal and the heavy fighting in the Mormel Woods.

Undoubtedly, the high point of the fighting in France for him, however, was the heavy fighting involved in breaking through the Weygand Line on 23 June 1940. *Feldwebel* Fischer had been attached to an infantry battalion with his platoon, and this battalion came to a standstill outside of the well-constructed field positions of the French at Estrée Demencourt.

Feldwebel Fischer's platoon was called in. He knocked out eight antitank guns, one after the other. They, in turn, had fought bitterly in an effort to halt the advance of the German tanks. After the antitank guns had been dispatched, Fischer and his men turned on and eliminated the machine-gun positions. The infantry then advanced with the tanks. The effort to take the field fortifications and the village were crowned with success due to the close working relationship between the German armor and infantry.

As a result of this attack, Fischer was substantially responsible for reopening the lines of communication to German armored formations that had already broken through to the south. He was later awarded the Iron Cross, First Class, for this.

✠

On 21 September 1941, the *23. Panzer-Division* commenced its formation in the greater Paris area. Personnel and even whole units were sent from other armored divisions to form the cadre for the new division. The first division commander was *Generalmajor Freiherr* von Boineburg-Lengsfeld, who had received the Knight's Cross on 19 July 1940 for his role as commander of the *4. Schützen-Brigade. Panzer-Regiment 201* became the division's armored regiment. *Feldwebel* Fischer was transferred to this regiment at the beginning of 1941. Initially employed again as a platoon leader in the *8./Panzer-Regiment 201,* Fischer was soon promoted to *Leutnant.*

At the beginning of March 1942, the division received movement orders to the Eastern Front.

When the Russians launched an offensive on 12 May 1942, the division was alerted and attached to the *LI. Armee-Korps* of *Generalleutnant* von Seydlitz. At Point 206.2, in the vicinity of Kharkov, the 8th Company encountered Soviet tank forces for the first time. This round of tank fighting was the opening act of the defensive fighting for Kharkov, which lasted until 27 May 1942.

Later on during the fighting, Fischer's battalion, with its 36 operational tanks, took up positions along the ridgeline running from Points 218.6 to 226.3. The enemy was attacking with the far superior T-34. *Leutnant* Fischer succeeded in setting one of the tanks ablaze. In the course of the fighting, eight T-34's were destroyed. The Germans bought this success at a cost of 13 total losses of their own.

Leutnant Fischer and his platoon were involved in numerous engagements in the weeks that followed. The German summer offensive broke through the Russian front and the pursuit to the Don started. The mighty river was reached at Nowo Uspenska on 7 July. An order from the corps gave further orders: "Turn south and pursue the enemy through Ostrogoshk to Olchowatka!"

The advance along the middle Don had begun.

Up through 18 November, *Leutnant* Fischer took part in all of the fighting as a platoon leader. He was used over and over again to conduct combat reconnaissance far in front of his own battalion. He worked together with combat engineers to clear lanes in minefields. His light platoon performed magnificently in conducting combat-outpost missions, bringing up supply elements and functioning as a liaison element. The nighttime screening of the main supply route was one of his specialties.

Fischer was promoted to *Oberleutnant* and assumed acting command of the 8th Company.

The *23. Panzer-Division* set up for defense at Ordshonikidse around 20 November 1942, when the *6. Armee*, some 500 kilometers farther north at Stalingrad, started its dramatic struggle for survival. The *23. Panzer-Division* was pulled out of the line and attached to the *LVII. Panzer-Korps* of *General der Panzertruppen* Kirchner. Together with the *6. Panzer-Division* (coming from France) and the *17. Panzer-Division*, this corps was allocated to the *4. Panzer-Armee*. It was intended for it to move along the rail line from Kotelnikowo to Stalingrad to relieve the encircled field army.

The battalion, under the acting command of *Hauptmann* Tilmann at this point, was issued 22 *Panzer IV's* with the long-barreled 7.5-centimeter L48 main gun in Ssalsk. The attack order was issued on 11 December 1942 at the command post of the *6. Panzer-Division* in Ssemitschnaja by the commander of the *4. Panzer-Armee*, *Generaloberst* Hoth. Present from the *23. Panzer-Division* were both the division commander, *Generalleutnant* von Boineburg-Lengsfeld, and the commander of *Panzer-Regiment 201*, *Oberstleutnant* Heydebreck. (Heydebreck would later be awarded the Knight's Cross as an *Oberst* while serving as the commander of *Fallschirm-Panzer-Regiment "Hermann Göring."*) The objective was to break the ring of encirclement around Stalingrad.

By 21 December, *Panzer-Regiment 201* lost the majority of its tanks in heavy fighting while attempting to carry out this mission. On 23 December, the lead armored elements were just 48 kilometers from the Stalingrad pocket, when they received the order to call off the attack. The high losses in both personnel and equipment, as well as the extremely heavy enemy resistance, made the prospects for success in continuing the attack to appear hopeless. In addition, elements of the attack force were needed at other critical sectors of the front, and the defenders in Stalingrad were expressly forbidden to attempt to break out. In the withdrawal movements that followed, *Oberleutnant* Fischer and his company were employed as a rearguard.

On 20 March 1943, the division was withdrawn from this sector of the front.

The *II./Panzer-Regiment 201*, which was redesignated as the *II./Panzer-Regiment 23*, was sent to Erlangen, where it received new-equipment training on the *Panther*. It was in Erlangen that *Hauptmann* Fechner reassumed acting command of the battalion after recovering from wounds suffered on the Eastern Front.

On 28 August 1943, the battalion was sent back to the Eastern Front by rail. It was already fighting by 4 September. Leading his 8th Company from the front, *Oberleutnant* Fischer rolled east of Kirowo against the Soviets, who were attacking the *306. Infanterie-Division* of *Generalleutnant* Koehler. The stupendous power of the long-barreled 7.5-centimeter L70 main gun of the *Panther* allowed a rapid victory. Sixteen T-34's were knocked out. On 7 September, Fischer's company attacked from Awdejewka in the sector of the *355. Infanterie-Division*. This time, six T-34's and one KV-I were knocked out.

When the Soviets crossed the Dnjepr 40 kilometers north of Saporoshe on 16 September, *Oberleutnant* Fischer was placed under the operational control of the *257. Infanterie-Division* with four *Panthers*. He succeeded in reducing the Russian bridgehead. It was not until November, however, that the main event for Fischer's company would arrive.

On 14 November, the Soviets moved out to attack the positions of the *23. Panzer-Division* with elements of four rifle divisions and 80 tanks from the XX Tank Corps. They intended to take Kriwoi Rog. They succeeded in taking Nowo Iwanowka, which was defended by a battalion with only 300 men from *Panzergrenadier-Regiment 128*. The battalion had been directed to defend six kilometers of frontage on both sides of the town. It was attacked by 40 tanks and two regiments of infantry.

Armored elements of the division that had been positioned in Glijewatka under the command of *Major* Fechner were told to advance to conduct an immediate counterattack and eject the enemy from Nowo Iwanowka. In addition to elements from *Panzer-Regiment 23* of *schwere Panzer-Abteilung 506*, a *Tiger* battalion had been attached in support. *Oberleutnant* Fischer, who was supposed to head to the trains area to recover somewhat from the last series of engagements, received a radio message during the night of 13/14 November 1943: "*Oberleutnant* Fischer is to report to the regimental command post and assume command of the *Panther* group."

He immediately headed to the command post in his beat-up *Schwimmwagen.* It was practically impossible to get through Kriwoi Rog. Finally, he arrived at Glijewatka. His old hands greeted him: "The shit has hit the fan up front, *Herr Oberleutnant.*" They came from a few *Panthers* that had returned from a forward firing position.

"The Russians will be attacking soon, *Herr Oberleutnant!*" the tank commanders reported. They had heard the sound of tanks in no-man's-land. But the attack did not come right away. It was not until 0200 hours that *Oberleutnant* Fischer was summoned to see *Major* Fechner.

"Fischer, the latest reports dictate that you take off immediately. I want you to take all 11 *Panthers* along the main supply route to Nedai Woda to the tactical assembly area at Hill 140.7. The field-army's assault battalion is there, and that is where the enemy's attack is expected."

The wiry *Oberleutnant* with the combed-back hair and the wrinkled forehead got ready. He moved at the head of the 11 *Panthers* in a command *Panther.* He stood in the open commander's hatch in order to establish the direction of march in the darkness.

Once they reached their initial destination, he issued orders: "*Oberfeldwebel* Elsner will establish a combat outpost. Three tanks will cover him!"

The four vehicles moved out.

Fischer turned to one of his crew members: "Let's dismount. I want to take a look at the terrain before it becomes light, so we can fight a good jump-off point."

"Good idea, *Herr Oberleutnant!*" the *Feldwebel* replied.

But things quickly changed. *Oberfeldwebel* Elsner had reported back on the radio.

"What's going on, Elsner?"

"It's swarming with Russians in a *balka*² in front of me. They are in the process of bringing mortars into position."

"That means the Russians have already run through our thin lines, Elsner. The Russians are to the rear of the 128th [*Panzer-Grenadier-Regiment*]. Get back here immediately!"

A few minutes later, Elsner and the other tanks had returned.

---

2. Translator's Note: Defile. The Germans adopted the Soviet word for a defile and used it almost universally.

Fischer summoned all of the tank commanders, once Elsner's group was back.

They met in front of the command tank. Fischer had known all of them for a long time. They formed a cohesive team with their tanks. There were tank commanders you could depend upon.

"Here's what's happening! The Russians are already behind the assault battalion. We have to reestablish contact with our mechanized infantry immediately. Four vehicles will advance to the left of the road; the rest will move on the right in the direction of Nedai Woda. The tank farthest to the right—you, Berger—will screen in the direction of Points 122.5 and 138.5. Elsner, you will take your platoon on the left of the road. Let's move out!"

A few minutes later, the tanks moved out. When they got to Hill 140.7, they were received with heavy antitank-gun fire.

"Elsner: Move along the *balka* and towards the Russian infantry! Everyone else follow me to the northeast. We're attacking the AT positions!"

Gerhard Fischer scanned the terrain through his vision port. It had become light in the meantime. "Move through the depression." He hoped to engage the enemy antitank guns from a good reverse-slope position by doing so.

"Up front, *Herr Oberleutnant!*" the driver suddenly called out. In roughly the same moment, Fischer also saw the enemy tanks that were in the depression about 900 meters ahead. They were engaging Elsner's platoon.

Fischer radioed Fechner's command post: "Russian tanks—type T-34— have advanced to a depression southeast of Nedai Woda in the direction of Hill 140.7. A Russian battalion has likewise infiltrated during the night into the *balka* south of Nedai Woda. As a result, contact with *Panzer-Grenadier-Regiment 128* has been lost."

Immediately following his situation report, Fischer called his tank commanders: "All vehicles are to immediately engage the enemy tanks!"

Fischer's command tank advanced. The first T-34 came into sight; it was destroyed with two rounds from the long main gun of the *Panther*. Elsner's platoon turned towards the enemy. All 11 tanks fired as rapidly as their loaders could load and their gunners could aim and fire. First three, then four T-34's were set alight. Then one of Elsner's tanks took a direct hit and was knocked out of commission.

When one of the T-34's turned and started to aim at the command tank, Fischer's driver immediately stopped and jerked the *Panther* around in the general firing direction. The gunner corrected his sight picture somewhat and the round that spit out of the main gun hit the T-34 just before it was about to fire. The round left the Soviet tank a burning torch.

A loud crack was heard from the direction of Elsner's platoon. The subsequent explosion told Fischer that anther of Elsner's tanks had been hit. Elsner reported: "Two vehicles out. My cupola blown off by an AT round; will continue to engage."

Suddenly, Fischer's driver was yelling into the intercom: "*Herr Oberleutnant,* 11 o'clock . . . AT . . . AT . . . AT!" He had already seen several muzzle flashes and had observed that the barrel was turning in the direction of their tank. Without waiting for orders, he jerked the vehicle around into the direction of the antitank gun. Fischer was about to curse when a mighty blow struck against the *Panther.*

"We've been hit, but it was HE!"

The gunner depressed the firing mechanism, and the direct hit from the *Panther's* main gun silenced the antitank gun.

In the middle of this difficult engagement, five *Tigers* of *schwere Panzer-Abteilung 506* appeared. They moved forward along the road west of the high ground.

"You're attached to me! Move out wide on my open right flank and screen against enemy tanks."

"We're on the way!"

The five *Tigers* turned. Their 8.8-centimeter main-gun rounds raced towards enemy targets—every one of them deadly if they hit a T-34. The five *Tigers* were in exactly the right spot to engage a newly arrived Russian tank battalion. Within a few minutes, they had knocked out 20 T-34's. The burning wrecks littered the battlefield.

Fischer issued new orders: "Turn in, move through the Russian positions and get to the old MLR[3]."

All of the tanks turned. When Fischer saw grenadiers emerging from their foxholes and trenches to both sides of him, he had his tank halt. He jumped down from his tank while still receiving enemy machine-gun fire and waved the grenadiers over to him. His *Panthers* and the five *Tigers* continued to roll forward.

"Follow my tank until we reach your main body. Then retake the old positions."

The aggressiveness of the *Oberleutnant* and his fellow tankers buoyed the grenadiers. They fell in behind the *Panther.* Ten minutes later, they reached the other tanks, which had come to a standstill in the face of an enemy antitank-gun belt.

"Roll through it! Run over anything that stands in your way!"

The tanks penetrated into the Russian positions. Antitank guns that had just fired collapsed under the weight of the steel giants moments later. Other

3. Translator's Note: Main line of resistance.

antitank guns were taken out with rapidly placed aimed fire. The tanks then reached the *balka* with the Russian battalion.

"HE . . . MG . . . engage at will!"

The Russian battalion and the mortar group were wiped out in a few minutes. Those who survived ran away in a wild panic. The ground soldiers reached their former positions and reestablished themselves.

Fischer then received another alarming report: "*Herr Oberleutnant,* there is a two-kilometer gap between the southeast edge of Nedai Woda to a point one kilometer west of Hill 138.5."

"We'll plug the gaps with the *Panthers.*"

By doing so, Fischer was undertaking a thankless task. He had to widely disperse his tanks in order to fill the gap. In addition, his vehicles offered good targets. On top of all this, the Russian artillery started to take the German lines under fire. Despite these obstacles, everything turned out well for *Oberleutnant* Fischer and his men.

✠

After more than 100 previous armored engagements, *Oberleutnant* Fischer had been decisive in deciding the outcome of the fighting at this location. He had mastered a critical situation through his own initiative. Thirty-one enemy tanks were left destroyed on the battlefield. Four additional ones had been immobilized and abandoned. In addition, 12 antitank guns had been eliminated and a number of others overrun. The division's war diary recorded the events as follows:

> *Oberleutnant* Fischer, a company commander in *Panzer-Regiment 23,* contributed significantly in the defensive success of the day. As the leader of the *Panthers* of *Gruppe Fechner,* he led the counterattack at Nowo Iwanowka to a complete success through his clever leadership and personal bravery. He will be recommended for the Knight's Cross.

Oberleutnant Fischer's *Panthers* remained in their exposed positions for several days. During the nights, Russian tank hunter/killer teams attempted to destroy the vehicles with satchel charges and Molotov cocktails. These ground incursions had to be turned back with hand grenades and submachine guns. *Leutnant* Mengel had an especially hard time of it. He had to bring supplies and ammunition forward to the *Panthers* at night in a prime mover.

On 28 December 1943, *Oberleutnant* Fischer was awarded the Knight's Cross.

On 4 January 1944, Fischer's battalion marched to Vinnitza to be issued 70 new *Panthers*. Subsequent to this, the battalion did not return to the division for a long time. It was allocated to the *1. Panzer-Armee* in order to counter the threatening situation that was developing southwest of Kiev. Together with *schwere Panzer-Abteilung 503*, the battalion was incorporated into the *ad hoc* armored regiment that was known as *schweres Panzer-Regiment Bäke*.

✠

On 10 January 1944, the recently promoted Fischer moved out under conditions of mixed snow, rain and frost to attack to the east. His battalion was instrumental in establishing a defensive position along the Bug. Other companies of the battalion were successful in this round of encounters as well. The 4th Company under *Oberleutnant* Kujacinski was able to knock out 10 enemy tanks without any friendly losses. (*Hauptmann* Kujacinski would later receive the Knight's Cross on 18 November 1944 as a company commander.) The 5th Company was able to knock out 15 enemy tanks. During the fighting on 28 January 1944, *Hauptmann* Fischer was wounded in the face and hand by shrapnel. He had himself treated at the clearing station and remained with his soldiers.

On 29 January, the battalion attacked to the west to open the main supply route, which had been cut off. One *Panther* was lost in an engagement with Russian assault guns, and two other ones were damaged. Three of the Soviet assault guns were eliminated.

Schweres Panzer-Regiment Bäke was then moved via Babin to Frankowka. From there it proceeded to the area around Uman, where it was attached to the *III. Panzer-Korps* of *General der Panzertruppen* Breith.

On 26 March 1944, the *Panther* battalion was bypassed by Soviet forces to the west and the south. The acting battalion commander, *Hauptmann* Esser, attempted to find a way out along with *Leutnant* Wassen. Neither officer returned from this reconnaissance.

Hauptmann Fischer unofficially assumed acting command of the battalion. He had to issue the order to blow up the *Panthers*, because there was no longer any routes open. He made his way back with his battalion on foot to friendly lines. The last elements arrived in Lemberg (Lvov) on 14 April, where 59 new *Panthers* that had been earmarked for the battalion were waiting for it. *Hauptmann* Fischer was officially named the acting battalion commander there.

Following this was the difficult defensive fighting in the Carpathian foothills at Stanislau, in southern Poland and in the area around Jassy. In the fighting for Zywaczow, *Hauptmann* Fischer attacked with 30 *Panthers*. In the process, the battalion surgeon was mortally wounded. The attack objective was taken; the advance continued as far as east of Harasymow. It was in the high ground there that Fischer's battalion encountered heavy Soviet tanks of a hitherto unseen type—they were "Josef Stalins." The battalion succeeded in knocking out two of them.

No fewer than 15 *Panthers* were lost in this round of heavy fighting. During fighting on 17 May to regain the Hungarian main line of resistance, *Hauptmann* Fischer was again wounded by shrapnel. An artillery shell had impacted next to his tank and a piece of shrapnel penetrated into his hand. Despite his wound, he remained with his soldiers.

On 4 May, the battalion returned to the division at Jassy, where the division commander, *Generalmajor* Kraeber, appointed *Hauptmann* Fischer as the official commander of the *II./Panzer-Regiment 23*.

At the beginning of August, *Hauptmann* Fischer assumed command of the division's *Panzergruppe*. A few days later, he was even given temporary command of *Panzer-Regiment* 23 in the Mielec Woods. On 24 August, Fischer's battalion was credited with the destruction of 8 T-34's, 2 KV-85's, 1 assault gun, 12 antitank guns and 4 field pieces. One day later, Gerhard Fischer was caught in a Russian air attack. A piece of shrapnel from a bomb hit him in the nose. Once again, he remained with his soldiers. Later on, he received the Wound Badge in Silver.

The division was transferred to Transylvania in September. In the weeks that followed, *Hauptmann* Fischer fought with his battalion at the hot spots in Hungary. He participated in the large-scale armor operations in the *pustza*,[4] which reached their high point on 13 and 14 October 1944. The *23. Panzer-Division* had been put to a hard test. *Major* Rebentisch, the acting commander of the regiment, and *Oberleutnant* von Oechelhaeuser, the adjutant of the *II./Panzer-Regiment 23*, were mentioned by name in the Armed Forces Daily Report, both receiving the Honor Roll Clasp.

On 16 October, the *III. Panzer-Korps* ordered both armored groups of the division to conduct an attack east from the area around Berettyo, Ujfalu and Derecske. *Panzergruppe Rebentisch* and *Panzergruppe Fischer* moved out separately. Fischer's group crossed the bridge over the canal south of Konyar with its tanks and knocked out four out of seven T-34's there. During the fighting, Fischer's tank was hit several times, but it remained operational. Fischer's group then got involved in a firefight with superior enemy forces along the southern outskirts of Tepe. At this point, he had only three *Panthers* and four assault guns left.

"Attack! Fire and movement! Attack quickly!"

---

4. Translator's Note: Plains (Hungarian).

The seven vehicles moved out. Fischer radioed threatened tanks, brought forward vehicles and personally knocked out three T-34's. He also set a Josef Stalin alight. After an engagement lasting 20 minutes, 9 T-34's and 3 Josef Stalin's were eliminated, but Fischer's group also lost three vehicles.

Enemy formations then attacked Konyar from the south and cut off Fischer and his forces. The remaining four fighting vehicles with the crews from the three knocked-out ones then had to fight their way out.

"We have to break though, men! Move as fast as possible . . . everyone follow me!"

The four tanks rolled through enemy-occupied territory at high speed. Behind him, Fischer could hear other tanks being hit. Then his vehicle was hit; the round did not penetrate, however. Only his tank made it across the bridge south of Konyar. The three remaining vehicles bottomed out in the canal area when they were trying to evade enemy fire. The crews bailed out and had to defend themselves against Soviet infantry.

From Konyar, *Hauptmann* Fischer launched an immediate counterattack across the bridge on foot with the infantry that was still there. He did not want to leave his crews in the lurch. And he did the seemingly impossible: Most of the tank crews were saved.

Despite this, Fischer could not be happy. The fighting had cost him nine tanks.

In recognition of his magnificent performance of duty, Fischer was promoted to *Major* on 1 October 1944.

The fighting on 26 October stood out for its success. On that day, he moved out with eight tanks and *SPW*-mounted elements from the 2. and 3./ *Panzer-Aufklärungs-Abteilung 23* from the crossroads six kilometers north of Hajdu-Dorog on Nyiregyhaza. His lead elements were closely followed by the self-propelled artillery of *Panzer-Artillerie-Regiment 128* and *Panzergrenadier-Regiment 126* of *Oberst* John. Block by block, Nyiregyhaza was cleared of the enemy. Antitank guns were destroyed and the city taken through quick action. One thousand Hungarians and ten thousand Germans were freed from the Russians. This was the last major engagement of *Panzergruppe Fischer* in the *pustza.*

✠

In the period from 28 September to 28 October 1944, the *23. Panzer-Division* had knocked out or destroyed 228 tanks, 5 armored cars and 233 antitank guns, as well as numerous field pieces, mortars and other heavy support weapons.

At the beginning of December 1944, *Major* Fischer was awarded the highest level of the Tank Assault Badge, signifying more than 100 separate engagements. By this time, he had already exceeded that number by several score.

Major Fischer led from the front, as always, during the fighting in December at Mezö Komarom and Polgardi. It was thanks to him that the positions at Belsöbarand and Külsöbarand were taken back.

The first attack he led on 11 March 1945 at Sar Egres failed, however. The antitank defenses were too strong. He tried again with his armored group in the afternoon. The attack against enemy tanks and antitank guns came to a standstill; three *Panthers* were also lost. A third attack—this time with 17 *Panthers*—succeeded in breaking through to the road at Simontornya Cece, but the embankment south of the road proved to be an impenetrable tank barrier.

The attack could not be continued until the following day. The Soviet defenses were overrun and the Alsö farmstead taken. Fischer's group was able to knock out six Soviet assault guns on that day.

The Germans continued to pull back in a series of delaying actions. Unterdraubing was reached at the end of April. All of the tanks had been lost by then, mostly due to a lack of fuel and ammunition. *Major* Fischer was given orders at the beginning of May to secure the corps' rear area from partisans with his tankless crews. As a result, the battalion, which was divided into three companies for this purpose, was employed as infantry from 6 to 8 May 1945.

Major Fischer was designated as the local-area commander of Unterdraubing on 8 May 1945. His mission was to screen the withdrawals of the *68. Infanterie-Division*, the *71. Infanterie-Division*, the *118. Jäger-Division*, Pannwitz's Cossack Division and the *13. Waffen-Gebirgs-Division der SS "Handschar" (kroatische Nr. 1)*.

Kampfgruppe Fischer held its positions at Unterdraubing until the evening of 8 May 1945. *Major* Fischer turned down a demand that he capitulate. Attacking Bulgarian forces were turned back with bloody losses. In the vicinity of St. Veit, *Major* Fischer and his soldiers surrendered to British forces.

✠

Major Fischer is one of the few tank commanders of the Second World War—on either side—who participated in nearly 200 separate armored engagements.

Fischer was released from captivity in the summer of 1945. He initially worked in a nursery at Hessigheim on the Neckar River. In 1946, he moved to Oldenburg, where he became an administrator in a commercial enterprise.

From 1951 to 1954, he attended college-level courses and eventually received academic degrees.

On 1 April 1959, he entered the *Bundeswehr*, where he served as the executive officer of a tank battalion. He later was promoted to *Oberstleutnant* and served as a tank battalion commander, before entering retirement. As this book goes to print, he is one of the few armor officers whose careers are portrayed in this title who is still alive.

German infantry are supported by a *Panzer III* during an attack on enemy positions.

Major Hans Gradl sometime after the receipt of his Knight's Cross to the Iron Cross in late 1941. Gradl wears a non-regulation striped civilian shirt with his uniform.

CHAPTER 7

Oberst Hans Gradl

BRIANSK TAKEN BY SURPRISE

Late in the evening of 5 October 1941, *Oberst* Kurt Cuno,[1] the commander of *Panzer-Regiment 39*, returned from the headquarters of the *17. Panzer-Division* to his command post. The division's advance guard had formed a bridgehead over the Nerussa on the previous day, and the entire division was closing upon it.

The command vehicle stopped in front of the regimental command post, and Cuno entered the main room of the peasant hut. His battalion commanders were already waiting for him.

"Gentlemen," he announced after a short greeting, "we're moving on! *Generaloberst* Guderian was at corps this morning. We will be attacking at first light tomorrow, along with the *18. Panzer-Division*."

"Are we headed north?"

"The 18th will move along our right flank to the north. Our mission, however, is as follows: *Kampfgruppe Gradl* will be attached to *Schützen-Regiment 63*, where it will advance across the tank ditch at Akulowa, allowing the rifle regiment's second battalion to take Hill 237 and then take the Karatschew-Briansk road. The rest of the [tank] regiment will then follow behind on order of the division."

"I hope the engineers have leveled the damned ditch!" *Major* Gradl interjected. He had just been promoted to field-grade rank on 1 October and, at the same time, entrusted with acting command of the 1st Battalion of *Panzer-Regiment 39*.

The 38-year-old officer, whose sharp features were set off even more by his prominent nose, smiled. When he smiled, the crow's feet in the corners of his eyes became even more prominent. The thick eyebrows above his eagle eyes drew together as he thought about the mission. Cuno knew that Gradl had not just jested when he made the comment. He replied: "The lanes will be cut. Engineers and support forces are already leveling two areas."

---

1. Translator's Note: *Oberst* Kurt Cuno received the Knight's Cross to the Iron Cross on 18 January 1942 in his capacity as commander of *Panzer-Regiment 39*. He survived the war, passing away in Munich on 14 July 1961.

"That's necessary, *Herr Oberst*! We got hung up there yesterday. The Russians could take their time firing at us—and they fired with everything they had." Gradl's tanks had run into a ditch that was six meters wide and five meters deep. No tank could get through that.

"Don't worry, Gradl! The lanes will be there in the morning. The attack will start at 0415 hours!"

✠

"Another two minutes, Hintze!"

Gradl, standing in the cupola of his command tank, looked around. The tanks of his battalion and those of the attached *Panzer-Abteilung 100*,[2] were roaring to life and getting warm. Through his binoculars, Gradl observed to the far side of the tank ditch and on to Hill 237. The Soviets had dug in there and were controlling the road to Briansk. Somewhere farther to the west had to be the command post of the Soviet commander-in-chief, General Jeremenko. Gradl's force and those of his division and the entire *XXXXVII Armee-Korps (mot.)* were in the rear of the enemy. Orel had been taken three days previously by the tanks of *Kampfgruppe Eberbach* of the *4. Panzer-Division*. By then, it was already 200 kilometers to the rear.

The hands of Gradl's watch jumped to the appointed hour and minute. He extended himself upward along with his right arm thrust his balled fist three times into the air. The tanks moved out in two columns towards their designated lanes. Guides showed the columns of steel the routes to take. In the pale morning light, the lanes were hard to identify.

The orders remained unchanged: across and on to the hill!

The tanks were able to make it through the lanes without difficulty. The assault groups of *Schützen-Regiment 63* linked up with the tanks, and the force moved out through the low vegetation. The men started to receive fire from the high ground. Gradl dropped down into the relative safety of the turret and slammed his hatch closed.

"Button up! . . . Continue to move!"

Gradl's loader reported that the main gun and machine gun were loaded and ready to fire; the gunner began traversing back and forth for targets. The tanks clanked forward through the bushes. They soon started to climb the slope. Through his optics, Gradl could see lances of flame from atop the

---

2. Translator's note: *Panzer-Abteilung 100* was a general headquarters flamethrower tank battalion. It was attached to Cuno at the time of the operations described here. In December, it was detached, redesignated as *Panzer-Regiment 100* (although the "regiment" consisted of only the one tank battalion) and reorganized. In February 1942, it was used to form the principal cadre for the formation of *Panzer-Abteilung "Großdeutschland."*

hill. The trajectories of the rounds took them over the tops of the tanks—a common problem when shooting down a slope.

Gradl issued orders to disperse further and smoke out the enemy's pockets of resistance as the tanks reached the crest of the hill. Gradl saw a machine-gun nest just off to his right. A quick order to the driver and the machine gun was turned to junk under the tracks of the tank a few seconds later. Gradl then saw deadlier foe: "Four-zero-zero . . . 11 o'clock . . . " He waited for his gunner to identify the target, a light tank. Once the enemy vehicle was in his sights, he fired almost as soon as Gradl ordered him to. The round was short: "Add 20 meters!" The next round was a direct hit, perfectly placed between turret and hull.

The riflemen assaulted forward behind the tanks. They occupied the captured or abandoned bunkers and machine-gun positions. After some more resistance, the first Soviets started to crawl from their holes to surrender to the riflemen. Gradl ordered his forces to reorganize on the north side of the hilltop. Once that was done, there were new orders: "Follow me to advance north on Karatschew!"

The battalion commander did not want to lose any time. He radioed his company commanders and gave them their individual objectives. Then the force moved out downhill.

The Soviet resistance turned weaker. Occasionally, some elements defended from field fortifications. Three antitank guns were knocked out.

"It looks like the Russians have decided not to play!" Gradl's adjutant called out, excitedly, when the first houses of Karatschew came into view. At the same moment, Gradl's radio operator reported he had just received an order from the division. Division intelligence had reported that the bridge ahead of the tanks had been blown up. The division ordered Gradl's force to stop its attack on Karatschew and, instead, reorganize and attack to the northwest along the road to Briansk.

Gradl quickly adapted to the changed situation. He had *Leutnant* Begemann conduct route reconnaissance as far as the new axis of advance. The young officer immediately headed out with two of his scout platoon vehicles. All of the tankers of the battalion were experienced in their trade, and their commander was one of the first men to volunteer for the fledgling *Panzertruppe*. His short, clear directives were quickly and meticulously followed. A few minutes after the new orders had been radioed, the formation swung into the new direction of march. Begemann radioed that the road to Briansk appeared clear of the enemy.

Gradl's armored *Kampfgruppe* started to hit the enemy from the rear, since it was now approaching from the east. At Gluschy, the commander in the trail tank radioed that the riflemen were not keeping pace. Gradl had his force halt in a patch of woods momentarily; he sent *Leutnant* Körber back to establish contact with the riflemen and act as a liaison officer. Gradl wanted the motorized infantry to close up as rapidly as possible; without them, his tanks were vulnerable.

Gradl had the division notified that he had to halt momentarily at Gluschy. *General* von Arnim, the division commander, instructed Gradl to await the arrival of the division's operations officer. Von Arnim had just returned to command of the division in September, after being forced to convalesce due to wounds received at Stolpce.

It did not take but half an hour for *Major* von Bonin to arrive. The operations officer informed Gradl that the taking of Briansk by surprise was still possible that morning. A frontal attack was impossible due to the improved and deeply echeloned field positions there, but *Kampfgruppe Gradl* was in a position to take everything from the rear.

Gradl countered by saying that it would be impossible to advance along the Karatschew-Briansk road. Begemann's continued reconnaissance had confirmed that there were field positions and heavy enemy traffic there: "They'll pick up on us right away!"

Von Bonin offered an alternative: "Then advance through the woods between Briansk and Sarewo. I'm sure they'll be strong forces there, too, but if you come by surprise down the road in the woods, you can do it. The bridge over the Desna is really important."

"I'll do it! As soon as the riflemen have closed, I'll have them mount up on the vehicles and enter Briansk through the road in the woods."

"Good, Gradl! May God be with you!"

Major von Bonin went back to the division. Gradl took stock of his operational forces: Six *Panzer III's*, seven *Panzer II's*, four troop transporters and two *Flak*. Some of them were only conditionally combat capable due to battle damage sustained in the previous fighting. But their presence was needed to help magnify the combat power of the force and add to its shock effect.

The riflemen arrived and were parceled out among the vehicles. Gradl announced the new objective: "Men, we're going into Briansk! I expect everyone to do his best!"

That was all the commander needed to say. His men trusted him implicitly; he had always led from the front from the very beginning of the campaign in the Soviet Union.

The route led the force west over marshy terrain that alternated with dry, dusty spots. In the middle of the woods at Sarewo-Seimischtsche, the *Kampfgruppe* encountered a Soviet horse-mounted patrol and took it prisoner.

This T-34 was flipped over by unknown means, but not before it had wreaked havoc on German wheeled vehicles, as evidenced by the smashed truck to the viewer's left.

"Let's go, men! We'll do it. I know we'll do it!"

The tanks entered the woods. The heavier *Panzer III's* led the way. All of a sudden, the tankers saw vehicles off to the left in the woods: more and more of them! The Soviets abandoned their vehicles in a flash, when they saw the unexpected German tanks. The tankers saw radio antennae in the clearing ahead. A large radio center began to emerge.

"Shoot it to pieces!" That was Gradl's only command.

The tanks led the trail in the woods. Their main guns began to bark. The firing thundered through the woods for three minutes. The radio center and its attendant trucks and other vehicles were destroyed. Pockets of resistance and machine-gun barrels that swung towards the tanks and the mounted riflemen were eliminated. The documents found there, which were taken to Gradl, showed that they had driven into the headquarters of a field army general. Later on, he discovered that it had been General Jeremenkow's command post and that his tanks had only missed the general by 50 meters. It was only by chance that the future Soviet field marshal was spared capture.

"On to Briansk!"

The *Kampfgruppe* started to rumble onward. After advancing another several kilometers, it encountered a fuel column led by a Soviet lieutenant. It was captured, along with a second one that was following closely behind. Then the woods started to clear. The first large buildings of a military base could be seen.

The Soviet sentries that moved along their designated routes did not pay any attention to the approaching tanks initially. They certainly had not counted on German tanks approaching them from the rear. It was not until the riflemen had dismounted and taken the Soviets prisoner and disarmed them that they realized what was happening. At the railhead behind the post was a train unloading a company of Soviet infantry.

"Let's get them, *Herr Major!*" his adjutant called out.

"Leave the railhead alone. The bridge is what counts . . . let's pick up the pace . . . everyone follow me!"

Moving quickly, the tanks advanced along the asphalt road towards the bridge over the Desna. Off to the side, Gradl saw a *Panzer IV* and a *Panzer II* through his binoculars that had been captured by the Soviets and which they had apparently intended to use to guard the bridge. He ordered his men to overpower the guards and man the tanks. The men succeeded in surprising the Soviet guards and Gradl soon had two more tanks at his disposal.

The German force approached the bridges. The guard force started to tumble out of its dugouts. Gradl ordered his men to open fire. The Soviets were covered with main-gun and machine-gun fire from the tanks and small-arms fire from the riflemen riding along. Gradl's tank soon hit the wooden planks of the bridge and started to rumble across, closely followed by the others. For a split second, Gradl wondered if the bridge had been wired and what would happen if the engineer decided to press the igniter. But he reached the far side intact, as did the rest of his vehicles. He moved a but farther forward and had his *Kampfgruppe* start to secure the bridgehead into the western part of the city. Vehicles moved out, weapons at the ready. The advancing dismounted riflemen took a hundred Soviets prisoner from a military facility off to the left of the Briansk-Rosslawl road. A Soviet truck column approached the German vehicles. A few rounds caused it to halt, whereupon it was captured. To Gradl, it seemed as though he were in a dream. The riflemen attached to his force had already taken 400 prisoners.

Gradl instructed his radio operator to contact the division: "Desna Bridge taken. Bridgehead expanded to the western part of Briansk. Request support!"

The division received the message and von Arnim immediately ordered *Oberst* Rübsam, the commander of *Schützen-Regiment 63,* to send two companies in Gradl's direction. Rübsam designated the two companies and went with

The bridge over the Desna that was taken by Gradl and his men in a bold surprise action in October 1941.

them. It was 1700 hours when they arrived, also advancing along the same route as Gradl's men had done earlier in the day.

"Congratulations, Gradl! A damned fine job!" the regimental commander told Gradl, not sparing any praise.

Gradl then had his vehicles pull back to the near side of the river, where they engaged and eliminated two Soviet antiaircraft guns that were positioned 800 meters north of the bridge.

Starting at 1800 hours, mighty detonations could be heard coming from the north. The skies turned black. The Soviets had started to blow up their giant reserves of fuel, ammunition and rations in the area around the city.

✠

As it turned light on the morning of 7 October, the Soviets tried to cross the Desna over an auxiliary bridge near the main bridge. The guard force posted there by the riflemen was soon in a tight spot. Gradl's tanks had to help out on numerous occasions, moving right into the middle of the desperate Soviet forces. More reinforcements were brought forward and then taken across the river. All the while, the bridgehead was under heavy Soviet artillery and small-arms fire.

The Soviets attempted with all the means at their disposal to retake or destroy that bridge of decisive importance. In a preemptive strike, Gradl attacked with his tanks at 1015 hours and delivered a decisive blow to the Soviet forces. The western part of the city was cleared of Soviet forces, and an antitank gun and an antiaircraft gun were captured. That ensured that

the bridge would remain in German hands. It was the type of surprise raid
that did not succeed all too often in the Soviet Union. When all was said and
done, *Kampfgruppe Gradl* accounted for the following enemy resources during
its raid on the bridge:

17 tanks (including 4 weighing 44 tons)

14 artillery pieces (including 4 of 15.2-centimeter caliber)

8 antitank guns

100 trucks

1 aircraft

10 prime movers

The battle group also captured more than 1,000 prisoners.

✠

Briansk, the city that had been especially fortified and protected;
Briansk, the sphinx in the flank of *Panzergruppe 2*; Briansk, the city in which
General Jeremenkow resided—it had fallen. A small battle group under the
determined leadership of a cleverly operating and tactically proficient officer
had brought about the miracle.

The 100,000 Molotov cocktails that had been stockpiled in the depots for
the men of the GPU formations were blown sky high. *Major* Hans Gradl had
taken the city with its all-important railway hub.

On 15 November 1941, he received the Knight's Cross to the Iron Cross
for his decisive action. The following could be read in the recommendation
for the award:

> As the result of his decisive, rapid deeds and his unflappable
> aggressiveness, *Major* Gradl not only took the crossings over the
> Desna, which were extraordinarily important for the continued
> operations of the division, but he also deprived the numerous Soviet
> divisions fighting west of Briansk of their main logistics point, cut off
> their route of withdrawal and, as a result, effected the final closing of
> the pocket of Briansk at a decisive place.

✠

Hans Gradl was born the son of an officer on 8 December 1903 in
Nuremberg. Just shy of 21, he volunteered for the 4th Company of *Fahrabteilung
4* in Landberg am Lech. Thus he was preordained for the *Panzertruppe*,
since these early motorized transportation battalions were considered the
forerunners of the *Panzertruppe*.

After a year of training at the infantry school in Dresden and a detailing to the artillery school at Jüterbog as an officer candidate, he was transferred to *Artillerie-Regiment 7* in Wurzburg. Newly commissioned a *Leutnant*, he was transferred to *Kraftfahr-Abteilung 7* in 1930. He served as a platoon leader in the motorcycle infantry company and then in the antitank company for four years. In the course of his platoon-leader time, he also served as an instructor in armored tactics at noncommissioned officer courses. On 1 April 1934, he was promoted to *Oberleutnant.*

Around that time, the *Panzertruppe* started to be formed. On 1 May 1934, Gradl was detailed to Special Course for Combat vehicles in Wustrow (Mecklenburg). He was then transferred to the Motorization Command at Ohrdruf, where he served simultaneously as a battalion adjutant and platoon leader.

He became one of the first tank company commanders of the German Armed Forces on 1 October 1936, when he assumed command of the 5th Company of *Panzer-Regiment 4 (2. Panzer-Division)*. He then served for a period in Berlin, where he was assigned to the committee in charge of reviewing the award of military driver's licenses. One year later, he returned to troop duty. He was given command of the 4th Company of *Panzer-Regiment 4*, the battalion's medium company. In March 1937, he was promoted to *Hauptmann.*

When the war started in September 1939, Gradl was assigned to a military school in Dresden as a tank tactics instructor. After some inquiries, he was able to regain command of a tank company in the middle of October 1939. He participated in the campaign in the West as commander of the 2nd Company of *Panzer-Regiment 4*. After that campaign, he was awarded the Iron Cross, Second Class.

On 1 July, he was transferred to *Panzer-Regiment 39* of the *17. Panzer-Division*, where he went with the division into the war against the Soviet Union. Initially, he was the regimental adjutant. On 29 July, he received the Iron Cross, First Class. One month later, he was designated as the acting commander of the 1st Battalion of *Panzer-Regiment 39*. The fighting at Putiwl, Belopolje, Cholopkowo and Gluchowo remained indelibly etched upon his mind. At the last place, Gluchowo, Gradl successfully relieved the encircled defenders with his tanks.

✠

Gradl continued in his battalion command with the *17. Panzer-Division* until March 1942. On 1 April of that year, he received transfer orders, putting him in command of the newly forming *Panzer-Abteilung 129*, which was to become the divisional tank battalion of the newly forming *29. Infanterie-Division (mot.)*.

On 21 June, the division arrived at its staging area north of Kharkov, where it was allocated to the *XXXX. Panzer-Korps* of *General der Kavallerie* Stumme. The corps was given the mission of advancing from the area around Kharkov-Woltschansk to the northwest in the direction of Woronesch, where it was to link up with the *4. Panzer-Armee* of *Generaloberst* Hermann Hoth.

As a result of the cloudbursts of the last days of June, the division's advance was delayed until the start of July. By the evening of 1 July, however, the division had already reached the Osskol. It formed a battle group there under the command of Gradl. Augmenting his battalion as the divisional motorcycle battalion, *Kradschützen-Bataillon 29*, a battalion of the divisional artillery, the *III./Artillerie-Regiment 29 (mot.)*, a company from the divisional antitank battalion, the *2./Panzerjäger-Abteilung 29* and a company of divisional engineers, the *3./Pionier-Bataillon 29 (mot.)*. Around 0600 hours on 2 July, the battle group crossed the Osskol. Hans Gradl led his force with his characteristic élan through the marshy bottom lands. Enemy columns that were attempting to escape encirclement were caught by the tanks and destroyed.

Gradl's force stormed ahead of the division until 4 July. That day, the division was turned by the corps in the direction of Ostrogoshk. The division commander, *Generalmajor* Fremery, rode with Gradl in his command vehicle. The after-action report that Gradl wrote at the time survived the war:

> 0245 hours: Commander's call at the division in Rasschowezkoje. *Kampfgruppe Gradl* received the mission to advance in the direction of Ostrogoshk via Chemelnowo, Kamyschenka and Polnokowo, exploiting the success of *Infanterie-Regiment 71.* It was to take the bridges over the Tichaja Ssossna by surprise and establish a bridgehead.
>
> 0330 hours: The unit leaders attached to the battle group assembled for an orders conference. The advance guard of the battle group was formed under the command of *Hauptmann* Mutius, the commander of *Kradschützen-Bataillon 29*.
>
> The advance guard moved out at 0430 hours. The main body of the battle group followed at 0530 hours. The lead elements of the advance guard reached Point 105.2 at 0645 hours. The leader of the advance guard decided to leave the axis of advance, which was occupied by the enemy and, moving about 2.5 kilometers to the south, rejoin the road at the nursery.
>
> In spite of great difficulty negotiating the terrain, the nursery was soon reached. The movement was continued, with the pace picking up. The motorcycles rode along the road; the tanks and the armored cars to the left and right of it. Enemy motorized and horse-drawn

columns were passed on the road and scattered. Any flare-up of rifle fire was soon silenced.

Trains elements, some of them heavily armed, were to be found in the woods, nurseries and localities on both sides of the main axis of attack. They were passed at high speed. Fighter-bombers accompanied the march from the air. All of a sudden, they signaled a tank warning. Enemy tanks approached us from the right. We went past them without stopping. An enemy motorized column, heading for the city, entered along the road that led into the main attack axis coming from Korotojak, 3 kilometers north of Ostrogoshk. Working together very well with the tank company, the enemy force was stopped. The crews fled into the bottom land, where they were engaged by the fighter-bombers.

Around 0910 hours, the lead elements of the advance guard had reached the southwest outskirts of Ostrogoshk. They immediately moved another 500 meters along the road into the city. There was a short period of house-to-house fighting, but it was intentionally kept to the bare minimum. An enemy T-34 was eliminated with hand grenades.

Leaving behind a platoon of tanks to screen to the east and another platoon to the west, the rest of the advance guard turned southeast so as to take the bridge 800 meters northwest of Gniloje.

The continued advance in the direction of the bridges proved difficult.

The soldiers waded through the water, chest high in some places. At 1000 hours, the southern bridge was in our hands, intact.

One tank under the command of *Oberleutnant* Kurt Müller, along with the lead platoon of *Oberfeldwebel* Drexler, stormed the main bridge—consisting of six bridges, one after the other—at the same time. They also took it about 1000 hours.

A firefight against the Soviets was initiated.

Gradl then took the main body of his battle group and entered Ostrogoshk proper. It took the city at 1100 hours. An airfield to the southeast of the city fell into the hands of the battle group. Three aircraft were shot down through concentrated machine-gun fire and another two were forced to abort their take-offs.

Once again, Gradl and his men had achieved considerable success. Six T-34's and two T-60's had been destroyed; twelve guns and numerous other weapons captured or eliminated. Five hundred prisoners were counted. In addition, there were 100 prime movers and a freight train with 70 cars loaded with ammunition. The division later received a radio message from the corps: "Thanks and recognition to the leaderships and the soldiers for the great success—Stumme."

An advance that started on 16 July with the object of taking the bridge over the Don at Zymljanskaja and establishing a bridgehead posed Gradl with difficult challenges again.

The field positions at Zymljanskaja were taken. The force then crossed a tributary of the Don along a sandy ford. By the time it turned dark, however, the Don still had not been reached. *He 111's* were called in, which dropped flares and other pyrotechnics. Gradl ordered his forces to prepare all-round defenses. He sent patrols forward to the Don and his advance guard, again under the command of *Hauptmann* Mutius. Two hours later, firm contact was established with Mutius.

On 21 July, the riflemen were sent across the Don in assault boats. The forces that crossed were soon subjected to numerous enemy attempts to dislodge them. It was not until 31 July that the division was able to break out of the bridgehead and continue its advance on Stalingrad. Serving as the division's advance guard, *Kampfgruppe Gradl* reached Kotelnikowo on 3 August. When it approached Abganerowo—the first defensive belt surrounding Stalingrad—it received heavy fire.

Two days later, during an attack on a Soviet field position, the commander's command tank was penetrated. Gradl was badly wounded. He was sent from the main clearing station to a military hospital in Dresden. He stayed there to convalesce and was later sent to Garmisch for additional treatment. It was not until 1 July 1943, 11 months after being badly wounded, that he was fit for duty again. He was sent to the armor school at Berlin (Zossen), where he was responsible for organizational and supply matters. He performed those duties until 1 June 1944.

He volunteered for frontline duty again and was selected for regimental command, attending a command course at the armor school at Bergen-Belsen. On 1 July 1944, he was designated as the commander of *Panzer-Regiment 4* in the *13. Panzer-Division*. On 1 September 1944, he was promoted to *Oberstleutnant.*

Gradl served as a *Kampfgruppe* commander in Romania and experienced the defensive fighting in the Carpathian Mountains as a regimental commander. He fought in the Budapest area in December 1944, where all of the tanks were lost. His men were then committed as infantry, and the final fighting demanded the utmost of all in self-sacrifice and determination. In the fighting around Budapest, the *13. Panzer-Division* was effectively wiped out.

Gradl was then placed in charge of the remaining combat elements of the division and led them all the way back into Slovakia , serving as a *Kampfgruppe* commander until 27 March 1945. At that point, he was transferred to the *21. Panzer-Division* to assume command of *Panzer-Regiment 22.* When he arrived at that division's location, it was involved in heavy fighting in the Forst-Cottbus area. Gradl was badly wounded again at Forst and was able to be evacuated to the hospital in Kalua after a dramatic journey. From there, he was evacuated to Leitmeritz and, finally, to Franzensbad. On 26 April 1945, he was notified that he had been promoted to *Oberst.*

On 1 May, he was captured by the Americans while in the hospital. He was sent to the camp at Eger. Gradl was released from there on 18 June 1945, after being treated with great respect by his captors. He passed away at Neuhaus am Schliersee on 10 March 1980.

Heinz Guderian, the man credited with the creation of the *Panzerwaffe*.

CHAPTER 8

Generaloberst Heinz Guderian

FATHER OF THE PANZERTRUPPE

On 24 June 1941, at the headquarters of *Panzergruppe 2, Generaloberst* Guderian prepared to move to Slonim. A radio message had stated that the *17. Panzer-Division* of *Generalmajor* von Thoma had taken the city. When the command vehicle approached Slonim, it encountered Soviet infantry elements, which were taking the road under fire. Inside were the commander-in-chief, his aide-de-camp, *Major* Büsing; a visitor from the Replacement Army, *Oberstleutnant* Feller; and a messenger. The motorcycle infantry of the division and a battery of its artillery were in the process of eliminating the resistance. Guderian was apparently not too happy with the way the fighting was being conducted, however. To the horror of those accompanying him, Guderian had his command half-track swing in the direction of the enemy.

"Fire when ready, Meiners!"

The junior noncommissioned officer behind the machine gun opened fire. The motorcycle infantry joined in with the fire from the *SPW*, and they succeeded in driving back the enemy riflemen. It was only at that point that the motorcycle infantry discovered that it was none other than their commander-in-chief who had joined them in the fight and led from the front.

His acumen at the command post, the *élan* with which he rallied the men in the attack and his leadership close to the front were what brought him success after success.

✠

When Guderian reached von Thoma's command post at 1130 hours, he also saw the commanding general of the *XXXXVII. Armee-Korps (mot.)*, *General der Panzertruppen* Lemelsen. As the men were talking, the sounds of fighting reached a crescendo. Guderian turned and observed down the road to Bialystok. Initially, he only saw clouds of smoke and flames that were shooting from a burning German truck. All of a sudden, two enemy tanks appeared form out of the smoke. Firing from their main guns and machine guns, they were headed for Slonim. The commander-in-chief could see *Panzer IV's* following them, also firing.

All of a sudden, the two enemy tanks turned towards the group of officers. Muzzle flashes could be seen coming from the main guns. Guderian, von Thoma and Lemelsen immediately dove to the ground. *Oberstleutnant* Feller and *Oberstleutnant* Dallmer-Zerbe, the commander of the antitank battalion of the *17. Panzer-Division, Panzerjäger-Abteilung 27*, were a second too late. Both were hit, collapsing to the ground, badly wounded. The German tanks finally caught up with the two Soviet interlopers and knocked them out.

But the event-filled day was not over yet for the commander-in-chief. After visiting the front lines at Slonim, he climbed aboard a *Panzer IV* and moved through no-man's-land to the location of the *18. Panzer-Division. Generalmajor* Nehring was not surprised to see his comrade of old with him in the front lines. They had served together on numerous occasions and knew each other well.

Guderian directed Nehring to move his division in the direction of Baranowiyze. At that point, Guderian returned to his command post. All of a sudden, he was in the middle of Soviet riflemen. They had just dismounted from a truck, part of the Soviet effort to retake the doomed city.

Guderian ordered his driver to step on it. The *SPW* moved through the middle of the surprised enemy ranks. His vehicle was followed by some machine-gun and small-arms fire, but it negotiated its way out of the danger zone without sustaining any battle damage.

A few days later, there were reports in both the Soviet and Swiss press that Guderian had been killed in the advance. The German high command requested Guderian correct the error by giving a short statement for the radio; that he did with a smile.

These small episodes from the life of the great leader, officer and soldier Guderian illustrate the character of the man. His soldiers called him "fast Heinz." He earned the nickname the first time during the campaign in France, when he passed the march columns of the *1. Panzer-Division* on 16 May 1940. The men were exhausted, but Guderian succeeded in rallying them as he roared forward: "No hesitation . . . no stopping!"

Guderian knew that all the signs were there for a decisive breakthrough. *Oberstleutnant* Balck's men saw their commanding general, cheered and called out: "There's the Old Man!" "It's 'fast Heinz'!"

The soldiers had plenty of opportunity to see him. They recognized him immediately. His image was indelibly burned into the consciousness; a medium sized but broad-shouldered man with gray hair and mustache. And if one of them did not know, then he was soon set straight. It was the creator of the mighty *Panzertruppe*. It was the general who had established the main operational principle of the fledgling armor arm: "Slam, don't slap!"[1]

---

1. Translator's Note: In German, *"Nicht kleckern, sondern klotzen!"*

That was the Guderian the fighting troops knew. But it went beyond that. It was he who had forged the mighty *Panzertruppe* and made it into a powerful instrument of combat. It was his concepts for the operational employment of armor that enabled the Germans with a force of some 2,200 armored vehicles to decisively defeat the combined French and British armies in the field in 1940 with their 4,800 armored vehicles.

✠

Heinz Guderian was born on 17 June 1888 in Kulm (Vistula). His father was a Pomeranian light infantry officer, the first officer in the family. Both of his grandfathers were the owners of large estates in Prussia. Since his father was frequently transferred and both sons—a brother, Fritz, was born in 1890—expressed interest in becoming officers as well, both were sent to a military academy for their education. On 1 April 1901, they were accepted into the military academy at Karlsruhe (Baden). Two years later, Heinz went to the main cadet academy in Berlin at Groß-Lichterfelde. He was graduated in February 1907 and entered the service as an officer candidate in *Jäger-Bataillon 10*[2] in Bitsch (Lothringen). Until December 1908, his commander was his father. A little more than a year after entering service, he was commissioned as a *Leutnant*. His battalion was moved back to its original garrison city of Goslar in October 1909. He made the acquaintance of Margarete Goerne there; on 1 October 1913, she became his wife.

He was blessed with two sons, the eldest of whom was born in Goslar in 1914. It was also in Goslar that the 65-year-old Guderian would also eventually find his final resting place on 14 May 1954.

Young Guderian followed his father's advice and was detailed to *Telegraphen-Bataillon 3* in Koblenz in 1912. It was there that he developed an appreciation for rapid, secure communications that were so necessary for the type of maneuver warfare he would later envision. At the start of the Great War, he was attending the military academy in Berlin to become a General Staff officer.

Upon mobilization, he was assigned to lead a communications center within his battalion, deploying to the field with the *5. Kavallerie-Division*. In 1917, he was assigned to the *4. Infanterie-Division* as the division's logistics officer. It was there that he experienced his first tank attack on 10 April. The enemy succeeded in breaking through with their tanks at Miettetal. In February 1918, he was assigned to the General Staff. He saw the end of the war in Italy, where he was assigned to the senior German military mission there.

---

2. Translator's Note: 10th Light Infantry Battalion.

After the armistice, Guderian served in the frontier forces in the east in Upper Silesia and, later on, in the Baltic region. When the 100,000-man army was formed, he was assigned as a company commander of the 3rd Company of *Jäger-Bataillon 10* in Goslar. Two years later, he was reassigned to the motorization directorate of the Defense Ministry in Berlin. Two years after that, he was assigned to the headquarters of the *2. Infanterie-Division* in Stettin. In 1927, he was reassigned to the Transportation Directorate of the Forces Directorate in Berlin. This signaled a milestone in the career of the young General Staff officer. In the fall of 1928, *Oberst* Stottmeister, the head of the Motorization Instructional Staff, asked Guderian to provide instruction on tank tactics to his officers.

Guderian, who had been promoted to *Major* on 1 February 1927, agreed to the assignment. From that point forward, his thoughts were constantly linked to the issues of armor, armored warfare tactics and operations and the arming of the force.

Since he had not even so much as sat in a tank up to that point, he immersed himself in every available printed source concerning armored warfare. He was especially assisted in his thought processes by English journals on the subject. Whenever exercises were conducted—early on with dummy tanks since real ones were not allowed by the Treaty of Versailles—he received considerable support from the commander of the 3rd Battalion of *Infanterie-Regiment 9, Oberstleutnant* Busch, a future field marshal. It was during that time that Guderian also made the acquaintance of another officer in the battalion with whom he would later work, the battalion adjutant, *Oberleutnant* Wenck, who later became a *General der Panzertruppen.*

In 1929, Guderian went to Sweden for four weeks of temporary duty, where he familiarized himself with armor while visiting the *Strijdsvagn-Bataillon II* of Colonel Burén. In Captain Klingspor's company, he drove a tank for the first time. Once he returned to Germany, Guderian started talking about the employment of armor at the division level.

A short time later, *Oberst* Lutz, who liked Guderian, asked him whether he would like to become the commander of a motorized battalion. He jumped at the chance and became the commander of the *3. (Preußische) Kraftfahr-Abteilung* in Berlin (Lankwitz) on 1 February 1930. With the help of *Oberst* Lutz, he was allowed to reorganize the battalion into an experimental force. He had four companies, which he organized as an armored-car company, a tank company (dummy tanks), antitank company and a motorcycle infantry company.

Guderian was promoted to *Oberstleutnant* on 1 February 1931. In the spring of that year, the inspector general of the Motorized Forces, *General*

Otto von Stülpnagel, told Guderian the following when he left his command: "Believe me, neither of us will ever see German tanks rolling!"

Replacing Stülpnagel in command was Lutz. Lutz was more optimistic about the future of armored forces and fetched Guderian to be his chief-of-staff in the fall of 1931. It was then that the actual pioneering work for the development of the *Panzertruppe* started. Guderian had visions of a branch of service that could operate independently at the division level at an operational level, exploiting its motorization capabilities to achieve decisive success on the battlefield. That was a new concept, since most of the other armies of the world—following the example of the British, who were considered the leaders in that regard—closely coupled the employment of armor with infantry, so as to give it greater local combat power. Consequently, the largest armored formation was the tank brigade.

Given the overall weight given to British concepts and the yoke of the Versailles Treaty, Guderian's concepts were rejected by the General Staff as too "utopian." It was the cavalry that proved to be especially resistant to Guderian's concepts. It only saw a potential for the use of armored vehicles in long-range reconnaissance.

During the planning stages for the expansion of the army in 1933, the questions surrounding the organization of the armored force and its operational employment became ever more heated. On 1 October 1933, Guderian was promoted to *Oberst*; a year later, he became the chief-of-staff of the command for motorized forces. Three motorized brigades were established. During field exercises held at the training area in Munster the following summer, there was a demonstration of an armored division. Present were general officers such as von Blomberg and *Freiherr* von Fritsch. All of them seemed satisfied with the results. When the end of the exercises was announced—signaled by the raising of a yellow balloon—the commander-in-chief of the army said in jest: "The only thing that's missing is 'Guderian's tanks are the best' on the balloon!"

General Lutz was named the commander of the command for motorized forces. Based on the lessons learned at Munster, the first three armored divisions were established on 15 October 1935. Guderian was designated as the commander of one of them, the *2. Panzer-Division*, in Wurzburg. Guderian went from theoretician back to practitioner. On 1 August 1936, he was promoted to *Generalmajor*. A few months later, his primer for armored forces, the book *Achtung—Panzer!*, was published. He covered the development of the German armored force in his book. At the end of his book, he wrote words that still have meaning today: "The stronger and more modern the leadership of an armed forces is in weapons, equipment and spirit, the more it guarantees the maintenance of peace."

After *Generalmajor*, Guderian assumed command of the *XVI. Armee-Korps (mot.)* on 4 February 1938 he was promoted to *Generalleutnant* 6 days later. On 10 March, Guderian received his first marching orders as a commanding general, when his corps, augmented by Hitler's personal bodyguard formation, the *Leibstandarte SS Adolf Hitler*, was ordered to march into Austria. The annexation of Austria into the *Reich* required a motorized march of nearly 700 kilometers by Guderian's forces, putting them to a practical test, which resulted in many lessons learned for the future. That fall, the *4. Panzer-Division* was formed under *General* Reinhardt in Wurzburg. It was followed by the *5. Panzer-Division* and the *4. leichte Division*.

The entry into the *Sudetenland* in October 1938 again saw *Generalleutnant* Guderian at the head of his corps. A month later, on 24 November 1938, he was named the *Chef der Schnellen Truppen* and, at the same time, promoted to *General der Panzertruppen.*

According to the duty description of his position, he possessed no command authority. Neither was he allowed to have manuals published under his authority. Thus, his sphere of influence was greatly reduced. Despite Guderian's protests that he was being "sent out to pasture," Hitler ordered him to take the position. Hitler assured Guderian that he would personally intervene if anyone tried to offer resistance to the expansion of the *Panzertruppe.* Guderian was assigned two General Staff officers as assistants. One was *Oberstleutnant i.G.* von le Suire, who would later distinguish himself by being awarded the Knight's Cross to the Iron Cross on 26 November 1944 for service while assigned as the commanding general of the *XXIV. Panzer-Korps.* His other assistant was *Hauptmann i.G.* Röttiger, who would later go on to become the first inspector general of the armed forces in the postwar *Bundeswehr.*

At the start of the campaign in Poland, Guderian assumed duties as the commanding general of the *XIX. Armee-Korps (mot.),* which had the *3. Panzer-Division,* the *2. Infanterie-Division (mot.)* and the *20. Infanterie-Division (mot.)* attached to it. Guderian, who stayed with the lead attack elements of the *3. Panzer-Division* at the start of the campaign, almost became a victim of friendly fire, when German artillery fired too short in a thick ground fog. The first impacting shells landed only about 50 meters in front of his command vehicle. The second salvo landed 50 meters to his rear. Guderian knew what was coming next and had his driver veer off to the right at high speed.

Given the unfamiliar terrain and the fact that the driver was nervous in his first combat situation, the wheeled vehicle promptly got stuck in a roadside ditch. As a result, Guderian was unable to directly participate in the initial successes of the forces he helped to create. The irrepressible armored commander soon found another vehicle and moved towards the sounds of the guns.

When the forces of Guderian's corps reached Brest-Litowsk, the bishop of Danzig, O'Rourke, and the head clergyman of the Catholic Church in Poland, Cardinal Hlond, were already there, having fled from Warsaw. Cardinal Hlond continued to flee to Rumania; Bishop O'Rourke, however, turned himself in to the German forces. He had an audience with Guderian, requesting his help, since he did not want to be handed over to the Soviets under any circumstances, which was a distinct possibility under the Non-Aggression Pact with the Soviet Union, especially since Brest was due to be handed over to the Red Army. Guderian provided him with an escort to Danzig, using forces from his logistics command. He later wrote to thank Guderian, wherein he singled out the chivalrous attitude of the German officer corps.

The campaign in Poland had brought tremendous lessons learned for the fledgling armored force. The ideas and concepts of Guderian had proven correct; they just needed fine tuning.

On 27 October 1939, Guderian was summoned to the *Reich* Chancellery. He was awarded the Knight's Cross to the Iron Cross, along with 24 other officers who had distinguished themselves in the first campaign of the war. Later on, Guderian wrote: "I saw in it [the award] a justification for my struggle to establish a modern armored arm."

The success of the armored forces in Poland seemed to make it advisable to establish more armored forces. The light divisions, which possessed a large number of wheeled vehicles, but little actual armor, were all converted to armored divisions.

For the campaign in the West, *General* von Manstein, the chief-of-staff for von Rundstedt's field-army group, proposed a plan that would have strong armored forces advance through Luxemburg and southern Belgium against the extension of the Maginot Line, which was not as strong as the portion that guarded the actual frontier between France and Germany. In November, von Manstein asked Guderian to review his plan for its feasibility in regard to the use of armored forces. Guderian assured the master strategist that the plan could be executed. When the original attack plan fell into the hands of the enemy during an emergency landing by a liaison aircraft on 10 January 1940, von Manstein's plan was finally accepted for execution.

At the start of the campaign in the West in May 1940, Guderian's corps had the *1. Panzer-Division,* the *2. Panzer-Division* and the *10. Panzer-Division* attached to it. Guderian's orders to his corps were simple: break through to the English Channel! On 10 May, the *1. Panzer-Division* crossed the border with Luxemburg at Martelange.

Guderian moved with his battle staff early on the morning of 12 May to Bouillon, which was attacked and taken by the forces of *Oberstleutnant* Balck's *Schützen-Regiment 1.*[3] While the commanding general continued on in the direction of the *10. Panzer-Division*, his chief-of-staff, *Oberst i.G.* Nehring, established the command post in the *Hotel Panorama* in Bouillon.

When he returned for the evening, an incident almost eliminated the commanding general from command, perhaps for good. As the general was making himself at home in the large work room that had been set aside for him, a German engineer column was attacked outside by enemy aircraft. The demolitions, mines and hand grenades went sky high, and the powerful explosion dislodged a gigantic boar's head trophy from the wall above where the general was sitting. It thundered to the floor, right next to the general officer. To add insult to injury, the large panoramic windows in the room were shattered by the explosions, sending shards of glass flying everywhere. Guderian emerged unscathed, however.

By the evening of that event-filled day, the *1. Panzer-Division* and the *10. Panzer-Division* had taken the fortress of Sedan. The general did not want to miss the assault across the Meuse by his riflemen on the morning of 13 May and crossed the river with them in one of the first assault craft. *Oberstleutnant* Balck greeted him on the far side of the river with the words: "Taking gondola rides on the river is forbidden!" Balck was referring back to a planning exercise where Guderian had said the exact same words in warning to his officers to dampen their rash eagerness somewhat. On 15 May, Guderian was privy to captured French military documents that came from the headquarters of General Gamelin, the French commander-in-chief: "The flood of German tanks has to be stopped once and for all!"

Guderian later wrote: "This order reinforced my conviction to carry on the attack with all forces available, since the will to resist on the part of the French forces seemed to be causing their senior command considerable worry. That meant no hesitation and no stopping at this point!"

Guderian met *Generalmajor* Kempf, the commander of the *6. Panzer-Division* from the neighboring armored corps, at the marketplace at Montcornet on 16 May. His division had reached the town at the same time as two of Guderian's divisions. The three divisions then continued their attack until they had consumed their last gallon of fuel. Their objective was palpably near. Therefore, it came as a complete surprise to Guderian on 17 May, when the field army ordered the advance to be stopped. A serious disagreement

3. Author's Note: He would later rise to the rank of *General der Panzertruppen* and be the 19th member of the German Armed Forces to be awarded the Diamonds to the Oak Leaves to the Knight's Cross of the Iron Cross (19 August 1944). Translator's Note: He was also the subject of some postwar controversy due to his disparaging remarks about the combat operations of the *Waffen-SS*.

ensued between Guderian and his superior, *Generaloberst* von Kleist. Guderian asked to be relieved of command. Rundstedt ultimately refused to accept the resignation and even encouraged Guderian to continue his movements by permitting him to conduct a "reconnaissance in force."

Guderian needed no further encouragement and continued his "reconnaissance-in-force." The *2. Panzer-Division* was the first armored division to reach the English Channel on 20 May. Two days were then lost, since the high command itself seemed surprised by the success and did not issue orders to continue the advance immediately. On 24 May, the *10. Panzer-Division* encircled Calais, but Hitler issued an order to halt on 25 May. The order read, in part: "Dunkirk is to be left up to the *Luftwaffe*. If it proves difficult to take Calais, then it will also be left up to the *Luftwaffe* [to reduce it]."

The army commanders were speechless. The stopping of the ground offensive gave the British the opportunity to embark at Dunkirk and escape capture and defeat. After only 17 days, Guderian's corps had successfully executed its mission, but the failure to eliminate the British Expeditionary Force at Dunkirk was a bitter pill to swallow, since Göring was unable to deliver on the flamboyant promises he had made concerning the abilities of airpower alone to defeat the enemy.

✠

Generaloberst Guderian watches his forces advance. He was not only a gifted theoretician of armor, but also an unflappable combat leader.

On 28 May, Guderian received instructions to form a *Panzergruppe*—the armored equivalent of a field army—to which he would received two corps, the *XXXXIX. Armee-Korps (mot.)* of *General* Schmidt and the *XLI. Armee-Korps (mot.)* of *General* Reinhardt.

The breakthrough towards the Swiss border started from the Rethel-Attigny area on 9 June. When *Generaloberst* List, the commander-in-chief of the *12. Armee*, to which Guderian reported, saw soldiers of the *1. Panzer-Division* setting up camp, cleaning their uniforms and bathing on 9 June, he expressed his displeasure to Guderian, who had just returned from the front lines. Guderian defended his soldiers. He stated that the failure of bridgeheads to be established at the crossing points could not be blamed on his tankers. In his chivalrous way, List immediately offered Guderian his hand as an apology. They continued to discuss the situation, without ever returning to the subject of the *1. Panzer-Division.*

Guderian's formations led the charge into the south of France and were the first to reach border, thanks to the up-front leadership of Guderian and his commanders. The use of the tanks in quick raids had spared the infantry a lot of casualties. Guderian's promotion to *Generaloberst* was announced in the *Reichstag* on 19 July 1940.

Guderian discusses operations with his division commanders after the taking of Roslawl.

✠

At the start of the campaign against the Soviet Union in 1941, Guderian's *Panzergruppe 2* advanced across the Bug to either side of Brest-Litowsk. Five armored divisions, three motorized divisions, one cavalry division and the elite *Infanterie-Regiment (mot.) "Großdeutschland"* reported to him. On 11 July, Guderian watched his forces cross the Dnjepr at Kopys.

Six days later, Guderian had become the 24th member of the German Armed Forces to receive the Oak Leaves to the Knight's Cross of the Iron Cross. *Oberst* Schmundt, Hitler's senior adjutant, personally brought it to Guderian's headquarters on 29 July. In the conversation that followed, Guderian asked Schmundt to argue for a straight thrust to Moscow, "the heart of Russia." He also advised against "delivering small blows that only caused casualties but did not decide anything."

On 1 August, Rosslawl was taken. Three days later, Guderian was summoned to the headquarters of *Heeresgruppe Mitte*. Hitler was to hold court at Nowy Borissow. All of the generals of the field-army group were of one voice in stressing the decisiveness of continuing the offensive directly towards Moscow. Hitler had the final word, however, and stated that the most important objective was the industrial region around Leningrad. It was only then that he could turn towards Moscow and the Ukraine.

On 21 August, orders were issued to conclude the encirclement of Kiev. The fighting, which ended on 26 September, was a great success, with some 665,000 Soviets being taken prisoner. The fighting had cost a great deal of time, however, that could not be recovered.

As a prelude to the assault on Moscow, the offence was then continued in the direction of Orel-Briansk. During the advance on Mzensk, *Panzergruppe Eberbach* encountered Soviet T-34's and KV-I's for the first time. Both tanks proved considerably superior to those the Germans fielded at the time. Despite the continued loss of valuable and highly trained forces, which could not be readily replaced, and the increasingly lengthy supply chain, German armored forces were able to advance into Mzensk on 10 October.

In the days that followed, the first snows—harbinger of one of the severest winters on record that was to come—fell. The roads, never good to begin with, were soon transformed into seemingly bottomless pits of mud. Any effort to advance seemed doomed to failure, although the attack on Tula, an important bulwark outside of Moscow, was ordered. Guderian had all available tanks assembled under the command of one of his ablest armor leaders, *Generalmajor* Eberbach, for the intended advance. Guderian personally accompanied the attack forces on 27 and 28 October. Pissarewo, 30 kilometers south of Tula, was taken. On 29 October, the lead armor elements closed to within 4 kilometers of the outskirts of Tula. It proved impossible to take the city in a *coup de main*, however.

The weather then proved to be an even tougher enemy. On 13 November, the temperature sunk to -22 (-7.6 Fahrenheit). The first damages caused by the killing cold occurred—both to equipment and personnel, neither of which were prepared to cope with the brutal temperatures. The enemy exploited the ability to maneuver again thanks to the hard-frozen ground and started to counterattack. New divisions were brought in from Siberia.

The *2. Panzer-Armee* moved out for a final assault on Orscha on 18 November. Although it had 12 and one half divisions on paper, its combat power had sunk dramatically. Guderian was up front with his forces for three days. On 23 November, he felt compelled to go to the command post of the commander-in-chief of *Heeresgruppe Mitte, Generalfeldmarschall* von Bock, to relay the conditions at the front: exhausted forces that had no adequate stocks of winter clothing and a logistics chain that had failed utterly. He did so with a heavy heart, but his professional conscience and the concern he had for the forces entrusted to him left him no other choice. He had never been one to risk his forces, even though he was always prepared to take bold steps and initiatives, and he recognized the bitter seriousness of the situation.

Von Bock, for his part, requested a change in the mission statement for his field-army group from the army high command. He wanted the attack orders rescinded and permission to fall back to a suitable winter position. The request was turned down by the army command. It was categorically stated that Tula must be taken. When further progress in the direction of Tula appeared even less likely, Guderian called off the attack on 6 December on his own initiative. The situation was becoming increasingly critical for his divisions. Guderian decided to go straight to the Lion's Den and flew to the *Führer* headquarters.

He landed at the Rastenburg air field on 20 December. There was a five-hour meeting with Hitler and a very heated exchange. As Guderian later wrote:

> Hitler: You are too close to the events. You're letting yourself be too influenced by the suffering of the soldiers. You have too much sympathy for the soldiers!
>
> Guderian: It goes without saying that it is my duty to lessen the suffering of my soldiers as best I can. But that is difficult when the men still do not have any winter uniforms and the infantry is running around for the most part in denim trousers. Boots, underwear, gloves, ear protection are either just not there or are in deplorable condition.

Hitler (flaring up): That is not true! The quartermaster general reported to me that the winter clothing had been released.

Guderian: Of course, it's been released, but it hasn't arrived yet. I am following its progress in detail. It's currently at the rail station in Warsaw and hasn't moved beyond that point for weeks. Our requests in September and October were brusquely turned down, and now it is too late!

No one had ever spoken to Hitler like that before. The quartermaster general, who was summoned, had to confirm what Guderian had said. When Guderian left the headquarters, Hitler turned to Keitel and said: "I have not convinced that man!"

The break between the two was complete. Guderian returned to his forces. He ordered a withdrawal to the Susha Position on 25 December. That was contrary to the express directive of Hitler that not a meter of ground was to be abandoned. It was considered to be "disobedience." Von Kluge requested that Guderian be relieved. The request was granted on 26 December, and he was discharged from active duty. *General* Rudolf Schmidt succeeded him in command.

The tankers throughout the force were depressed to hear of the relief. They were robbed of the leader they would have followed blindly anywhere and who had always commanded them well.

At the end of the year, Guderian's heart problems also became worse. He took a cure at Badenweiler at the end of March. One of the first officers to contact Guderian upon his return to Berlin was "Sepp" Dietrich, the commander of Hitler's bodyguard, the *Leibstandarte*. Dietrich had been a tanker in the First World War. He called Guderian directly from the *Reich* Chancellery to demonstrate, as he later recalled, to the people there that they had done wrong to the founder of the *Panzertruppe* and that he had had nothing to do with it. He was as good as his word and also expressed his displeasure to Hitler about the entire affair.

In the fall of 1942, Guderian's fragile heart condition worsened. At the end of November, he suffered a collapse, but he was able to recover under the care of the Berlin professor, Dr. Domarus.

On 17 February 1943, he was surprised to receive a call from the Army Personnel Office and summoned to a conference with Hitler at the latter's headquarters in Winniza. When he arrived, he noticed his books on top of Hitler's desk. Hitler cut to the chase and told Guderian he was naming him the inspector general of armored forces. Guderian demanded authority to go with the position; Hitler granted him his wishes. Now that it was practically too late, Guderian had the command authority over the force he helped create. He selected *Oberst* Thomale,[4] an experienced armor commander, as his chief-of-staff. He assumed his title of *Generalinspekteur der Panzertruppen* on 28 February 1943.

Guderian considered his most pressing duty the reorganization of the armored and mechanized infantry divisions. The new tables of organization and equipment were soon created. On 9 March, accompanied by Thomale, he briefed for four hours at the *Führer* Headquarters. One of the main requests that Guderian made was for the continued production of the proven workhorse of the *Panzertruppe*, the *Panzer IV*, while the newly introduced but still mechanically unreliable *Panther* was "ripe" for series production. After finishing his briefing, he lost consciousness after leaving the briefing area and collapsed to the ground. Hitler was not informed of the attack; otherwise, Guderian may have been relieved of his duties again.

While Guderian was expending all of his energy to restore his beloved *Panzertruppe* to the vaunted and feared force that it once was, plans were already being made for the German summer offensive that would later enter the history books as Operation "Citadel." During the course of one of the planning meetings, in which the production of the *Panther* was discussed, Guderian held on to Hitler's hand during their handshake and requested he be allowed to speak openly to the *Führer*. Hitler took him aside, and Guderian implored him to forego any offensive operations on the Eastern Front that year. The chief of staff of the German Armed Forces, *Generalfeldmarschall* Keitel, inserted himself into the conversation and stated that an attack was necessary for political reasons. Guderian countered by saying that no one knew where Kursk, the campaign objective, was located. He continued, adding that it was completely immaterial to the world at large whether the German Armed Forces held Kursk.

Hitler responded: "You are absolutely correct! I get a queasy feeling whenever I think about this attack."

Guderian's final bit of advice: "Stay away from it!"

Despite that and similar warnings from a host of others, Hitler ordered the attack to go forward. After several delays, it started on 5 July 1943. In return for little perceived success, the newly reorganized and equipped armored divisions and mechanized infantry divisions were badly bruised and battered. In addition, the Soviets launched an immediate counteroffensive, with *Heeresgruppe Mitte* being pushed back. It was thanks largely to the iron wills of the respective commanders-in-chief, *Generaloberst* Model and *Generaloberst* Harpe, that the front eventually stabilized.

---

4. Author's Note: Thomale had received the Knight's Cross to the Iron Cross on 10 February 1942 as an *Oberstleutnant* and commander of *Panzer-Regiment 27* (*19. Panzer-Division*).

The heavy losses sustained in that winter's fighting on the Eastern Front, coupled with the imminent threat of an invasion by the Western Allies, placed ever-increasing demands on Guderian in his efforts to strike a balance and preserve his force. To counter the Allied invasion, Guderian succeeded in staging 10 armored and mechanized infantry divisions in the West prior to the start of the actual invasion on 6 June 1944. They were hampered by the Allied air supremacy and, worse, the fact that the Soviets started their summer offensive later in the month, on 22 June. The Soviet offensive was expected, but in a completely different area, and it caught *Heeresgruppe Mitte* off guard when 146 rifle divisions and 43 armored formations slammed into it. The Soviet quickly succeeded in establishing a deep breakthrough and creating a massive crisis on the Eastern Front.

On 20 July 1944, a bomb detonated in Hitler's briefing room at the Rastenburg *Führer* Headquarters. Guderian had been visiting antitank formations in Hohensalza that day and did not discover the news of the assassination attempt from *Generalmajor* Thomale until after he had returned to his home in Deipenheim. He was summoned to the *Führer* Headquarters. Guderian discovered from Keitel and Jodl what changes were being made in the composition of the general staff as the result of wounds sustained from the blast. Towards noon, Guderian personally reported to Hitler. Hitler asked him to become the chief-of-staff of the army, replacing *Generaloberst* Zeitzler. Guderian accepted the position in the hope that he might be able to use the powerful forces at his disposal as leverage in getting acceptable peace terms, since he no longer harbored any illusions about winning the war. He especially wanted to be in a position to thwart the Soviet advance from the east, which would be the main object of his attention, since the German Army General Staff was only responsible for directing operations in the East. Hitler had long since made the Armed Forces General Staff the arbiters of all operations in all other theaters of war. He was not seeking laurels; instead, he wanted to save what could be saved and create the prerequisites for a negotiated peace.

Guderian took tight control of the reins of the general staff. He designated *Generalleutnant* Wenck as the chief of the operations staff. Guderian's efforts to have Hitler voluntarily give up the Baltics fell on deaf ears. The Soviet offensive in that sector soon separated the northern German field forces from the rest of the Eastern Front and created what was later to become known as *Heeresgruppe Kurland*. Once those forces were contained, the Soviets made preparations for continuing their offensive to the west. The general offensive was launched on 12 January, reaching German territory by 20 January. Guderian attempted to convince the foreign minister, von Ribbentrop, that the war had to be ended. Guderian volunteered to personally approach Hitler on the subject. Von Ribbentrop turned him down.

When Guderian once again pleaded with Hitler for the evacuation of Kurland in February, it almost came to blows between the two, when the *Führer* stood in front of the chief-of-staff with raised, clenched fists. *Generalmajor* Thomale diplomatically pulled his boss away from the scene by the coattails.

A few days later, it again came to a violent argument when Guderian demanded that *Generalleutnant* Wenck be placed in charged of *Heeresgruppe Weichsel*, in place of the totally inept Himmler. Guderian was able to get his way on that issue, since even Hitler realized that Himmler was no field commander. Unfortunately, Wenck was injured badly in a crash on the way to the front and was never able to assume command there.

On 30 March 1945, Guderian left his headquarters in Zossen for good. Two days earlier, he had a final, irreversible break with Hitler. The *Führer* had relieved him with the following words: "*Generaloberst* Guderian, your health requires an immediate convalescent leave of six weeks."

When Guderian arrived home, his wife greeted him by saying how terribly late it was. Guderian replied that it was the last time he would be so late, since he had been relieved.

On 1 April 1945, Guderian entered a sanatorium at Ebenhausen, near Munich. He was accompanied by his wife. On 1 May, he went to the Tyrol, where the headquarters of the Inspectorate General for Armored Forces had moved. On 10 May 1945, he and his headquarters were taken into custody by American forces.

Guderian was assigned to various prisoner-of-war camps before eventually being transported to Nuremberg where, like most of the senior General Staff officers, he was acquitted of any and all charges. He was released from captivity on his 60th birthday, 17 June 1948. He remained in his adopted home state of Bavaria, since he was unable to return to his native region of Prussia, which was occupied by the Soviets and outlawed by the Allies. He turned to writing and in 1950 and 1951 turned out several books concerning the future defense of Western Europe. In 1951, his memoirs—*Erinnerungeneines Soldaten*[5]—appeared and immediately became an international bestseller, being translated into numerous languages.

Suffering from chronic heart problems, he passed away on 14 May 1954 and was buried in his old garrison town of Goslar.

---

5. Editor's Note: The English title of this excellent book is *Panzer Leader*.

A single A7V attacks with assault detachments at Charleroi (Belgium) on 6 September 1918. The Germans only produced about 20 A7Vs and the majority of their tank force consisted of captured British Mark IV tanks. Guderian was markedly influenced by the Aliied use of massed armor formations in the last year of the Great War.

Generaloberst Guderian (sitting) during a short pause in operations in the Soviet Union in 1941.

Generaloberst Hermann Hoth, a gifted armor commander.

CHAPTER 9

Generaloberst Hermann Hoth

COMMANDER OF ARMOR

When retired *Generaloberst* Hermann Hoth accepted the invitation of *Generalfeldmarschall* von Manstein to attend a German television broadcast in 1963 discussing the destruction of the *6. Armee*, a man stepped into the limelight that had heretofore only been known to professionals as a commander of large armored formations. During the broadcast, the retired general officer had this to say:

> For every military leader—whether noncommissioned officer or commander—the carrying of responsibility is the most difficult but unavoidable burden that he has to bear in war: the responsibility for carrying out the mission; the responsibility for the soldiers entrusted to him.
>
> No one can take that responsibility away from him, even those who give him orders. It is the heavy counterweight to the freedom to operate, which has always been the highest principle of Prussian leadership.
>
> Responsibility bore heavily upon all of the leading personalities that were caught up in the calamity of Stalingrad. And they carry that burden up to today. Their actions and inactions were marked by the knowledge of their responsibility before God and their conscience, not by a sense of responsibility to a dictator, who threatened them with the loss of honor, freedom or life.

The words that Hoth spoke were not empty platitudes; they came from a conviction that he proved on numerous occasions.

✠

Hermann Hoth was born on 12 April 1885 in Neuruppin as the offspring of a business and agricultural family. In 1896, after the death of his father, he attended the Prussian academy of cadets in Potsdam and Berlin (Lichterfelde).

In 1904, he joined the Thuringian *Infanterie-Regiment 72* in Torgau as an officer cadet, starting his military career.

One year later, he was commissioned. He served as battalion adjutant for three years and was sent to the War Academy in Berlin in 1910 for training as a General Staff officer. That was followed by six months in his old regiment as adjutant, before he received a new assignment that played a great role in his future military development: He was assigned to the General Staff, where he served under *Oberst* Nicolai, who led the secret intelligence service.

In 1914, he was permanently assigned to the General Staff, where he served according to the dictum of *Generaloberst* von Seeckt: "General Staff officers have no name."

Promoted to *Hauptmann*, Hoth served in Hindenburg's headquarters in 1914, where he experienced the Battle of Tannenberg and the fighting at the Masurian Lakes. During the advance through Mlawa and Grodno towards the Lesser Beresina in 1915, he was a General Staff officer for a corps headquarters. In a twist of fate, he would travel the same route again 26 years later.

In June 1916, the young *Hauptmann* was detailed to the air corps, where he made the acquaintance of the future *Generalfeldmarschall Freiherr* von Fritsch. As the acting commander of *Feldflieger-Abteilung 49*, he saw some of the first aerial fighting of the summer of 1916, before he was transferred to the headquarters of the commanding general for the air corps. Hoth experienced the rise of the new means of warfare first hand.

Shortly before the end of the war, he was assigned to the *30. Infanterie-Division* as its operations officer. He participated in the defensive fighting in the Champagne region, in Flanders and at Arras before the war ended.

After the war, Hoth remained on active duty. Initially, he was a company commander in *Freikorps Maerker*, followed by duty with *Infanterie-Regiment 18*. In 1920, he was assigned to the War Ministry. He was promoted to *Major*. After three years of duty in the ministry, he alternated troop and staff duty. When promoted to *Oberst*, he was placed in command of an infantry regiment in Braunschweig. He then performed staff duty as the senior infantry officer for a military district in Liegnitz, where he was also promoted to *Generalmajor*. One year later, he was promoted yet again, serving as the commander of the *18. Infanterie-Division* as a *Generalleutnant*. By November 1938, he was designated as the commanding general of the *XV. Armee-Korps* in Jena, where he was also promoted to *General der Infanterie*.

✠

In the campaign in Poland, Hoth's corps was employed on the right wing of the *10. Armee*. Hoth's forces succeeded in rolling up the enemy forces south of Tscenstochau and advancing rapidly on towards Lysa Gora. By doing so, his corps blocked the route over the Vistula at Putawy and Deblin to a strong Polish force assembling in the Radom area. His corps then had to fight on a reversed front, where it played a decisive role in the first pocket battle of the Second World War from 9 to 12 September. Seven Polish divisions were taken into captivity.

The success was largely achieved thanks to Hoth's own initiative. As a result, he was one of the first members of the German Armed Forces decorated with the newly instituted Knight's Cross to the Iron Cross at the end of the campaign (27 October).

In the ensuing fighting along the Bzura, Hoth's forces again shined, when they blocked the path of the Polish forces attempting to escape encirclement by moving into the fortress of Modlin. In the end, 20 Polish divisions capitulated.

In both battles, Hoth proved he not only understood the principles of modern maneuver warfare, but that he was also a master at executing them.

✠

During the campaign in the West, Hoth's corps, which was employed in the first wave, had the *5. Panzer-Division*, the *7. Panzer-Division* and the *2. Infanterie-Division (mot.)* allocated to it. Operating on the southern wing of von Kluge's *4. Armee*, it advanced through the northern part of the Ardennes and reached the destroyed crossings over the Meuse at Dinant. By 12 May, the commanding general was standing in front of the destroyed bridge. He ordered the construction of a provisional bridge across the river, to be ready by the morning of 13 May. The effort paid off, and the front of the opposing French 9th Army was rolled up in seesaw fighting on 13 and 14 May. The withdrawing enemy was then pursued.

During the night of 16/17 May, *Generalmajor* Rommel's *7. Panzer-Division* advanced on Avesnes. This paved the way for three corps—Hoth's *XV. Armee-Korps (mot.)* and two other motorized corps—to leapfrog their way in pursuit of the Allied forces fleeing back from Belgium.

A *Gruppe Hoth* was then formed, which consisted of his corps and Hoepner's *XVI. Armee-Korps (mot.)* and Schmidt's *XXXIX. Armee-Korps (mot.)*. Hoth's forces received instructions to screen the advance of *Gruppe von Kleist* to the Somme to the north and to deflect the enemy forces that were withdrawing to the southwest. On 21 May, the British attempted a relief attack at Arras, but it was turned back.

By 24 May, the La Bassé Canal was reached. It was there that Hitler's orders to stop halted the forward advance of the armored divisions. Hoth's bold leadership of his armored forces often appeared too risky to the high command in light of the fog of war that existed over the entire situation. As a result, there was frequent tension between his headquarters and those placed above him.

During the second phase of the campaign in the West, which started on 5 June, Hoth's corps, which had been further augmented by the *1. Kavallerie-Division* and the *11. Schützen-Brigade (mot.)*, was employed on the right wing of the *4. Armee*. Despite the loss of 100 tanks on 5 June, the corps succeeded in rolling up the center of the French 10th Army. On 7 June, the *5. Panzer-Division* and the *7. Panzer-Division* broke through the French lines at the Hornoy Plateau.

Two days later, Rommel's *7. Panzer-Division* was at the Seine at Rouen. The French IX Corps was encircled at St. Valéry. Elements of the British 51st Infantry Division were able to be evacuated by sea, while the French 2nd and 5th Light Cavalry Divisions covered their rear. General Berniquet died at his command post in St. Valéry-en-caux.

Hoth's next mission was to clear the northern French area between the Cotentin Peninsula and Brest. At the end of the campaign, he was promoted to *Generaloberst*, thus marking him for future field army command.

✠

At the start of the offensive against the Soviet Union on 22 June 1941, Hoth's *Panzergruppe 3* was employed with its two motorized corps and 840 tanks along the left wing of *Heeresgruppe Mitte*. Advancing from the Suwalki Triangle, it headed for the Njemen. Once there, it continued through Wilna in the direction of White Russia. On 28 June, the seventh day of the campaign, his forces took Minsk, some 400 kilometers from the frontier. At about the same time, *Panzergruppe 2*, advancing on the field-army group's right wing, arrived in the same area, having moved through Baranowitschi. The first pocket was formed, encircling three Soviet field armies.

On 30 June, *Generaloberst* Guderian flew to Hoth's headquarters at Krewo, where he was warmly received. Both of the commanders-in-chief, who were friends, discussed the continuation of operations. They were of one accord in how they saw their operational objectives. Hoth later wrote that they wanted "to continue sending the armored formations east so as to prevent the enemy from establishing a new front behind the Dnjepr and the Düna." The means to that end: a quick armored raid east.

Generaloberst Hoth then focused all his efforts in getting his forces freed up again after they had been tied down for a week in the pocket battle. In order to avoid having his ideas disapproved, Hoth merely reported on 30 June that he was going to head towards the Düna on 2 July with a force of only four divisions. Those divisions could be withdrawn from the encirclement without endangering its success.

During the subsequent advance on 2 July, *General* von Knobeldorff's *19. Panzer-Division* covered the 200 kilometers to the Düna in 24 hours, despite heavy rain. Hoth's *Panzergruppe 3* then fanned out across the Upper Düna between Polozk and Witensk. Hoth hoped to take Witebsk (Vitebsk) in a *coup de main.* Over the next few days, he discovered that he had not correctly interpreted the enemy situation. A powerful enemy defense held up his divisions, with the enemy going over to local counterattacks with fresh tank forces that had been diverted from the Moscow area.

Hoth personally took charge and oversaw the continued attack preparations for the taking of Witebsk. He decided to commit the *20. Panzer-Division* across the Düna between Witebsk and Polozk so as to then attempt to take Witebsk from the rear. He participated in the planning process for the forced crossing of the river. On the evening of 7 July, Hoth retuned from Ulla to his headquarters at Lepel. On the morning of the following day, the tanks rolled over the military bridge that had been set up across the river; they entered Witebsk the following day. By the evening of 10 July, three armored divisions of Hoth's forces were across the river, and Witebsk was firmly in German hands.

Hoth's operations had brought about a decisive change. For the commanders-in-chief, it then became imperative to exploit the freedom of action they then enjoyed. Hoth, a cool-headed thinker and expert operational planner, reported his decision on the evening of 10 July to pursue the enemy across the Welish to the northeast with the *XXXIX. Armee-Korps (mot.)* of *General der Panzertruppen* Schmidt and across the Newel with the *LVII. Armee-Korps (mot.).*

On 13 July, Hitler's senior adjutant, *Oberst* Schmundt, arrived at the headquarters of *Panzergruppe 3.* Hoth briefed him and closed by saying:

> If the enemy continues to mine the roads and destroy the bridges in the same manner he has up to now, then the rapidity of motorized forces will not be able to be fully exploited; the attrition to the forces will be greater than their achievements. It must then be decided whether to wait for the closing of the non-motorized forces.
>
> If the impression is made that the advance is once again becoming more fluid, then every available vehicle has to be used in the pursuit to Moscow.

That same day, the decision was made at higher levels to hold back on the long-range operations of *Panzergruppe 3*—the headwaters of the Düna—and block the route to the east for the enemy forces located north of Smolensk. Hoth later wrote: "No one knew at the time that the decision would bring about an end to all long-range operations of *Panzergruppe 3* for months."

On 15 July, the *7. Panzer-Division* reached Ulchowo Sloboda, north of Smolensk. For the second time in three weeks it found itself on the Soviet main highway, blocking the most important road east for the enemy forces. The pocket around Smolensk started to form. The *29. Infanterie-Division (mot.)* of *Panzergruppe 2* entered the city from the west. Two days later, Hoth received the Oak Leaves to the Knight's Cross of the Iron Cross for his achievements. He was the 25th member of the German Armed Forces to be so honored. Hoth's forces had achieved the operation prerequisites for the assault on Moscow. But before the armored division could move out to do that, they had to wait for the arrival of the infantry divisions. In addition, the armored forces needed some time to rest and conduct urgently needed maintenance.

Panzergruppe 3 was positioned to the rear of the Smolensk Pocket, with the *7. Panzer-Division* west of Jarzewo and the *20. Panzer-Division* at Ustje (along the Wop). The Soviets attempted to break out in those areas many times over the next few days. It was not until the beginning of August that the *V. Armee-Korps* and the *VIII. Armee-Korps* were able to reduce the pocket enough to free up individual armored divisions.

Hoth took the opportunity at a briefing to Hitler on 4 August at Borissow to inform the *Führer* that the mechanized forces of his armored group had not had enough time to undergo battlefield reconstitution and that he had lost approximately 60% of his armored vehicles. He concluded: "If we have 10 day's time and replacement parts, we can get back to approximately 60 to 70% of our operational strength." Hoth had previously submitted that same information to his commander-in-chief, *Feldmarschall* von Kluge, in writing.

The German Army High Command was harboring hopes of being able to advance on Moscow in a decisive advance by *Heeresgruppe Mitte* by the end of August. Those intentions were shattered by a *Führer* directive: "Further attacks by *Heeresgruppe Mitte* in the direction of Moscow are to be stopped. *Panzergruppe 3* is to immediately give an armored crops to *Heeresgruppe Nord*, since the attack there threatens to bog down."

Despite that transfer of forces, the German Army High Command presented Hitler with a plan to attack Moscow on 18 August. Hitler briskly disapproved the recommendation on 20 August, even though on 12 August he had personally ordered the taking of Moscow before the onset of winter. Hitler stated that the capture of Moscow was not the most important objective of the upcoming operations; instead, it was the taking of the Crimea, the taking of the industrial and coal regions along the Donez and the interdiction of Soviet oil imports from the area of the Caucasus.

The largest envelopment of the war resulted from Hitler's decree of 20 August. With it came a spectacular feat of arms, but it had no decisive impact on the war and made it questionable whether Moscow could be reached as a result of the wear and tear on the forces in the field. It was not until 26 September that the pocket battle of Kiev was ended with the capitulation of four Soviet field armies.

Panzergruppe 3 did not move out again to the east until the beginning of October. The advance on Moscow had been ordered, but it was much too late.

Generaloberst Hermann Hoth in consultation with Romanian officers at his headquarters in 1942.

Hoth's forces were employed along the left wing of *Heeresgruppe Mitte* as part of the *9. Armee*. In the Battle of Wjasma, Hoth's forces formed the northern pincer. On 7 October, elements of Hoth's forces linked up with elements of Hoepner's *Panzergruppe 4* approaching from the south. That created a prerequisite for a continued advance on Moscow.

The Soviet rain period then started, which softened the roads and trails, making it impossible for large-scale troop movements. The forces had to wait for a frost, so that the roads would again become trafficable for heavy vehicles. At that point, Hoth was summoned to take command of the *17. Armee* in the area of operations of *Heeresgruppe Süd*. He led that field army through the difficulties of the mud period and advanced it as far as the middle Donez. Operations then came to a standstill, with the Soviet regaining the initiative by launching counterattacks, which rolled up the front on both sides of Isjum and threatened all of the field-army group.

For months on end, everything was on a knife's edge. It was only through the art of improvisation that the field army was able to master the situation, despite insufficient forces.

On 15 May 1942, Hoth assumed command of the *4. Panzer-Armee*. It was largely thanks to Hoth's forces that the situation along the front was stabilized again after the backhanded victory of the pocket battle of Isjum-Kharkov. At the same time, the victory created the prerequisites for the summer offensive of 1942.

Heeresgruppe Süd of *Generalfeldmarschall Freiherr* von Weichs moved out to launch its offensive on 28 June 1942 with the *2. Armee*, the Hungarian 2nd Army and Hoth's armored field army. The *4. Panzer-Armee* advanced from the area around Kursk in the direction of the Don. It was the main effort of the field-army group, and Hoth had the *XXXXVIII. Panzer-Korps* of *General der Panzertruppen* Kempf lead the way. In a bold move, the corps took Woronesch on 6 July, with *Generalmajor Ritter* von Hauenschild's *24. Panzer-Division* leading the way. Moving downstream from Rossosh, the *4. Panzer-Armee* found itself in the enemy's rear again and reached the Don above the mouth of the Donez on 21 July. During the last remaining days of July, the armored field army was pivoted to the northeast in the direction of Stalingrad while still south of the Don.

During that phase of the fighting, Hoth demonstrated both tactical and operational prowess without equal. His forces—an armored corps, an infantry corps and Rumanian elements—advanced across the Aksai, past Tundutowo and into the area just west of the city by 2 September.

As the result of Hoth's successful efforts, the *6. Armee* received significant relief, when it was subjected to intense Soviet counterattacks north of Stalingrad and was forced to go over to the defensive. Once Hoth's efforts began to be felt, the *6. Armee* was free to continue its offensive. At the same time, the *4. Panzer-Armee* continued its assault in the direction of Stalingrad.

The execution of the attacks by Hoth's forces on Abganerowo and the high ground at Tundutowo, the southern bulwark of the inner defensive ring around Stalingrad, must be considered masterpieces of tactical and operational leadership. Let us examine them a bit more closely.

✠

The *Generaloberst* studied the maps at his command post. His chief-of-staff, *Oberst i.G.* Fangohr assembled and evaluated the latest reports. The commander-in-chief had just been at Kempf's command post and had gone with him to the command post of the *24. Panzer-Division*. Hoth had likewise visited the *14. Panzer-Division* and discussed the situation with *Generalmajor* Heim at the rail station at Tinguta, forming his assessment of the situation. Back at his headquarters he was engrossed in determining what everything meant. A short while later, he turned to his chief-of-staff: "We've got to tackle this differently, Fangohr! We are bleeding ourselves white in front of the high ground. That's no place for tanks. We need to reorganize and continue the attack at a completely differently at a place far away!"

Without wasting time or words, he established his new objectives and intention. The narrow face with the intelligent features had become even more lank and ascetic over the many weeks of fighting. Only his eyes continued to sparkle. When he had finished his plan, he called up field-army group and presented it to *Generaloberst Freiherr* von Weichs. The field-army group command-in-chief gave his blessing.

Hoth then shifted from operational planner to tactician. He pulled his motorized and armored forces out of the front lines and moved them at night, replacing them with infantry divisions. At Abganerowo, 50 kilometers behind the front, he had his mechanized might reassemble and form up into a new attack wedge.

On 29 August, Hoth had his attack force slam into the flank of the Soviet 64th Army. He intended to bypass the strong enemy fortifications along the high ground at Beketowka and Krassnoarmeisk, then pivot and envelop the high ground to the south of Stalingrad. On 30 August, the mechanized formations, supported by infantry formations from the *IV. Armee-Korps*, broke through the Soviet defensive ring around Stalingrad at Gawrilowka. By evening of the second day, the *24. Panzer-Division* was on the Stalingrad-Karpowka rail line, representing a penetration of 20 kilometers through the Soviet defenses.

At that point, the *6. Armee* only needed to advance south with its mechanized forces to form a pocket. The bold operations of Hoth had created the prerequisites for the elimination of the Soviet forces that were covering Stalingrad. Von Weichs issued corresponding orders to Paulus's *6. Armee*, which read, in part:

> As a result of the decisive success of the *4. Panzer-Armee* on 31 August, the opportunity has presented itself to defeat the enemy decisively by attacking his forces located west of the Stalingrad-Woroponowo-Gumrak rail line. It is imperative to quickly establish contact between the two field armies and then advance into the city center.

But before the *6. Armee* could move out on 2 September, Colonel General Jeremenkow had pulled his head out of the noose and pulled back with his two field armies. The two German field armies linked up on 3 September, but the enemy had already disappeared.

The field-army group then ordered the two field armies to exploit the situation and advance into Stalingrad as quickly as possible. The attack on the city started and, by 14 September, Hoth's forces had taken the southern part of the city. On 17 September, the German Army High Command placed the *6. Armee* in charge of reducing the city, whereby Hoth also lost one of his corps, the *XXXXVIII. Panzer-Korps*, to the command and control of *General der Panzertruppe* Paulus.

The Soviet counteroffensive, which started on 19 November, only hit a portion of Hoth's forces. Positioned south of the Volga, only the northern wing of Hoth's field army, the *IV. Armee-Korps*, was pushed into the pocket. Hoth employed his *29. Infanterie-Division (mot.)* under *Generalmajor* Leyser against the elements of the Soviet 57th Army that had broken through south of Stalingrad. The Soviet efforts in the Germans sector were stopped, but the Soviet 51st Army, employed against the Rumanian VI Corps, broke through with its IV Motorized Corps in the lead. The Soviets headed in the direction of Sety.

Hoth was planning on hitting that Soviet force in the flank, when orders arrived from the field-army group that he was not to conduct the attack. Instead, he was to establish defensive positions to protect the *6. Armee*. The *29. Infanterie-Division (mot.)*, as well as the *IV. Armee-Korps*, were reallocated to the *6. Armee*. On 22 November, Hoth and Paulus met in Nischnij Tschirskaja to discuss the situation. On 24 November, a *Führer* order arrived affecting the forces in the pocket: Stalingrad had to be held under all circumstances, and the *Luftwaffe* was directed to supply the pocket from the air.

Hoth's armored divisions were always in the thick of things. As the commander-in-chief of an armored field army, he was feared by the enemy.

Heeresgruppe Don, which had been formed for the crisis situation, was placed under the command of *Generalfeldmarschall* von Manstein. Hoth's forces were allocated to von Manstein's command. Hoth's forces were directed to relieve the encircled forces in Stalingrad. On 12 December, they moved out, with the initial objective of establishing a supply corridor to the trapped forces 100 kilometers away.

In intensive fighting against superior enemy forces, Hoth's men gave their utmost. He attacked with the *LVII. Panzer-Korps*, the only German force he possessed. The remaining forces of his field army consisted of two Romanian corps. As was to be expected, the Soviet drew forces away from the *6. Armee* to combat the relief effort. After seven days of indescribable fighting and effort, Mischkowka was reached, which meant there were only 60 kilometers left between the two forces.

Von Manstein gave the *Führer* Headquarters two options: either bring up new, fresh forces from the Caucasus or have the *6. Armee* attempt to break out from Stalingrad and link up with Hoth's forces. Both of the recommendations offered the opportunity for success and both were rejected.

The relief forces were able to cover another 10 kilometers towards the beleaguered Stalingrad force. Hoth and every soldier of his force waited and hoped for four days for the *6. Armee* to try to break out. But the leadership of the *6. Armee* felt itself compelled to follow Hitler's directive until it was too late.

When the Soviets broke through in the sector of the Italian 8th Army in the middle of December and were soon in the rear of the field-army group, Hoth was forced on 23 December to release his *6. Panzer-Division*, which had been in the thick of the relief effort, to help prevent an even greater catastrophe: "It was an important decision, since it meant the last, albeit weak hope of relieving Stalingrad had to be given up. To prevent an even greater defeat, however, it was necessary."[1]

With a heavy heart, Hoth had to pull back his *LVII. Panzer-Korps*. The *6. Armee* was lost. The Soviets then concentrated their efforts against Hoth's weak field army. The front held by the Romanian 4th Army, which was under the command and control of Hoth, collapsed. Only the *LVII. Panzer-Korps* possessed sufficient combat power and willpower to prevent a catastrophe. With its exhausted forces, and the belated introduction of two fresh motorized infantry divisions, Hoth prevented the Soviets from enveloping *Heeresgruppe Don* from the south and preventing the *1. Panzer-Armee*, which was echeloned forward to the east of Rostow, from having its withdrawal route blocked.

Let us turn to the qualified opinion of Erich von Manstein to see how this unqualified masterpiece of command and control was executed:

---

1. Author's Note: See Horst Scheibert, *Zwischen Don und Donez*.

Generaloberst Hoth accomplished that mission with similar quiet, decisive and agile leadership. He understood how to delay the advance of the enemy forces pressing hard to his front without running into the danger of being defeated by holding on to a position for too long. Moreover, by means of sharp blows from both of his wings by quickly assembled forces he was always able to thwart the intention of the enemy to envelop his field army.

It was through his operations that Hoth was able to save the German forces along the northern banks of the Don. But the Soviets always had enough reserves that they were able to keep up incessant attacks. No less than four Soviet field armies—with strong armored forces in the lead—were able to break through to the field-army group's rearward lines of communications to the south of Slawjansk on both sides of Isjum and along a line running from Kharkov to Bjelgorod.

During the German counterattack launched on 22 February 1943, magnificently planned by *Generalfeldmarschall* von Manstein, it was Hoth's *4. Panzer-Armee* that again formed the main effort. In several phases, the enemy was thrown back from Isjum and Kharkov across the Donez. By the end of March, the Germans had reestablished a defensive front.

✠

During Operation "Citadel," which started on 5 July 1943 and had the elimination of the salient around Kursk as its objective, Hoth's armored field army and *Armeegruppe Kempf* formed the southern arm of the pincers, while Model's *9. Armee* attacked from the north.

In the first five days of the offensive, Hoth's forces penetrated the deeply echeloned Soviet defensive belt, but the *9. Armee* ran into difficulties from the outset, and its attack finally came to a standstill. At the high point of the fighting, with von Manstein still having an armored corps in reserve on the southern part of the front, the German Armed Forces High Command called off the offensive. The threats emerging in other theaters of war did not allow any more attrition of combat power.

After the stalemate at Kursk, the Germans were never again able to achieve the operational initiative in the East. In August, the Red Army launched its summer offensive along a broad front. The *4. Panzer-Armee* was forced back into an area on both sides of Kiev. It was there that it defended against the attacks of the 1st Ukrainian Front at the beginning of November. Kiev was lost; the Soviets reached a line running Fastow-Shitomir-Korosten. It appeared that the Soviets might be able to envelop *Heeresgruppe Süd* from the north and eliminate it.

Hoth was given reserves, with which he was able to interdict the Soviet intentions. The enemy's penetration was reduced through counterattacks, although it could never be completely eliminated. Both Dnjepr and Kiev were lost.

On 15 September, Hoth became the 35th member of the German Armed Forces to receive the Swords to the Oak Leaves to the Knight's Cross of the Iron Cross. A few days later, he was relieved of command by Hitler, who stated that Hoth needed some time to recuperate. He only assumed command of active forces again at the very end of the war, where he was assigned to command forces defending the Harz Mountains.

✠

Following the war, Hoth was charged with war crimes at the U.S. Military's post-Nuremberg trails and sentenced to 15 year's imprisonment. His sentence was commuted and he was released in 1954. Not shaken by the specter of imprisonment, Hoth proceeded to rebuild his life. He went to live in Goslar, where he wrote on a variety of topics concerning military matters. He was also a popular lecturer within the *Bundeswehr* and in military history circles.

Hermann Hoth passed away in Goslar on 25 January 1971.

Even after the Germans were forced onto the defensive, Hoth's forces always skillfully engaged the enemy.

Major Willy Jähde, while serving as commander of *schwere Panzer-Abteilung 502 (Tiger)*.

CHAPTER 10

Major Willy Jähde

IN THE EAST AND WEST WITH TANKS

"*Herr Major*, you're supposed to report to the CG immediately!" the adjutant said to his commander as he entered the command post of *schwere Panzer-Abteilung 502 (Tiger)*.

Major Willy Jähde's forehead wrinkled under the black overseas cap he was wearing cocked over his left ear. He had just returned from visiting his 2nd Company at the front.

"Another Russian breakthrough, Meier?"

Jähde turned around and got back into his *Kübelwagen* staff car. Ten minutes later, he was at the corps command post, where he removed the lamb fur coat he had been wearing to keep warm, before reporting to the commanding general of the *L. Armee-Korps.* Wegener's corps was employed in the northern sector of the Eastern Front just to the south of Leningrad.

The general officer greeted the commander of the regional "fire brigade," as the heavy tank battalion was known. *General* Wegener was a highly decorated and competent officer, who had earned the Oak Leaves to the Knight's Cross in service to his country.

"Jähde, I want you to form a *Kampfgruppe* with the operational elements of your battalion, the 2nd Battalion of *Grenadier-Regiment 377* and *Panzerjäger-Kompanie 240.* I want you to hold the Woronowo-Ssjaskelweo sector against the anticipated Soviet offensive. Your position will be the bulwark of the defenses north of Gatschina."

"I'll need more infantry for that, *Herr General.*"

"Take whatever you can find up there. You're in charge!"

Jähde drove back to his command post. It was night by the time he reached the area of operations. The *Tigers* had been alerted and were on the move. Early on the morning of 21 January 1944, Jähde was in his new sector. Elements of the *9. Luftwaffen-Feld-Division*[1] were there, which Jähde promptly

---

1. Translator's Note: When the *Luftwaffe* started having excess ground personnel due to a loss of aircraft, it was directed to turn its personnel into ground combat formations. Göring, not wanting to cede personnel to the army, arranged for his men to be formed into divisions under *Luftwaffe* command and control. The results were initially disastrous until experienced army personnel could be transferred into the divisions to take over command and control positions.

impressed into his command. He also received engineers from a front-line combat engineer school. Augmented by those infantry elements, Jähde was able to establish an outpost line along the sector he had been assigned. The outposts were directed to interdict any other forces that might be falling back to the rear and send them forward again. That morning, several hundred stragglers were intercepted and either returned to their units or integrated into Jähde's force.

During the evening of 22 January, around 2200 hours, Soviet T-34's broke through the thinly held lines at the northwestern outskirts of Woronowo. When Jähde heard the sound of fighting at the outskirts of the village from his command post in the village center, he ran to the door and told his adjutant to hold out while he got a *Tiger*.

He ran outside and had to head straight for the enemy tanks to get to the positions of the *Tigers*. He started to draw the enemy's attention, and soon there were bursts of machine-gun fire arcing over his head. He took a zigzag course and threw himself to the ground on several occasions. When he saw mounted infantry on the rear deck of the third enemy tank, he brought his submachine gun into position and cleared the deck with a long, well-aimed burst.

The first enemy tank closed to within 10 meters of Jähde and then passed him. He jumped up, only to hear the rattle of Soviet submachine-gun fire. Rounds whistled past his ears. He fired a burst in return and continued on his way to get his tanks.

Once he had passed the third tank, he breathed a sigh of relief, since there were no more enemy tanks to be seen. He made his way to the positions of the 1st Company, where he saw *Leutnant* Ruwiedel, the leader of the battalion's recovery section.

"Where's the closest *Tiger*, Ruwiedel?"

"Over here, *Herr Major!*" *Feldwebel* Haumann called out.

"Follow me! I'll guide you. Three T-34's have broken through!"

"Lead the way, *Herr Major!*"

The tank's engine exploded into life. The tank turned and followed the commander on the ground. As Jähde left, he instructed Ruwiedel to send another *Tiger* as well.

The *Tiger* moved along a side road. All of a sudden, the first T-34 was in sight. Jähde took cover behind a low wall. The T-34 fired. Its round screamed above the turret of the *Tiger*. Haumann's gunner took aim and fired. The round slammed into the broad side of the turning enemy tank and tore it apart in a thunderous explosion.

"Let's go . . . on to the main road!" Jähde called out.

When they reached the main road, Jähde found himself facing the second T-34. The tanks were so close to one another that Haumann was unable to traverse his turret. The third T-34, which was right behind the second Soviet tank, started to back up to be able to engage the German vehicle.

Just at that moment, the second *Tiger* arrived. It was back far enough that it could engage. Its first round dislodged the turret from the hull of the T-34. The second round took care of the T-34 moving in reverse.

That was the not the end of it, however. The sound of fighting could be heard echoing over from the main line of resistance. Jähde had both tanks follow him.

The two *Tigers* followed closely behind. Jähde led them to a field, where they had a clear field of fire into the area where the Soviets were attacking. The *Tigers* fired 10 high-explosive rounds apiece, before the Soviets decided that they had had enough for the time being.

Jähde knew the respite would be short. He ordered his forces on full alert before he returned to his command post and submit a report to the corps.

As it turned first light on 22 January, Jähde was in the front lines again. He visited the elements attached to him, as well as the individual positions of all of his *Tigers*. All of a sudden, an artillery barrage started falling on the German positions. Jähde felt a blow to his right hand. Blood started flowing, when he raised his hand to take a look at the wound.

His adjutant called out: "*Herr Major*, you need to go to the rear!"

"Nonsense, Meier, dress my wound!"

As the officer had his wounds dressed, the Soviets started attacking the right-hand portion of his defensive sector. Jähde's reaction was instantaneous: "Get the reserve company, Meier!"

When Meier brought the men forward, Jähde's orders were brief: "Follow me!"

When the men reached the lines, the Soviets had already advanced as far as the initial dugouts and positions. Jähde charged forward with his submachine gun, the rest of the men following. The Soviets were turned back and the main line of resistance restored.

Later that day, the Soviets increasingly fired on Jähde's command post, which had evidently been discovered. Jähde ordered his headquarters to move 800 meters to the rear. Just as the men reached the new position, the artillery fire increased to a mighty crescendo on the location of the old command post. There was no doubt about it: The Soviets were going to attack again and soon.

Jähde needed to go up front. He asked his adjutant whether the *Kübelwagen* was ready.

"Ready to go, *Herr Major!*" Meier knew the "old man" well enough to realize he would always head towards the sound of the guns. Jähde headed out to his forward companies in the unarmored staff car. He stopped in a depression, dismounted and continued on foot. He made his way towards a machine-gun platoon, where he experienced the violent Soviet attack. When one of the gunners was wounded, Jähde took up position behind the machine gun, despite his wounded hand. He continued firing until a replacement could be brought forward.

The fighting lasted through the night. Towards first light on 23 January, the Soviets advanced with tanks. Most of them were T-34's, which were intended to clear a path for the Soviet infantry through the German positions. But Jähde had positioned his *Tigers* in such a fashion that they could fire on the enemy tanks from the flanks. The mighty "88" once again proved its superior ability to penetrate any known armor on the battlefield. The hydraulics of the turret were so exact that a good gunner never needed to make any corrections after traversing. On 22 January, 12 enemy tanks were left as burning hulks in front of the German lines; on the morning of 23 January, another 11 would be added to the number.

As the fighting was going on, Jähde received a report that the Soviets were attacking the infantry company employed at Ssjaskelewo for the second time, this time in regimental strength. Jähde ordered Kerscher's *Tiger* platoon to report to him. *Feldwebel* Kerscher of the 2nd Company moved forward with his four tanks. *Major* Jähde mounted up with the tanks and soon they were racing towards the threatened sector. It was not a minute too soon when they arrived, since the forward Soviet assault forces, supported by tanks, were already entering the trenches and the village.

A deadly duel ensued. Kerscher, one of the most experienced tank commanders of the battalion and a later recipient of the Knight's Cross, knocked out seven T-34's with his *Tiger*. His remaining three tanks were likewise very successful. The Soviets started streaming back and the area in front of the positions was littered with the smoking wrecks of Soviet armor.

For these actions, *General* Wegener later recommended Jähde for the Knight's Cross. In his recommendation, he wrote:

> *Major* Jähde firmly led his *Kampfgruppe* in defending against numerous enemy attacks—some of them in regiment strength and with heavy tank support—with a great deal of audaciousness, which he repeatedly demonstrated in critical situations. As a tanker, he was able to force his will upon three infantry battalion commanders. As a result, it is solely thanks to *Major* Jähde that this important bulwark of the defense was held.

Two *Tiger I's* advance in battle formation. The *Tiger* at the rear is covering the flanks of the lead vehicle.

✠

Willy Jähde was born in Helmsdorf in the Sorau region on 18 January 1908. He attended school at Forst in der Lausitz and then entered the *Reichswehr*. He was eventually assigned to the 2nd Company of the Prussian *Kraftfahr-Abteilung 6* in Hanover.

After attending the Military Academy in Dresden, he was commissioned a *Leutnant* in 1934. He initially performed duties in the signal corps in Breslau, but he never felt that was quite the branch for him. It was not until he was assigned to the 3rd Company of *Panzer-Abteilung 66* that he felt he had found his military home. The tank battalion was part of the *2. leichte Division* and under the command of *Oberstleutnant* Sieckenius.

Oberleutnant Jähde participated in the campaign in Poland as part of the battalion and division, which had been allocated to *General* Hoth's *XV. Armee-Korps (mot.)*. On the first day of the war, the battalion advanced as far as Kosiecin. Early in the morning of 2 September, Jähde received his baptism of fire. Leading his company, Jähde advanced into Woischnik. For his part in the taking of the town, Jähde was later awarded the Iron Cross, Second Class.

That engagement was followed by the bitter fighting to take Kielce on 5 September. It was the tanks of Sieckenius's battalion that decided the engagement, and the town was in the hands of the division by 1930 hours.

During the fighting in the woods in the Lysa Gora, the tanks were not employed. Instead, they were held in reserve for the division around Bezin. In the subsequent fighting at Szydlowiece, they engaged Polish tanks for the first time. That was followed by the capture of Radom and bitter fighting west of the Vistula on 12 and 13 September. Jähde again distinguished himself, later earning the Iron Cross, First Class, for his actions there.

Following the campaign in Poland, on 18 October 1939, the *2. leichte Division* was deactivated and reformed as the *7. Panzer-Division*. It was determined that the light divisions were too lightly armored for the missions intended for them, with the result that all four of them were converted into armored divisions. The divisional tank element was *Panzer-Regiment 25*, and *Panzer-Abteilung 66* was absorbed into that formation. The regimental commander was *Oberst* Rothenburg, a officer with First World War experience, who had been awarded the *Pour le mérite* during that conflict. Sieckenius's old battalion was redesignated as the 3rd Battalion of the regiment. Jähde, who had just been promoted to *Hauptmann*, was given command of the 9th Company.

Starting on 12 February 1940, *Generalmajor* Rommel took over the reins of command of the division. He was also an experienced officer from the First World War, who had also been honored with the *Pour le mérite*.

The next station in Jähde's career was the campaign in the West. He fought as part of Rothenburg's force that assaulted Haversin on 12 May and advanced to the high ground west of Leignon. On 15 May, Cerfontaine was taken.

The *7. Panzer-Division* formed the main effort of the *4. Armee* of *Generaloberst* von Kluge. The division assaulted far in front of the field army at Cambrai and Arras and took the important high ground east of le Cateau. It was there that Jähde's tanks engaged a superior tank force and knocked out four enemy vehicles. During the evening of 17 May, he experienced firsthand a typical orders conference—Rommel-style—at the high ground near Pommereuil: "Continue to march: Le Cateau–Arras–Amiens–Rouen–Le Havre!"

That same day, the tanks had blasted a path through the Maginot Line. Bunkers, tank traps, field positions and deeply layered wire obstacles had been overrun. It was not without cost: Several German vehicles were lost in the operation. At Cambrai, the 3rd Battalion encountered heavy enemy obstacles. Jähde and his crew just barely escaped being knocked out.

Rommel was rewarded for his audacious operations with the bestowing of the Knight's Cross to the Iron Cross on 27 May 1940. That was followed by the award of the Knight's Cross to *Oberst* Rothenburg on 3 June. Another famous personage of the regiment, Adalbert Schulz, then a *Hauptmann* and commander of the regiment's 1st Company, received the Knight's Cross that fall, on 29 September.

After the campaign in the West, Jähde was reassigned to the Armor School at Putlos, where he was a class advisor to the Noncommissioned Officer Academy. Many young noncommissioned officers benefited from Jähde's experience and sage advice at the school. He stressed loyalty to the chain-of-command and the soldiers placed in one's trust as well as tactical prowess.

Upon his promotion to *Major*, Jähde was sent to the 1st Battalion of *Panzer-Regiment 29* of the *12. Panzer-Division*, where he assumed command. That division was one of the few armored divisions employed in the northern sector of the Eastern Front, terrain that was generally unfavorable to the large-scale employment of tanks. When Jähde arrived at the division's location, it was in the process of undergoing a battlefield reconstitution. When it returned to combat operations, Jähde found himself and his battalion employed between Puschkin and Urizk in August and September. Jähde quickly learned of the different conditions that were prevalent there. Beside the restrictions of the terrain, the limited number of German tanks were often faced with vastly superior quantities of Soviet armor. Consequently, the tanks often fought defensively or were only employed for local counterattacks. Nonetheless, Jähde scored significant success at the Pogostje Pocket and in the area around Tottolowo, and his superiors took notice.

In the fall of 1943, Jähde was reassigned to *schwere Panzer-Abteilung 502 (Tiger)*, replacing *Hauptmann* Oehme. His baptism of fire with the battalion was during the defensive fighting at Newel in November 1943. When things

Knocked-out enemy tanks on the Eastern Front. In the foreground is a Lend-Lease British Valentine infantry-support tank. In the background is a T-34/76. The Russians appreciated the relatively heavy armor of the Valentine but not the puny (40 mm) main gun. The T-34 was a markedly superior tank in all respects, but the Russians were desperate for armored vehicles.

started turning critical in the Gatschina area, the battalion was rail-loaded and expedited there.

Despite Jähde's efforts to avoid having his battalion split up, the 1st Company was immediately committed from the railhead before the rest of the battalion arrived, since the Soviets had broken through with superior forces in the area between Leningrad and Gatschina. One axis of attack for the Soviets was along the shore banks, while the other was east of Gatschina and in the direction of Puschkin.

What Jähde feared would happen happened. The Soviets surrounded the 1st Company along the road. *Leutnant* Mayer's platoon was eliminated. When the Soviets attempted to take Mayer prisoner, he shot himself.

A few days later, Gatschina had to be abandoned. The withdrawal moved along the Gatschina-Wolossowo-Narwa road. Whenever the situation threatened to become critical, Jähde and his men showed up. Jähde was also known as a selfless commander, who did everything for his men.

That was the case, for instance, when *Leutnant* Carius's platoon had to serve as a rearguard and two of his vehicles developed mechanical problems. Jähde summoned the vehicles back and also went forward to help escort them, even though he had to move through Soviet elements that had already reached the road just outside of Wolossowo. He linked up with the vehicles on a trail south of the main road, which had been rendered trafficable due to the frost.

"A *Kübelwagen* approached us," Carius recounted later, "at first light. It was *Major* Jähde, who didn't think twice about coming out by himself to link up with us, despite the danger, and, if necessary, getting us out, even though there was not a German soldier to be seen near or far. He hugged me and admitted that he had already written us off. He was really happy to see that we had towed the two broken-down vehicles along."

Jähde informed Carius that the road outside of Wolossowo was already occupied by the enemy. Without Jähde's warning, they would have moved right into the midst of the enemy.

The men decided to head south after it had turned dark, bypassing the marshland and the Soviets and then swinging back towards Wolossowo. The main guns of the disabled tanks were turned to 6 o'clock in case any Soviets decided to pursue them.

When it turned dark, Jähde boarded Carius's tank and took up a position at the loader's feet. He took a quick nip from his flask and ordered the force to move out. When the tanks reached the area south of the marshland, they suddenly started to receive antitank-gun fire from the rear. One of the towed tanks was hit in the turret. *Feldwebel* Wesely, who was towing that tank, then eliminated the enemy antitank gun with his own main gun. The trouble was not over, however. Soviet infantry then assaulted the tanks, aided by the darkness. They tried to knock out the tanks with bundled charges and Molotov cocktails. Carius and his tankers drove back the attackers with hand grenades and crew served weapons. After the harrowing experience, they finally reached Wolossowo, where the rest of the battalion was located. Jähde was talking to the local commander, *Oberst* Wengler,[2] when Soviet armor attacked.

The immobile tanks were positioned along the flanks to provide covering fire. The two operational tanks then engaged the attacking Soviet force. The Soviets were driven back in the nighttime fighting, leaving behind a number of burning wrecks. Just after midnight, however, they attacked again. Jähde counted 26 tanks, mostly T-34's. The fighting started anew. The tanks ran low on ammunition and eventually only Jähde's tank and that of his adjutant had ammunition. Nevertheless, they continued the fight, even launching an immediate counterattack.

Jähde proved himself not only an able battalion commander but also an excellent tank commander. He narrowly missed being knocked out or destroyed on several occasions. He maneuvered, halted, fired and advanced again, with his machine guns also engaging the accompanying Soviet infantry. The two *Tigers* rolled through the Soviet forward positions, crushing machine guns mounted on sleds and flattening antitank guns. At such close range, every round fired by the *Tigers* was a deadly hit. The two *Tiger* crews worked together in unison; the crews practically robotic in their precision movements. Jähde's crew knocked out a total of nine Soviet tanks; eventually, his tank was hit and rendered combat ineffective. He and his adjutant, whose tank had knocked out six Soviet armored vehicles, rolled back to Wolossowo. Jähde had been wounded, but he refused to go to the rear. He stayed up front with his men. It was his seventh wound.

Three hours later, the Soviets attempted another attack. Once again, strong infantry elements were preceded by armor. They attacked from both the west and the southwest. But they were turned back once again. The road, which the enemy had occupied in places, was cleared, enabling the withdrawal to the west to continue.

Right after receiving the Knight's Cross, Jähde received a new assignment. After convalescing from his wound, he was to take command of the training units for tankers at the Noncommissioned Officer Academy. Although the new assignment was considered a step up the career ladder, Jähde did not

2. Author's Note: Wengler was the commander of *Grenadier-Regiment 366*. He was the 123rd member of the German Armed Forces to be honored with the Oak Leaves to the Knight's Cross to the Iron Cross on 21 January 1945. He was killed in action in the spring of that year while serving as a *Generalmajor* and commander of the *227. Infanterie-Division*.

look forward to it. He would have preferred to have remained as commander of the battalion. The battalion also did not want to see him leave. He was a commander after their own hearts. Jähde had a hard time suppressing his tears when he shook hands with his men for the last time in Pleskau.

✠

Jähde remained at the school until just before the end of the war, when he was ordered to form a *Kampfgruppe* with cadre, students and stragglers. He led his battle group into the area around Kassel and the Harz Mountains, where he was eventually captured by the Americans, who eventually released him from captivity later that same year. He returned to his home region, which was occupied by the Soviets. In Eisenach, they tried to accuse him of war crimes, but were unable to produce a single bit of evidence against the blameless officer.

In August 1961, Jähde escaped from the Soviet zone into the west, abandoning everything behind him. He reestablished himself in Munich and passed away in Dillingen on 25 April 2002.

Jähde shares a lighter moment with his *Tiger* crew.

General der Panzertruppen Walter Kempf was successful in command at both division and corps level.

CHAPTER 11

General der Panzertruppen
Werner Kempf

FROM NAVAL CADET TO ARMOR COMMANDER

The 12th of May 1940 was transitioning to dusk as the long columns of the *6. Panzer-Division* made their way towards the Meuse. At 1640 hours, a messenger from the division communications center brought a radio message to the command vehicle of *Generalleutnant* Kempf. According to the message, the lead elements of *Generalmajor* Rommel's *7. Panzer-Division*, which were racing ahead of the other elements of *Generaloberst* Hoth's *XV. Armee-Korps (mot.)*, had reached the Meuse at Yvoir.

The division commander immediately headed towards his lead elements, where he ordered them to move as rapidly as possible to the Meuse. Advancing as part of *General* Reinhardt's *XXXXI. Armee-Korps (mot.)*, Kempf also wanted to play a role in conducting the decisive effort.

One of his aides turned to him: "It's getting dark, *Herr General*. The advance is coming to a standstill, because the routes cannot be identified."

Without hesitation, Kempf replied: "Order the advance guard to turn on its lights and move as rapidly as possible!"

On the far bank of the Meuse, the French defenders suddenly saw an illuminated snake of steel that was approaching the point where the Semois spilled into the Meuse.

The French commander in the sector, General Potzert, thought he was observing a torch-lit parade. He wished he had ground-support aircraft available to support him; they could not miss such an inviting target. Instead, he had to rely on his own resources—the 102nd Fortress Infantry Division.

Of course, the fact that they were such inviting targets was not lost on the men in the vehicles, either. Even *General* Kempf was not sure he had made the right decision, but he saw a golden opportunity and he did not want to miss it.

The general from Eastern Prussia, his somewhat broad face serious and reserved, led from the front. He spurred on the lagging motorized riflemen and guided his tanks true to the principles of maneuver warfare that he had been among the first to advocate along with Lutz and Guderian.

One of his liaison officers recommended he needed to get some rest. His answer was quick and to the point: "Our men can't do that . . . that's why we'll continue to move up front with them."

Whenever he looked behind him, the general saw the torch-lit parade, as the men had begun to refer to their night march. But they made their way to the river without incident. No bombs fells; no one blocked their route.

The divisional reconnaissance assets, which had been sent to the front, reported that they had reached the banks of the Meuse at first light. Kempf ordered his tanks forward to provide covering fire; he then had the combat engineers brought forward to prepare for an assault crossing.

The general issued his orders without wasting any words. The 54-year-old general officer did not feel tired. For him it was imperative to act quickly and decisively. He needed to attack quickly, break through the enemy front and then employ the principles of maneuver warfare he had advocated for so long.

The general raced forward to the river in his command tank, closely followed by a radio vehicle. A section of *Panzer II's* followed the general to give the mobile headquarters some protection. The sun had started to rise on that morning of 13 May and its rays beamed down on the silver band of the river. A few French artillery batteries had already stated to fire from the far side.

"Where are the engineers?"

"They're heading here at top speed, *Herr General.* They have to be here shortly!" Machine-gun fire whipped across the river towards the group around the general, forcing the men to take cover.

"Have the tanks eliminate the machine-gun nests and artillery positions; have them move behind the embankment to give covering fire to the riflemen."

"The 3rd Rifle Battalion is just arriving, *Herr General!*"

"Have the riflemen cross in the dead angle. They are to take the village of Montherme on the hill on the river bend."

The riflemen started to arrive, while the tanks waited for them from their concealed positions along the river bank. The engineers also started to arrive and got their assault craft ready.

Kempf ordered his tanks to start providing covering fire. Once the fire was opened, the riflemen raced towards the water and jumped into the available craft. The motors of the boats sprang to life and the vessels started to head for the opposite bank.

The boats started to receive machine-gun fire. Wherever the tanks could make out muzzle flashes, they immediately took the enemy forces under fire with their main guns and machine guns. The enemy positions were slowly eliminated, and only one of the assault craft was sunk. The passengers were able to swim to safety on the near shore.

The riflemen ran into a brigade of the French 102nd Division, consisting of colonial forces. Machine guns were still firing from Montherme. The men reorganized to eliminate the enemy forces in the village.

The division artillery ranged on the village and soon covered it in a hail of fire. The first fires started to tongue their way skywards from stricken buildings; soon, the entire village was in flames. A pyrotechnic was fired into the air just outside of the village and arced its way through the sky, indicating the riflemen had reached their attack positions. The tanks ceased firing into the village, and the riflemen stormed ahead.

The crossing point was soon secure and the division began moving to the other side. Kempf crossed with his forces and reorganized for the continued attack. He sent his advance guard out and the division followed closely behind.

In a breathtaking advance, Kempf's forces rapidly gained ground to the west. The general avenue of advance took them towards Mon Idée. Whenever the enemy attempted to put up any resistance, Kempf's agile leadership and employment of maneuver warfare techniques soon eliminated him.

By the evening of 13 May, the French front lines had not only been penetrated, but Kempf's tanks were already 65 kilometers west of the Meuse. Later on, Kempf would receive the Knight's Cross for the stupendous feat-of-arms (3 June 1940).

✠

Werner Kempf was born on 9 March 1886 in Königsberg.[1] He was born to be a soldier and entered the corps of cadets at the first opportunity, entering his active-duty service with *Infanterie-Regiment 149* in Schneidemühl. In 1912, the young *Leutnant* was transferred to the marine infantry and was assigned to the 2nd Sea Battalion, which was commanded by *Major* von Lettow-Vorbeck.

He was soon assigned with the task of training the naval cadets on the training ship, the *Vineta*, and spent the next two years on voyages that took him around the globe, from the West Indies to South America.

When a revolution broke out on Haiti, the ship sent its marine infantry cadre ashore, and Kempf was entrusted with leading it for several weeks. When the war started in 1914, Kempf was named as the adjutant of *Marine-*

---

1. Translator's Note: Königsberg, sometimes referred to as Kaliningrad, is still held by the Russian military and used as a naval base. It is restricted territory to this day, and Russia considers it part of its country, even though separated from its territory by the Baltic States.

Infanterie-Regiment 2, which had been formed out of his old battalion. The regiment was committed on the Western Front, where it was inserted into the hot spots of the fighting. In January 1916, Kempf was promoted to *Hauptmann* and earmarked for General Staff officer training. At the beginning of 1918, he was assigned to the headquarters of the marine infantry corps of *Admiral* von Schröder in Flanders. After the war, he served in a free corps as part of *Marine-Brigade Erhardt.*

Kempf was accepted into the 100,000-man army of von Seeckt, where he served as a company commander in *Infanterie-Regiment 4* in Stargard. Two years later, he performed staff duties in Schwerin/Mecklenburg.

Until the spring of 1926, Kempf had had little to do with motorized elements. That was to change dramatically, when he was asked whether he wanted to be assigned to a motorized battalion. He agreed and was sent for practical training to *Kraftfahr-Abteilung 1.* He was then assigned to the Directorate of the Inspector General of Motorized Forces, led by *General* von Bockelberg, on 1 October 1928 as its operations officer. In that capacity, he became one of the driving forces behind the creation of what was to become the *Panzertruppe.* He later wrote:

> The necessity for a modern army to possess tanks was clear. We were forbidden to have them. Did it make any sense for the *Reichswehr* to use dummy vehicles and train the forces in that manner in fighting with and against tanks? The questions was very controversial. We answered without hesitation in the affirmative and it led us to procuring . . . mock-ups.

First under von Bockelberg, and then under his successor, *General* von Stülpnagel, Kempf worked closely with the chief-of-staff of the Directorate, *Generalmajor* Lutz. Lutz had originally served as a Bavarian engineer officer, who was designated as the motorization officer of a field army in the First World War. He continued his interest in the issue of motorization after the war and later became the Inspector General of Motorized Forces. He was the first general officer to bear the title of the newly created rank of *General der Panzertruppen* (1935). As his chief-of-staff, he selected another name that would become synonymous with the creation of the *Panzertruppe, Oberst* Heinz Guderian.

Oberstleutnant Kempf was sent to Munich to command *Kraftfahr-Abteilung 7.* He served in command from February 1932 to the end of June 1934. During the maneuvers of 1932, he served as the commander of an *ad hoc* motorcycle battalion that impressed all with its speed and maneuverability.

He then served as the chief-of-staff for the Directorate of Motorized Forces, succeeding Guderian. Kempf later wrote:

> The struggle in the Ministry of the Armed Forces, which had already been initiated by *General* Lutz and Guderian, centered around two issues:
> a) The tank was not an auxiliary arm of the infantry. Instead, it was the main weapon of separate, full motorized armored divisions.
> b) Motorization, in general, needed to be pushed forward at an even greater tempo. The engine was vastly superior to the horse. The cross-country mobility of the motorized vehicle was sufficient (proven by the summer and winter terrain trials).
> At the time, no one even perceived that a few years later (in 1944), the Americans and English would land in France without bringing a single horse.

With regard to *General* Lutz, Kempf had the following to say:

> I worked together with *General* Lutz as both operations officer and chief-of-staff in perfect harmony. The service *General* Lutz performed in motorizing the army was extraordinarily large. His unflappable nature was a great counterpoint to the temperamental Guderian, who affronted those responsible in the ministry with ease.
> Despite that, Guderian was the driving force. Above all, he recognized early on the importance of armor in future conflicts; later on, he was the advocate for the fully motorized armored divisions.

On 1 October 1937, Kempf was given another armored command, this time the *4. Panzer-Brigade* in Stuttgart. When the start of the war, Kempf, who had been promoted to *Generalmajor*, was given command of an *ad hoc* armored formation that was referred to as *Panzer-Division Kempf*. Army elements, joined by formations of the *SS-Verfügungstruppe*, the forerunner of the *Waffen-SS*, were shipped to Pillau and committed to the campaign from there.

Kempf led his formation with distinction, advancing across the Narew and Bug Rivers and demonstrating the value of a large armored force in conducting raids.

After the campaign in the West, *Generalleutnant* Kempf was given command of the *XXXXVIII. Armee-Korps (mot.)*. The armored corps was allocated to *Generalfeldmarschall* von Rundstedt's *Heeresgruppe Süd* and was employed north of Krystinopol to cross the Bug, whereupon it advanced in the direction of Uman.

On 1 July, Kempf was promoted to *General der Panzertruppen*. His forces— the *9. Panzer-Division* of *Generalleutnant Dr.* Hubicki, the *16. Panzer-Division* of *Generalmajor* Hube and the *25. Infanterie-Division (mot.)* of *Generalleutnant* Clößner—broke through the Stalin Line at Ljubar. Later on, Hube was awarded the Knight's Cross to the Iron Cross for his role in those operations (1 August 1941).

Kempf drove his corps forward through a series of rapid raids. Uman was bypassed to the north. On 1 August, Kempf's forces were at Nowo Archangelsk. There were then three Soviet field armies in the pocket that had been formed—the 6th, 12th and 18th Armies. The classic battle of envelopment with a reversed front yielded a net of 103,000 prisoners.

That was followed by the pocket battle of Kiev. It was Kempf's corps that led the charge at the front of von Kluge's *Panzergruppe 1*. He led from the front, frequently going from division to division. He led as he had taught during the formative years of the *Panzertruppe*. On the evening of 10 September, in the middle of a powerful summer thunderstorm, his forward elements reached the Dnjepr. Kempf did not rest on his laurels. He had his forces immediately attempt to cross the mighty river.

While Kempf had already established his reputation in France, his forces went on to even greater success in the Soviet Union.

By the next day, his corps engineers had thrown bridges across the river. The lead elements of the *18. Panzer-Division* were the first ones to cross. With them was the commanding general. Despite the deplorable road conditions, the advance was also continued at night. The new avenue of advance was aimed at Lubny, east of Kiev, which was to the rear of the Soviet forces concentrated in front of the German armies. In the space of 12 hours, the *16. Panzer-Division* churned its way 70 kilometers through the mud, closely followed by the *9. Panzer-Division*.

Kempf ordered the division to take the bridge over the Ssula in a *coup de main*. The division engineers of the *16. Panzer-Division—Panzer-Pionier-Bataillon 16*—moved out with its 1st Company to conduct the surprise attack. Firing smoke to conceal their movements, the men reached the bridge and charged into Lubny on the eastern side. Once the bridge was secure, *Schützen-Regiment 64* followed closely behind. The fighting continued all of 13 September, and the final Soviet elements did not lay down their arms until Sunday, 14 September.

Kempf then sent elements north to link up with Guderian's forces advancing south. At 1820 hours on 14 September, the two armored forces met, closing the ring around Kiev, some 200 kilometers east of the city. Kiev itself fell on 19 September. Budjenny's field army group had been effectively destroyed, although the field army commander and his political advisor, Nikita Khrushchev, escaped by air.

Kempf's corps took in some 109,000 prisoners by the end of the operation. In all, some five field armies surrendered, yielding the Germans 650,000 prisoners.

Moving though seas of mud, the corps reached and took Kursk at the beginning of November. The corps stopped its offensive operations for the winter, renewing them in 1942. Kempf's corps was employed as the main effort of Hoth's *4. Panzer-Armee*. The *24. Panzer-Division* formed the spear, while the *16. Infanterie-Division (mot.)* brought up the left and *Infanterie-Division "Großdeutschland"* the right. The armored division was directed by Kempf to take the important city of Woronesch in a *coup de main*. *Generalmajor Ritter* von Hauenschild understood his orders. Kempf had demanded an "unswerving advance" and that's what he got. Kempf also allowed his division commander the latitude to make decisions that seemed appropriate for the situation. Ten days after the advance started, the city fell to the *24. Panzer-Division*. The operations of the division are still studied in Germany today as an example of how to conduct offensive armored operations.

With the taking of Woronesch, the Don had been reached. It was crossed west of Remontnaja. Kempf's corps had cleared the way for the rest of the *4.*

Panzer-Armee. It then started its pursuit of the withdrawing enemy in the large bend of the Don.

On 10 August, Kempf was honored with the Oak Leaves to the Knight's Cross to the Iron Cross. He was the 111th member of the German Armed Forces to receive the high award. By the end of August, his corps was near the southern approaches to Stalingrad. On 1 September, Kempf personally led the *14. Panzer-Division* and the *29. Infanterie-Division (mot.)* in the direction of Pitomnik. On the previous day, the *24. Panzer-Division* had achieved a 20-kilometer-deep penetration and reached the Stalingrad-Karpowka rail line. It was an effort to encircle the Soviet 62nd and 64th Armies. *General der Panzertruppe* Paulus's *6. Armee* only needed to pivot south to form the northern arm of the pincers. Unfortunately, it moved too slowly and the Soviet forces, which later became the mainstays of the defense in Stalingrad, were able to escape.

At that point, Kempf was summoned to the *Führer* headquarters to receive his Oak Leaves from the hand of Hitler. Once there, Kempf was informed that he was to remain in Germany, recover from the strain of the continuous fighting and await new command orders. He was granted a few months of respite and thus escaped the hell surrounding Stalingrad.

On 15 February 1943, Kempf was given command of an *ad hoc* field-army detachment. *Armee-Abteilung Kempf* was given the task of clearing up the dangerous situation around Kharkov, which he did in masterful fashion. Later that year, his field-army detachment became part of the southern arm of the German offensive geared at retaking the salient around Kursk. His forces included the *XI. Armee-Korps* of *General der Infanterie* Raus and the *III. Panzer-Korps* of *General der Panzertruppen* Breith. His forces were given the mission of covering the flanks of the main effort of Hoth's *4. Panzer-Armee.*

The offensive started on 5 July. Raus's corps crossed the Donez and created the prerequisite necessary for Breith's corps to close up to the right wing of the *SS-Panzer-Korps* of *General der Waffen-SS* Paul Hausser. Bitter fighting broke out between Kempf's forces and those of General Vatutin's Woronesch Front, with its 5th Guards Tank Army and the 5th Guards Army. On 12 July, the offensive was called off, despite signs of promise in the south, because of the Allied invasion on Sicily and the signs of a Soviet counteroffensive to the north around Orel.

On 8 August, Kempf's forces were reorganized and redesignated as the *8. Armee.* It became Kempf's mission to hold back the forces of General Vatutin heading for Kharkov. After coordinating with *Generalfeldmarschall* von Manstein, Kempf proposed to evacuate Kharkov in a timely manner to reduce casualties and the losses of irreplaceable materiel. Hitler, however, considered the recommendation as a sign of weakness and disloyalty. He relieved Kempf of his command and placed him in the unassigned officer manpower pool. Kempf was never given another command again.

✠

After the war, he resettled in Bad Harzburg. He participated in the rebuilding of the German armed forces in the postwar years and was a frequent visitor to military schools. When he passed away on 6 January 1964, soldiers of the *Bundeswehr* served as an honor guard over his coffin, which was covered with the flag of his East Prussian homeland.

Kempf in command of an *Armeeabteilung*, an ad hoc formation between a corps and field army in size, along with his chief-of-staff at the time, *Generalmajor* Speidel, who would later be instrumental in rebuilding the German Armed Forces after World War II.

Oberst Willy Langkeit, most famous as the commander of *Panzer-Regiment "Groß-deutschland."*

CHAPTER 12

Generalmajor Willy Langkeit

ARMORED BATTLE GROUPS IN THE ATTACK

The *14. Panzer-Division* had started its preparations for the attack on Rostow on 19 October 1941. There was a deeply echeloned system of bunkers and field fortifications that extended around the city. Through scissors scopes, the German officers could see that there were still thousands of Soviets, mostly women, still busy improving the positions.

In addition to the *14. Panzer-Division*, which formed the main effort in the center, there were two other German formations participating in the planned attack: On the right was the *13. Panzer-Division*; on the left was the reinforced brigade of the *Leibstandarte SS Adolf Hitler*. Command and control of the operation was the function of the *XIV. Armee-Korps (mot.)*.

The attack, which was launched on 20 October, bogged down, however. Hours of rain had softened up the roads and trails, which were not in good condition to begin with, in addition to making cross-country movement almost impossible, even for tracked vehicles. The situation did not change over the next few days.

Because of the inclement weather, the attack was delayed until the middle of November. After the orders conference on the evening of 16 November, *Hauptmann* Willy Langkeit hurried back to his battalion. Ever since the battalion commander had been wounded on 21 August, Langkeit had assumed acting command of the 2nd Battalion of *Panzer-Regiment 36*. He summoned his two company commanders for the attack; only two, since all of the tanks of the regiment had been consolidated into the two companies that formed the tank component of *Kampfgruppe Langkeit*.

"Comrades, we're finally moving out again tomorrow! Our mission is to penetrate the Soviet field positions south of Generalskoje and Nesswetaj at first light and roll through to Rostow."

"Who's attacking with us, *Herr Hauptmann?*"

"*Oberst* von Falkenstein is leading the 1st Battalion of the 103rd from the north to Generalski-Most; the rest of the brigade is advancing with us.

Overall command is with *Oberst* Jesser. Intermediate objective for tomorrow is Bolschilije Ssaly . . . "[1]

After issuing detailed instructions, Langkeit dismissed his company commanders so they could start making their preparations.

✠

"Panzer . . . marsch!"

Langkeit heard the radioed order from von Jesser and raised his hand and pumped it vigorously three times in the air. The tanks of his battle group started to move, followed closely by the trucks and the few *SPW's* carrying the riflemen. The roar of the tanks echoed through the pale light of breaking dawn on 17 November. The sound of the tank engines was reinforced by the sound of crunching ice as the tracks moved across the frozen landscape. The command tank reached a small depression. When it emerged out the other side 100 meters farther on, it was greeted by furious fire from the Soviet field positions.

The tank hatches slammed shut. The two companies spread farther apart and started their methodical bounding and firing to advance towards and break through the field positions. The tanks started to pick up speed as they neared the first line of defenses, which were spewing fire in their direction.

The first few enemy positions were silenced. The enemy antitank guns on the flanks were engaged by the tanks that had been held back for that purpose. The positions were barely 20 meters away, when one of the antitank guns fired directly at the command tank of Langkeit. Fortunately, the round struck the reinforcing armor plate on the front of the tank and howled skywards. The gunner responded immediately, and the antitank gun blew apart in a violent explosion. The tanks then reached the trench line, which they then collapsed with their tracks. The Soviets jumped up and ran to the rear, followed by the machine-gun fire of the pursuing motorcycle infantry, who were clearing the trench line and the dugouts.

"Keep going!" Langkeit ordered.

The tanks then took on and overcame the second and third lines of defense. They had punched through, but were still receiving flanking fires from the positions that had not been eliminated to the flanks. They had to be engaged and eliminated as well, if the riflemen hoped to advance. They were taken out one by one, and the Germans slowly advanced meter by meter.

---

1. Translator's Note: Von Falkenstein was the commander of the division's *Schützen-Brigade 14*, which consisted of the two motorized rifle regiments of the division, *Schützen-Regiment 103* and *Schützen-Regiment 108*. *Oberst* von Jesser was the commander of *Panzer-Regiment 36*.

Soviet tanks started to appear. In the midst of the melee that had erupted in the Soviet defensive positions, there was then the cacophony of tank engagements. Two T-26's fired at Langkeit's tank. Fortunately, the rounds ricocheted harmlessly. The first enemy tank went up in flames; the second T-26 turned to pull back, but Langkeit's gunner hit it in the flank and it started to burn.

The other Soviet tanks started to flee. Langkeit had the tanks of his force pursue. By evening twilight, they had reached the day's objective: Bolschije Ssaly. The battle group commander ordered his forces to set up an all-round defense, known as a hedgehog.

That night, the Soviets poured continuous fire into the defensive perimeter. Artillery shells plowed up the ground. The tank crews were forced to remain in their vehicles.

At first light on 18 November, the Soviets launched a counterattack from out of the city, supported by tanks. Langkeit ordered his tankers to wait until the enemy force had closed to within 600 meters. Like a mighty peal of thunder, the tanks opened fire when the enemy had approached to within the designated range. In addition to T-26's, there were also the considerably deadlier T-34's. Then, a handful of KV-I's and KV-II's appeared.

Von Manteuffel visits his forces during the hard defensive fighting around Jassy (Romania) in May and June 1944. At his side is the regimental commander, *Oberst* Langkeit.

Langkeit ordered one of his platoon leaders, Bergmann, to interdict some enemy tanks attempting to break though on the right flank. The heavy platoon pivoted in the direction of the new threat and started to engage. The fight lasted about three minutes, with the reports of main guns echoing through the air. The hit enemy tanks were engulfed in smoke and flames. The Soviet tanks then scattered and described a wide arc as they headed for the protective concealment of the neighboring woods. Langkeit's men had turned back the first enemy counterattack.

Two more enemy tank attacks were likewise turned back. In the end, there were 17 enemy tanks immobilized, knocked out or completely destroyed on the battlefield.

The German attack could not be continued, however, since the Soviets were counterattacking all along the front—from the south, southeast and southwest. The Soviets manhandled heavy guns forward to engage the German tanks. Maneuvering cleverly, the Germans were able to approach the guns and knock them out. In all, the armored battle group accounted for 17 tanks, 36 artillery pieces, 2 antiaircraft guns and 2 antitank guns on that 17 November. In addition, numerous prisoners were taken. *Oberst* von Jesser discussed operations for the next day with Langkeit that evening: "Langkeit, I want you to attack with the tanks in the first wave at first light. Approach the edge of the city directly and break through the enemy to the south! The city will be cleared by the riflemen who will follow!"

Initially, the attack the next day went well. While the tanks penetrated through the enemy, von Jesser brought the riflemen forward. The enemy started to pull back to the northern edge of the city.

The tank obstacles on the outskirts of the city were effectively engaged by concentrating the fires of all the vehicles. The riflemen were able to close up rapidly to the tanks. By 1330 hours, Langkeit's tanks were at the edge of the city, but he was soon faced with strong Soviet tank concentrations. The Soviets succeeded in knocking out a few of the German vehicles. A bitter firefight ensued. Heavy Soviet tanks attempted to destroy Langkeit's relatively small force, but the German tankers started to heavily attrite the attacking Soviets. Finally, the Soviets pulled back their forces to the protective cover of a railway embankment, leaving behind 12 knocked-out tanks.

A pause in the fighting followed, during which the men of the battle group could hear the sounds of fighting coming from the sector of the *SS* brigade, which had been reinforced with *Panzer-Regiment 4* of the *13. Panzer-Division.*

That evening, von Jesser confidently predicted to Langkeit they would enter Rostow the following day.

At 0800 hours on 20 November, the tanks moved out again in a steel wedge. Leading his men in his command tank, Langkeit approached the railway embankment, soon entering the enemy minefields. A few mines went up with fearful explosions behind him when some of his tankers ran over them. They also received flanking fire from the Soviet field positions. Suddenly, however, they were in the midst of the Soviet positions they had approached. Langkeit's tank caved in a trench line. All of a sudden, there was an ear-deafening crack and a blinding flash of light. The tank had received a direct hit and came to a shuddering halt; there were cries from within the vehicle. Langkeit and the gunner were able to bail out; everyone else had been killed.

As they dismounted, they started to receive fire from the other trenches. Pistols in hand, Langkeit and the other man ran back to the positions of their tanks, closely followed by exploding shells and the whip crack of small-arms fire. Miraculously, neither of the two was wounded. Langkeit mounted a tank and continued to direct the fight from there.

Towards noon, the tanks entered the city. The riflemen started engaging the enemy in bitter house-to-house fighting. Enemy fighters and fighter-bombers entered the fray; three Soviet bombers were shot down by the divisions' antiaircraft elements. The fighting raged back and forth.

The next day, the tanks continued to lead the assault against the Soviet positions within the city. Followed by the riflemen of *Schützen-Regiment 108* and the motorcycle infantry of *Kradschützen-Bataillon 64*, they took the bridge over the Don that had been prepared for demolition. They then advanced through several more enemy positions until they reached the southern edge of the islands in the Don.

That ended the first phase for the fighting for the important city. On 28 November, from the division's winter positions along the Mius, Jesser recommended Langkeit for the newly created German Cross in Gold for his role in the fighting. His recommendation read, in part:

As early as the defensive fighting along the Tuslow and east of Pokrowskoje, Langkeit had repeatedly demonstrated exceptional bravery. With the few operational tanks he had available, he turned back ever-renewed breakthrough attempts by the enemy in front of the division. It is largely thanks to his tireless personal efforts that the defensive effort succeeded. After he lost his command vehicle, he directed his tanks without regard for his personal safety from his *Kübelwagen.*

On 21 November, demonstrating verve and exemplary pluck, he took the bridge over the Don that had been prepared for demolition and advanced through new enemy positions to the southern part of the island.

The enemy's strength and the harshness of the fighting are reflected in the success garnered by his decisive leadership. Destroyed were:

31 tanks; 45 guns; 13 antitank guns; 9 antiaircraft guns; 10 mortars; 1 armored train; 1 freight train; 1 aircraft; 1 steamer; 1 tug. In addition, 1,500 prisoners were taken.

For his part in this round of fighting, von Jesser received the Knight's Cross to the Iron Cross on 18 January 1942. For whatever reason, the recommendation for Langkeit's German Cross in Gold was initially not approved.

✠

Willy Langkeit was born in Schluchten, near Treuburg in East Prussia, on 2 June 1907, the son of a farmer. At the age of 17 in 1924 he entered military service in *Kraftfahr-Abteilung 1* in Königsberg. He was commissioned and served the normal officer duties, first as a platoon leader and then as a company commander in the 8th Company of *Panzer-Regiment 36 (14. Panzer-Division)* in Schweinfurt.

He was awarded the Iron Cross, Second Class for his actions during the campaign in Poland. During the initial stages of the campaign in the West, he continued to command his 8th Company. Starting on 5 June 1940, he was given acting command of the 2nd Battalion of the regiment. That same day, he forced the Weygand Line with his formation. It was there that his regimental commander characterized him on an efficiency report as "Decisive; brave in character; aggressiveness; and extraordinary devotion to duty." On 1 August, he was awarded the Iron Cross, First Class, for his actions in penetrating the French defenses.

At the start of the campaign in the Soviet Union, he returned to command his 8th Company, from the crossing of the Bug to the advance to the Don. The division fought as part of *General* von Mackensen's *III. Armee-Korps (mot.).* A few kilometers outside of Dnjepropetrowsk, his battalion commander, *Oberstleutnant* Schmielauer, was wounded. Langkeit assumed acting command, leading the battalion through Alexandrowka and Mariupol in the direction of Rostow. On 1 December 1942, he was promoted to *Major* and given official command of the battalion. After months of occupying defensive positions along the Mius, German offensive efforts renewed in the late spring after the end of the mud period.

Attacking on both sides of Andrejewka, the *14.Panzer-Division* reached the Suchij Torez on the first day of the attack, 17 May 1942, by advancing through Saporo Marjewka. On 22 May, Langkeit's tanks closed the pocket south of Kharkov, when he took Bairak on the Don early in the afternoon and established contact with the *6. Armee.*

From there, the division was directed to advance east again on 7 June. Due to the heavy rainfall, it was impossible to advance and the attack was postponed. It was not until 10 June that *Gruppe von Mackensen* was able to move out. On 14 June, the Burluk was reached. *Panzer-Regiment 36* and, by extension, Langkeit's battalion distinguished themselves in a series of flank and rear attacks on enemy armored forces.

On 1 July 1942, Langkeit finally received the German Cross in Gold. At the time, the division was undergoing battlefield reconstitution in the vicinity of Stalino. At the same time, *Generalmajor* Kühn was reassigned, being replaced by *Generalmajor* Heim at the helm of the division. Heim had previously been the chief-of-staff of the *6. Armee.*

On 8 July, the division moved out to pursue the withdrawing enemy in the direction of the lower Don. On 11 July, there was the first enemy contact of the pursuit, when Soviet tanks were engaged at the bridge over the Donez at Schachta. On 17 July, the corps had the *14. Panzer-Division* pivot south with a new objective of Nowtscherkassk. It proved impossible for the motorcycle infantry battalion, supported by two tanks, to take the city on the hill by surprise. They were greeted by guns of numerous calibers when they approached.

Generalmajor Heim reorganized his forces to retake the city, with the movements not being completed until 23 July. Late in the afternoon of that day, Langkeit led his battalion against the city from the west. The tanks assaulted the Soviet lines and took bunkers and field positions. The bitter fighting, which resulted in heavy casualties on both sides, lasted until the night. The Soviet pulled back slowly, and every meter of ground had to be taken. Langkeit's forces succeeded in holding the terrain they had taken until the riflemen were able to relieve them and the artillery could be brought far enough forward to provide support.

Early on the morning of 24 July, a flattened tank ditch was breached. The tanks—Langkeit in the lead—advanced across some additional, smaller ditches, through minefields and over barricades. The riflemen followed, cleaning up and occupying the taken terrain. They reached the western portion of the city. Houses were on fire and walls were tumbling down with thunderous roars. Langkeit had his forces engage the antitank guns, which were firing down the straight streets. Under his leadership, the tanks reached the northern edge of the city and established contact with the division's motorcycle infantrymen—*Kradschützen-Bataillon 64*—whose attack on that sector had bogged down.

By 25 July, all of the city was in the hands of the division. Langkeit had contributed significantly to the taking of the historically important city of the Don Cossacks. When *Generaloberst* von Kleist came to visit the troops shortly thereafter and recognize them for their efforts, Langkeit's name came up for possible recommendation for the Knight's Cross to the Iron Cross. Von Kleist concurred, and Langkeit received the high award on 9 December 1942.

Oberst Theodor Kretschmer, the regimental commander at the time of the assault on Nowtscherkassk, later said the following about his battalion commander:

> *Generalleutnant* Heim asked me when I was transferred[2] to the Personnel Office to attempt to have *Major* Langkeit earmarked for command of *Panzer-Regiment 36*. That was out of the ordinary at the time, since Langkeit had just become a *Major*—as I recall, he was the youngest *Major* in the entire *Panzertruppe*—and the request [for command] was founded on the extraordinary devotion to duty and the noteworthy bravery of that tested and true front-line officer.

That same month, Heim placed Langkeit in acting command of the regiment. Eventually, the Personnel Office made him officially the commander of the regiment.

At the start of the defensive fighting around Stalingrad on 19 November—when Soviet forces launched a large-scale offensive in the area around Kletskaja at 0400 hours—the *14. Panzer-Division* was positioned as a ready reserve in the great bend of the Don behind the Romanian forces.

Langkeit's regiment was soon put to a severe test. It was thanks to the efforts of Langkeit and his men that encircled formations were hacked out again and again from the Soviets. He was promoted to *Oberstleutnant* ahead of his peers at the end of November for bravery in the face of the enemy. His accomplishments in command during that difficult period proved that Heim had made the right choice in Langkeit for regimental command.

During a break in the fighting, Langkeit was presented with the Knight's Cross to the Iron Cross at an awards formation on 24 December. It was followed by an open-air Christmas service.

On 29 December, the Soviets broke through the lines of the *376. Infanterie-Division* in the Dimitriejewka area. Langkeit and his tankers were committed

---

2. Author's Note: Kretschmer was transferred to the Army Personnel Office in September 1942 after having replaced von Jesser in regimental command in May of the same year.

to seal off and eliminate the Soviet penetration. He was also reinforced with elements from other divisions to accomplish that mission.

That night, there were tank-on-tank engagements. Of the 23 tanks that Langkeit had at his disposal, he lost 9 for various reasons. Two were complete write-offs, however, because of direct hits. Nonetheless, the Soviets were pushed back, and the infantry division was able to reoccupy its former positions.

Langkeit fought in the pocket—in the vicinity of the last remaining open airfield at Stalingradskij—until 19 January, when he was flown out along with *Hauptmann* Wagemann, *Major* Seidel and *Oberstabsarzt Dr.* Kindermann. All of the officers were either wounded or sick. The men left on 23 January on the last aircraft that left the pocket.

The division was effectively destroyed in the fighting. A few groups of soldiers, who had not been caught in the pocket initially, were able to escape the devastating blow to the Germans. Among them was one of Langkeit's battalions, the 1st, which was under the command of *Major* Bernhard Sauvant. *Kampfgruppe Sauvant* seemed to perform miracles in the fighting between the Volga, Don and Dnjepr Rivers in November and December 1942. Sauvant received the Knight's Cross to the Iron Cross in 30 November 1942 for his actions and later went on to become a successful *Tiger* battalion commander, as well as a recipient of the Oak Leaves to the Knight's Cross (260th recipient on 28 July 1943).

In the middle of March 1943, the reconstitution of the *14. Panzer-Division* started in France. In September, *Generaloberst* Guderian visited the division in Nantes in his capacity as inspector general of the armored forces. A final series of exercises conducted on 1 and 2 October 1943 demonstrated that the division was ready for deployment. The new division commander was *Generalmajor* Sieberg.

On 17 October, the division started heading by rail to the east. It later detrained at Kamenka-Snamenka, some 2,500 kilometers distant. Since an enemy attack with large armor elements in support was expected, Sieberg had all of the armored elements of the division form under *Kampfgruppe Langkeit.* In addition to Langkeit's *Panzer-Regiment 36*, there was also the 1st Battalion of *Panzergrenadier-Regiment 103*, the division's *SPW* battalion, the 1st Battalion of *Panzer-Artillerie-Regiment 4*, the division's self-propelled battalion and the 3rd Company of *Panzer-Pionier-Bataillon 13*.

The battle group assembled just west of Wladimirowka on 28 October. It advanced along the rail line to the north until it reached the way station of Tschabanowka. The first enemy resistance was encountered there, and it was quickly broken. Langkeit then summoned his commanders to discuss his intent for the continuance of operations.

The officers gathered behind his command tank. The commander in his black *Panzer* uniform seemed to radiate confidence. They turned their eyes on the man with the sharply chiseled features and the alert dark eyes. The commanders knew that fortune seemed to follow him. At that moment, a liaison officer came running up to Langkeit: "message from the reconnaissance platoon!"

"Let me see it!"

Langkeit read the message then turned his eyes back to the group of officers: "Gentlemen, the reconnaissance platoon has made the decision for us. Strong enemy infantry and armored forces are around the settlement of Pawlowka. We're attacking. Mount up and head left!"

Langkeit mounted his vehicle and stood in the commander's hatch. The remaining crew buttoned up. The tanks started to move out and head west, approached the enemy with a steel fist.

After moving 2 kilometers, the outlines of some T-34's could be identified. The first muzzle flashes could be seen in the light fog; followed by massed fires coming from the long hedgerow that extended in front of the German tank column about 800 meters away. Antitank rounds hissed overhead.

Orders were issued to the companies; voices buzzed in the headphones. Langkeit's tank also started to fire and moved ahead by leaps and bounds. The sounds of main guns firing and the resultant impacts rose to an ear-deafening crescendo. Smoke and flames covered the landscape. Looking through his binoculars, Langkeit could see the enemy start to pull back.

"Move out . . . attack!"

The tanks rumbled across the green, frozen ground. The dismounted grenadiers started to fan out behind the tanks. The artillery was already ranging on the village. The hedgerow was reached by the tanks. They burst through and then engaged their counterparts head on.

Firing, moving and advancing, the tanks entered the fray. A short while later, some 20 T-34's and KV-I's were reduced to flaming hulks on the battlefield. The command element then rolled into the village with a *Panther* company. Enemy tanks continued to appear, and antitank guns fired from ambush positions. By then the grenadiers were in the village, however, and had started to mop up.

Langkeit received a report that the Scharowka collective farm was still resisting. He had the 1st and 2nd Tank Companies attack the collective farm head on, while the 3rd and 4th Companies were sent to both flanks. The fighting flared anew at the collective farm. Tank-versus-tank engagements were the order of the day, mixed in with duels against antitank guns. The two flanking companies then hit the farm, followed by grenadiers. The tanks assisted in eliminating pockets of resistance, while the sounds of small-arms fire and exploding hand grenades from the grenadiers filled the air. The Soviets put up a bitter resistance, but eventually they either surrendered or fell back. The collective farm was in German hands.

Langkeit's battle group had scored an impressive success. It had eliminated or captured 33 tanks, 6 antitank guns and 12 trucks. In addition, a large number of prisoners had been taken. But that did not mean the fighting north of Kriwoi Rog was over—not by a long shot.

Three days later, *Kampfgruppe Langkeit* received orders to attack east across the Ingulez so as to disrupt Soviet concentrations that had been identified there. After the commander's conference at the Kuzowka rail station, the armored group moved out at 0700 hours. It broke through the first enemy field position and rolled up the antitank-gun belt behind it, thus opening the way for the second attack wave. Supported by *Stukas*, the grenadiers of *Panzergrenadier-Regiment 108* entered Wodjana.

The good news of the success was tempered by the fact that *Generalmajor* Siebert and his operations officer, *Oberstleutnant* von der Planitz, were badly wounded by antitank-gun shrapnel on the high ground at Tolstaja. The division commander succumbed to his wounds on 2 November. *Oberst* Unrein had assumed acting command on 30 October.

For his part in the decisive fighting in and around Wodjana, Langkeit was later awarded the Oak Leaves to the Knight's Cross of the Iron Cross. He became the 348th member of the German Armed Forces to receive the prestigious award (7 December 1943).

On 20 November, Langkeit's battle group attacked north from the Gannowka area. A large-scale tank engagement developed, in which 22 enemy armored vehicles were knocked out or destroyed. On 26 November, the battle group was credited with eliminating 21 enemy tanks, even though it only had a total of 36 tanks at its disposal. In addition, on the same day, it turned back an enemy attack conducted by the equivalent of two regiments.

On 1 January 1944, Langkeit was promoted to *Oberst* on 1 December 1943, again ahead of his peers, for the continued demonstration of bravery in the face of the enemy. He did not participate in the fighting for Kirowograd. He had been summoned back to the homeland for the presentation of the Oak Leaves. When he returned, he discovered that the *14. Panzer-Division* had almost been wiped out.

He was entrusted with building a new *Kampfgruppe* with what remained of his regiment—seven *Panzer IV's*, four assault guns and four flamethrower tanks—the 1st Battalion of *Panzergrenadier-Regiment 103* and the 1st Battalion of *Panzer-Artillerie-Regiment 4.*

Langkeit's hastily assembled force moved out for the first time on 24 January to attack. Its mission was to throw back the lead elements of the

Soviet 4th Guards Army, which had pushed back the *389. Infanterie-Division* in the area between Krassnossilka and Balandin with its rifle divisions, and was attempting to break through with the tank elements it had pushed forward.

Advancing through Kamenowatka, Langkeit's forces took possession of Rossochowatka and the high ground to the northwest. That sealed off the enemy's penetration. Hard fighting then developed around the Rossochowatka area over the next few days. The village was lost, only to be retaken by Langkeit's men.

In the end, however, the Soviets succeeded in breaking through. After the hole had been punched through the sector of the *8. Armee*, the enemy pushed through strong forces to the west. In the second phase of their offensive, the Soviets advanced with General Rotmistrow's 5th Guards Tank Army in the direction of Swenigorodka. The fact that the *XI.* and *XXXXII. Armee-Korps* were not completely encircled and eliminated was thanks to the fact that General Koniev halted his operations on 29 January and pulled back his lead elements. On 6 February 1944, the Soviet mud season started.

Langkeit participated in the subsequent withdrawals to Romania with his division. In the middle of March, however, he was reassigned to *Panzergrenadier-Division "Großdeutschland"* to assume command of the division's tank regiment. *Major* Bernau, one of his battalion commanders, took over command of *Panzer-Regiment 36.*

On 26 April, the Soviets attacked between Pruth and Moldau with around 20 rifle divisions and several tank divisions to kick open the door to Romania through the Sereth Valley. The Soviets attacked in the sector of *Panzergrenadier-Division "Großdeutschland"* with nearly 400 tanks. (The fighting is also covered in some detail in the chapter on Hasso von Manteuffel, who was the division commander at the time.) The battle is considered a masterpiece of a mobile defense, and Langkeit played no small role in its successful outcome. When he discovered that the Soviets were committing their heavy tanks, the "Josef Stalins," on the flanks, he committed *Hauptmann* Klemz's *Tiger* battalion against them.[3] The *Tigers* knocked out three of the Soviet steel monsters; the rest turned back. Klemz was later awarded the Knight's Cross to the Iron Cross (4 June 1944) for staving off potential disaster to the division along its flanks.

The defensive battle lasted four days before the Soviets reached their culminating point. They had lost 150 tanks by then. Von Manteuffel decided to counterattack.

---

3. Translator's Note: *"Großdeutschland"* was the only army division that had a battalion of *Tiger* tanks organic to it. It was the regiment's third battalion. All of the rest of the *Tiger* battalions in the army were separate formations that were employed as general headquarters formations.

Langkeit's regiment staged 2 kilometers behind the main lines. Von Manteuffel visited the regiment at 0335 hours early Sunday morning. The officers greeted one another. Seventy minutes later, at precisely 0445 hours, the *Panzer IV's*, *Panthers* and *Tigers* moved forward from their assembly areas. The neighboring division also moved out to attack. The tanks moved out in long columns towards the valley. Von Manteuffel rode along in the center attack group.

The Soviets opened fire from the cliffs with their antitank guns on the tanks and the following grenadiers, who were led by Oak Leaves recipient *Oberst* Lorenz.

Von Manteuffel linked up with Langkeit on the high ground, where they had a good view of the battlefield. The division commander asked Langkeit how things were going.

"The Russians are slowly weakening. Rothkirch[4] reports that the Russian infantry in front of him is pulling back."

A liaison officer brought Langkeit a message, and he, in turn, had new orders radioed to von Rothkirch.

Von Manteuffel continued: "What's happening on Hill 256, Langkeit?"

The tanks heading up the hill have been hit by flanking fire and forced to stop half way up. The fusiliers[5] accompanying them have also bogged down."

"That's not good, Langkeit. I'll be up front with the fusiliers."

A short while later, von Manteuffel personally attacked with *Oberleutnant* Nocker's fusilier company to take the hill.

That got the attack rolling again, and the tanks moved out at speed to chase the enemy forces that were rapidly withdrawing. On 8 May, the Armed Forces Daily Report announced:

> The defensive operations that started on 26 April between Pruth and Moldau have come to a preliminary close. The desired breakthrough on the part of the Bolsheviks failed in light of the tough defense offered by the forces under the command of *General der Infanterie* Wöhler.
>
> In addition to suffering heavy, bloody losses, the enemy also lost 386 tanks, 92 guns and 100 aircraft.
>
> During the fighting, *Panzer-Grenadier-Division "Großdeutschland"* of *Generalleutnant* von Manteuffel particularly distinguished itself.

4. Author's Note: *Hauptmann* Hans-Siegfried *Graf* von Rothkirch und Trach was one of the tank battalion commanders.

5. Translator's Note: Within *"Großdeutschland"* there were two *Panzergrenadier-Regimenter,* however; one regiment was referred to as fusiliers, while the other one went by the term grenadiers.

For his decisive role in the battle, Langkeit received the Romanian "Order of King Michael the Brave" on 1 June 1944. His regiment had been responsible for 56 of the enemy tank losses. There was a short period of rest, before the division was shipped by rail to East Prussia. The enemy had advanced to the borders of the *Reich*.

Willkowischken, which the Soviets had taken on 3 August, was retaken by the division. The Armed Forces Daily Report of 11 August announced:

> South of Kowno, the city of Willkowischken was retaken in a counterattack. In the last two days of fighting, the enemy lost 69 tanks and assault guns, as well as 62 artillery pieces.

Langkeit during an orders conference at Schaulen in late 1944. He was later wounded during the fighting.

Langkeit was wounded in the fighting that took place in that area around Schaulen. He was hospitalized and sent to the homeland to convalesce, where he was placed in charge of the division's replacement brigade in Cottbus. But he was not able to hold out there for long.

By the end of January 1945, he was again leading armored forces, this time an element composed of forces from the replacement brigade, as well as cadre from the armor school in Wünsdorf. The *Kampfgruppe* was dispatched to the Eastern Front, where it reported to *General der Infanterie* Busse's *9. Armee*, which was facing the Soviets approaching the Oder.

At the time of Langkeit's arrival, the Soviets were rapidly advancing with two large armored forces in the Oder-Warthe Bend, the main effort directed at Frankfurt an der Oder and Küstrin. Immediately after his arrival, Langkeit received orders to move through Frankfurt towards Reppen and bring the Soviet forces there to a standstill. It was imperative that the high ground east of the Oder, which dominated the entire region, remained in German hands.

Langkeit advanced with his forces, reached the high ground and turned back the Soviet forces. Langkeit's actions were one of the few bright spots in the otherwise dismal situation facing the Germans all along that sector of the front. Busse later wrote about Langkeit's operation:

> The failure of the Soviet effort in that sector was primarily thanks to the noteworthy bravery of *Oberst* Langkeit, who personally got involved with complete disregard for himself and, as a result, helped rally the forces that had been hastily assembled and had not yet developed any cohesiveness. I personally witnessed his exemplary actions.

Langkeit's feat of arms prompted Busse to submit the armor officer for promotion to *Generalmajor* ahead of his peers: "for recently demonstrated leadership performance and again demonstrating extraordinary bravery."

On 20 April, the Armed Forces High Command approved the recommendation, especially since Langkeit had also been taking all of the forces pouring into his sector to form a new division—*Panzergrenadier-Division "Kurmark"*—which he was also earmarked to command. Indeed, he seemed the perfect choice for the upcoming struggle that was to decide the fate of Germany.

Generalmajor Langkeit experienced the final weeks of the war with his *ad hoc* division, first fighting his way out of encirclement west of the Oder and then taking it to Beelitz to the rear of *General der Panzertruppen* Wenck's *12. Armee*. During the last days of April, he received the third level of the Tank Assault Badge for having participated in 75 or more armored engagements.

On 7 May 1945, the young general went into captivity with his division, surrendering to U.S. forces.

Following the war, Langkeit entered the *Bundesgrenzschutz*—Federal Border Protection Service—in 1951. He helped form the coastal protective services of that agency and led them for a long time as a *Brigadegeneral.*

Willy Langkeit passed away in Bad Bramstedt on 27 October 1969.

SS-Obersturmbannführer Johannes-Rudolf Mühlenkamp, most famous as the long-time and successful commander of *SS-Panzer-Abteilung* (and later *Regiment*) 5 *"Wiking."*

CHAPTER 13

SS-Standartenführer Johannes-Rudolf Mühlenkamp

IN ACTION WITH THE 5. SS-PANZER-DIVISION "WIKING" AT KOWEL

"*Obersturmführer* Nikolussi-Leck, reporting as ordered!"

The 27-year-old company commander of the 8th Company of *SS-Panzer-Regiment 5 "Wiking"* looked at his commander inquisitively. "Hannes" Mühlenkamp took a step closer to his old comrade-in-arms, extended his hand and then told him: "Well, Nikolussi-Leck, you are to depart at 1500 hours and move to Tupaly with your entire company. You are attached to the *131. Infanterie-Division*. How many of your vehicles are operational?"

"I have 17 *Panthers*, 1 *Bergepanther*[1] (recovery version of the *Panther* tank) and 10 haulers available, *Obersturmbannführer!*" the young officer from southern Tyrol answered immediately.

"Outstanding," Johannes-Rudolf Mühlenkamp replied, who was not lavish with praise. Mühlenkamp was referred to by all of his soldiers as "Hannes." "You will receive some volunteer assault detachments from *Grenadier-Regiment 434*, which is led by *Oberst* Naber. They will mount up with you. I will head out at 1300 hours with *Standartenführer* Richter to take a look at the terrain."

The two comrades-in-arms took their leave of one another. It was only 15 minutes later on this 28 March 1944 when the commander of the 8th Company was rolling out with his tanks. Preceding him to the front was the regimental commander.

The *Panthers* of the company reached Tupaly without encountering the enemy. One tank became disabled along the way with clutch problems.

These movements were all on behalf of the encircled garrison at Kowel: a regiment of German militia, a regiment of *SS* cavalry, an artillery battalion, a *Flak* battalion and 300 German railway workers. This handful of soldiers was defending against approximately one dozen Soviet rifle divisions and a number of armored formations.

---

1. Translator's Note: The armored recovery version of the *Panther*. It had an open crew compartment and was fitted with an assortment of powerful winching and lifting devices for recovery of tanks under combat conditions. Usually these were *Tigers* and *Panthers* that were difficult to recover with the usual 18-ton *FAMO* half-track.

The soldiers of the *5. SS-Panzer-Division "Wiking"* had not been successful on their first try to relieve the garrison. As a result, higher commands were pressing even harder for the tanks of the division to press into the city.

It had been only 30 days since the remnants of the division had been able to escape from the pocket at Tscherkassy with 800 men. Those lucky 800 were only able to get out with their lives. No heavy equipment could be brought with them.

It was thanks to the fact that the newly forming 2nd Battalion of the division's tank regiment had been in Germany that the division was able to rebuild some combat power so quickly. On 12 March 1944, the division was ordered to form a *Kampfgruppe* of some 4,000 soldiers in order to support the German forces defending at Kowel.

It proved futile that the divisional commander, *SS-Gruppenführer* Herbert Gille, personally flew to the *Führer* Headquarters to persuade the senior leadership that his division was no longer suitable for combat operations. He was forbidden to personally speak to Hitler. Gille then returned to the front, where he had himself flown into Kowel to assume command of the defenses there.

Three days later the divisional *Kampfgruppe* was seeing action again. Two of the division's regiments—*SS-Panzergrenadier-Regiment 9 "Germania,"* whose 3rd Battalion was being reconstituted in Germany and *SS-Panzergrenadier-Regiment 10 "Westland"*—were *en route* by train through partisan-controlled territory from Cholm to Kowel. Like the tanks of Mühlenkamp's regiment, the infantry had to detrain over open track. It was this initial attempt to reach Kowel—advancing into the town in an attempted *coup de main*—that failed.

✠

The division then formed two *Kampfgruppen* for the planned relief action. One was led by *SS-Standartenführer* Richter, the other by *SS-Obersturmbannführer* Mühlenkamp.

The operation envisioned by the division, which intended to advance on Kowel via Hrubiszow and Turzysk, was not approved by the *4. Armee*. In fact, the field army then moved *Kampfgruppe Richter* to Cholm to deal with another crisis.

The *131. Infanterie-Division* of *Generalmajor* Weber was *en route* at this point. Also arriving to assist was *leichte Sturmgeschütz-Brigade 190*, which was attached to Mühlenkamp. He had it sent to the Lubomol sector of the Kowel front. By 28 March, Mühlenkamp's *Panther* battalion finally arrived. Mühlenkamp wanted to employ the battalion in an separate action to free Kowel by advancing through Lubliniec. This recommended course of action was also disapproved by the *4. Armee.*

This was the situation as we introduced this section. What would happen in Tupaly on the following day, 29 March 1944?

✠

Mühlenkamp was addressing Nikolussi-Leck again: "Go to *Oberst* Naber's location and report to him."

"What happened to *Sturmbannführer* Hack's attack, *Obersturmbannführer?*"

"Hack was only able to reach the outskirts of Nowe Koszary and Stare Koszary with his battalion[2] and the 190th. The infantry bogged down there. You will move out to attack at Stare Koszary at 1100 hours. You will advance on Kowel via Czerkasy and Moszczona. You will be given infantry, three groups of 10 men each. The divisional artillery of the 131st Infantry Division will support you. Hack's men will guide you when you get up front."

SS-Obersturmführer Nikolussi-Leck departed as ordered. He was guided into position by *SS-Sturmbannführer* Hack and received a directive to first take out the enemy antitank guns. But *SS-Obersturmbannführer* Mühlenkamp arrived a few minutes later and countermanded this order. Any attempt to eliminate the Russian antitank guns would cost heavy casualties, possibly of decisive

A *Wiking Panther Ausf. A* with accompanying infantry. Note the sniper leaning against the turret and preparing to fire.

_____

2. Translator's Note: *III./SS-Panzer-Grenadier-Regiment 9 "Germania."*

impact. He issued the following orders instead: "Nikolussi, move along the railway line to Czerkasy. After conducting reconnaissance, proceed towards Kowel via Mosczona."

Said, done. A few minutes later, Nikolussi-Leck bellowed into his throat mike: "*Panzer marsch!*"

The 16 operational *Panthers* of his company moved out as one. *SS-Hauptscharführer* Eugen Faas was in the lead vehicle of the 1st Platoon. *SS* combat engineers from *SS-Obersturmbannführer* Julius Weck's battalion had mounted up on the *Panthers*. The light snowfall that had started did not interfere with visibility. Rattling and rumbling, the tanks moved forward. When the first rounds of impacting Russian artillery landed to the left and right of the tanks and caused dirt and shrapnel to fling against the sideskirts, the tank commanders ordered their drivers to step on it.

SS-Sturmbannführer Hack's men joined the advance of the tanks to the right. They were supported by the 10 assault guns of the attached light assault-gun battalion. On the left flank were infantry from the *131. Infanterie-Division—Grenadier-Regiment 434* of *Oberstleutnant* Bolm. This regiment was supported by another seven assault guns.

The lead platoon of Nikolussi-Leck's company soon reached the lead field fortifications of the enemy. Off to the right, *SS-Hauptscharführer* Faas saw the muzzle flash from an antitank gun. Orders bellowed. Long, garishly red lances of flame shot out from the mouth of the long-barreled 7.5-centimeter main gun of his *Panther*. Hits were observed and fires started to break out. Jauss's and Scheel's platoon had likewise passed the confining section of marshy terrain by then and were employed by Nikolussi-Leck in flanking movements. The attack proceeded apace. Soviet soldiers ran from their fortifications.

The company commander ordered everyone to follow him.

The snowfall started to become thicker. The trail crews of the company could see barely three meters in front of them. All of a sudden, the lead *Panther* bogged down in a marshy spot. This was followed by four more *Panthers* that shared the same fate. Nikolussi-Leck had the bogged-down tanks assume right-flank security for the company.

A short while later, the lead vehicles ran into the blocking position established by the enemy 600 meters west of Czerkasy. It boasted 12 antitank guns. The tanks advanced against the obstacle in an inverted wedge. Three tanks were immobilized by gunfire. The remaining tanks were able to eliminate all of the enemy antitank guns.

Five minutes later, the tanks were on some high ground. The snowfall had become so thick that visibility was zero.

Nikolussi-Leck ordered his radio operator to send a message to the regiment: "Company positioned on the high ground 600 meters west of

Czerkasy. Enemy positions penetrated. Infantry still being engaged. Strong snowfall restricts visibility. As soon as the snowfall ends, I will continue to advance. Six vehicles bogged down in marshland. Recovery tanks requested. Send a surgeon for the wounded!"

At 1530 hours, *SS-Obersturmführer* Nikolussi-Leck moved out with his remaining tanks for the assault on Czerkasy. After a few dozen meters, an additional three *Panthers* were stuck in the ground. The company commander had his tanks veer left, move across the railroad tracks and then attack the village from the left.

In a firefight lasting 15 minutes, Nikolussi-Leck's remaining crews engaged antitank guns and artillery. The last eight tanks, some of which were hit but still operational, rolled into the village. The village was mopped up by the grenadiers of *Kampfgruppe Bolm*, who soon closed on the village as well. *SS-Obersturmbannführer* Mühlenkamp directed his company commander to remain in the village and screen to the north and the east.

During the night, three stuck tanks were recovered. This gave Nikolussi-Leck an operational strength of nine *Panthers* early on the morning of 30 March, when he was ordered to move out again in the direction of Kowel.

Faas was in the lead again. He was closely followed by the other eight tanks. It was still pitch black, when they started moving. The *Hauptscharführer* suddenly saw muzzle flashes 400 meters west of the Czerkasy rail station. He submitted a spot report and then opened fire. Faas and his crew knocked out a T-34. One hundred meters farther down the route of advance, however, Faas's tank ran over a mine and was immobilized with track problems. A second tank suffered the same fate. Faas formed a strongpoint with the two immobilized but still combat-capable tanks. He was joined by 16 grenadiers. Nikolussi-Leck continued the attack in the direction of Kowel with his remaining seven tanks.

Faas soon found his hands full with Russian attackers, while the rest of the company rattled towards Kowel. In contravention of an order that had been brought forward by a motorcycle messenger, Nikolussi-Leck continued the attack after having reached the lead Russian positions. He knew that to remain stationary was to invite trouble in this situation.

Moving together, the tanks then overran the enemy obstacles, knocked out enemy antitank guns and collapsed enemy fighting positions under their tracks. All at once, Nikolussi-Leck could see German helmets. They had done it! They had broken through and were in the Kowel pocket. Nikolussi-Leck stopped in front of the headquarters, and *SS-Gruppenführer* Gille stepped out into the open. Nikolussi-Leck reported to him: "*Gruppenführer*, I am reporting for duty with my 8th Company and its seven tanks."

This "*Panther* Pounce to Kowel," as it was later recorded in war correspondent reports, had succeeded in knocking out, destroying or capturing 16 antitank guns, 2 antiaircraft guns, 3 tanks, 40 antitank rifles, and an unrecorded number of mortars and infantry weapons. All of Nikolussi-Leck's stranded tanks were able to be recovered.

Mühlenkamp submitted Nikolussi-Leck for the Knight's Cross. Gille also recommended approval and the high decoration was presented to the young officer on 9 April 1944.

✠

Johannes-Rudolf Mühlenkamp, the regimental commander of *SS-Panzer-Regiment 5 "Wiking,"* was born on 9 October 1910 as the son of the governmental official Emil Mühlenkamp in Metz-Motigny.

In 1919, the family was expelled from Metz, which then belonged to the French. The fact that his father had been a frontline soldier from 1914 to 1918 had made his presence in the newly French region unacceptable. The family landed up in Braunschweig, the hometown of Emil. The young Mühlenkamp attended the college preparatory school there. He wanted to become a mechanical engineer. His apprenticeship was done in the field of automobile construction.

After attending a military-preparation camp, Rudolf joined the *SS-Verfügungstruppe* in 1934. He attended the officer-candidate school of the fledgling force in Braunschweig from 1934 to 1935. At the time, the school was under the supervision of former army general Hausser, whom Mühlenkamp would later serve under as adjutant.

In 1936, he went on an exchange program with the army and was assigned to the motorcycle battalion of the *2. Panzer-Division* (*Kradschützen-Bataillon 2*). When he returned to the *SS,* Mühlenkamp was assigned as the platoon leader of the motorcycle platoon of *SS-Infanterie-Standarte "Germania."* Mühlenkamp later attended the army's armor school at Putlos, where he further deepened his knowledge in the leadership of armored formations. In the spring of 1938, he became the company commander of the regiment's motorcycle company, the *15./SS-Infanterie-Standarte "Germania,"* in Hamburg.

When the Second World War broke out, Mühlenkamp continued as the commander of the motorcycle company in Poland. He was one of the first ones in the regiment to earn both levels of the Iron Cross in the short but difficult fighting. Following the campaign, Mühlenkamp became the regimental adjutant.

After the Polish campaign, the heretofore separately employed formations of the *SS-Verfügungstruppe* were consolidated into a divisional formation—the

SS-Verfügungs-Division (mot.). It was this division that later evolved into what became the *2. SS-Panzer-Division "Das Reich"* at the end of the war. Its first commander was *SS-Gruppenführer* Hausser.

At the start of the campaign in France, Mühlenkamp was again in command of the regiment's motorcycle company. Mühlenkamp was a familiar sight at the head of the division, where he frequently conducted rapid raids into the enemy's flanks and rear. He later became the commander of the division's advance guard battalion and was the divisional adjutant for a period of time. Hausser then selected the young officer to command the division's reconnaissance battalion.

Mühlenkamp led his men in the fighting for the Ijessl and Grebbe positions, the pursuit of the withdrawing enemy as far as the fortress of Utrecht, the breakthrough to the channel and the fighting between Arras and St. Omer. That was followed by the crossing of the Marne and the breakthrough to the Seine. During the pursuit to Dijon and the fighting on the Langres Plateau, Mühlenkamp continuously distinguished himself as a tactically proficient leader of the advance guard.

A period report concerning the forced crossing of the La Bassee Canal and the attack on Robecq shows how the *SS-Kradschützen* under Mühlenkamp's command operated:

> The company moved out to attack at 1030 hours. It received machine-gun and rifle fire as it approached the canal.
>
> With covering fire provided by the machine-gun section, elements advanced down to the left of the approach road. Using portions of a blown-up bridge, the 1st Platoon succeeded in crossing the La Bassee Canal.
>
> The machine-gun section and the 2nd Platoon, which had been employed with covering the right flank, were then immediately brought up. As the company approached the southern edge of Robecq, six enemy tanks attacked. The company took up positions in the buildings and in the basements and engaged these tanks. The two armored cars also participated in the engagement. The effect of the friendly 2-cm main-gun fire was minimal . . .
>
> A platoon from the antitank battalion finally arrived and also participated in the fighting. It was possible to bring one gun over the canal.
>
> After the enemy tanks turned around, the company penetrated further into Robecq and found two destroyed French fighting vehicles.

The company had forced a crossing over the La Bassee Canal and secured it for the formations of the division that were following.

In December 1940, the division was redesignated as *SS-Division "Deutschland"* only to be changed yet again in January to *SS-Division "Reich."*

After a period of training and occupation duties in southern France, the division was transferred to the Temesvar area of Rumania. Two days after its arrival, divisional patrols crossed the border into Yugoslavia, where the division suffered its first casualties in the Balkans. It was planned for the division to advance across completely marshy terrain towards Seleus and Alibunar. "Hannes" Mühlenkamp, who was the commander of the reconnaissance battalion during this campaign, continued to lead from the front. He was both a circumspect and aggressive leader. His superiors had known for a long time that Mühlenkamp was an officer who was preordained for higher levels of command.

After operations were concluded in the Balkans, the division was transferred into the area of Temeschburg. From there, it went to Linz, Eferding and Lake Traun. The reconnaissance battalion was billeted in Ebensee and Traunkirchen.

Starting on 5 June 1941, the division was moved again. At the time, no one knew the destination of the train movement. When the soldiers reached the area around Lublin, however, they knew they were going to secure the German border with Russia, at the very least.

SS-Division "Reich" was attached to the XXXXVI. *Armee-Korps (mot.)* of *General der Panzertruppen* von Vietinghoff-Scheel at the time. When the campaign in the Soviet Union started on 22 June 1941, the corps was initially held back as an operational reserve. By 25 June 1941, the division had moved up to the initial line of departure for the German offensive. On 26 June, *SS-Obersturmbannführer* Ostendorff,[3] the division's operations officer, was informed at the corps command post that the division was to prepare to attack as soon as the traffic conditions allowed it.

---

3. Author's Note: Ostendorff's entire career was with the division. On 13 September 1941, he was awarded the Knight's Cross to the Iron Cross, followed by the Oak Leaves on 6 May 1945, as the 848th member of the German Armed Forces so honored. He served as the last commander of the division. Translator's Note: At the time of the writing of this book, Ostendorff's award of the Oak Leaves was considered legitimate; however, recent research by Veit Scherzer (*Ritterkreuzträger, 1939–1945*) calls this into question, stating that there is no official records of the award and the claim that it was awarded by "Sepp" Dietrich in the waning days of the war has no legitimacy. Ostendorff is by no means the only person whose receipt of the Knight's Cross or one of its higher levels has been called into question by Scherzer. Editor's Note: The Association of Knight's Cross Holders actually does recognize the legitimacy of these later awards.

The division's operations in Russia started on the morning of 27 June 1941. *SS-Gruppenführer* Hausser was still in command, and he led his division against the crossroads at Pereszew. *SS-Hauptsturmführer* Mühlenkamp moved out with his reconnaissance battalion against the village of Szack. In a rapid assault, the village was taken, and several enemy tanks were eliminated in the process. From this day forward, the division was in uninterrupted, heavy combat.

During the advance to the Swislotsch and Beresina Rivers, the reconnaissance battalion was constantly up front. Mühlenkamp had an ability to "read" the battlefield, and he never let his soldiers advance without being adequately covered.

When he received the mission of conducting reconnaissance in the enemy-occupied area around Puchowiecze and eliminate any forces there, he initially led the movement with a strong advance element. The advance forces were able to identify the enemy positions to such an extent that the rest of the battalion was able to defeat the enemy in a daring attack on 1 July and open the way to the Beresina for the division. Early on the morning of 4 July, the first soldiers of the division were able to cross the river.

The next objective of the division was to break through the Russian positions along the Dnjepr and force a crossing of the river. Mühlenkamp's men reached the Druth on 6 July. On the next day, his battalion was once again far in front of the division. In the vicinity of Dosow, Mühlenkamp identified strong enemy forces supported by artillery. There were also strong enemy forces at Gorodischtje. The information that Mühlenkamp and his men were able to provide to Hausser allowed the division commander to deploy his regiments in a timely fashion.

✠

In the summer of 1941, the advance into the Soviet Union was so rapid that it appeared that Hitler's prediction of an early victory was valid.

It would take too much space within the context of this book to detail all of the operations Mühlenkamp participated in. Here are some of the highlights:

When the reconnaissance battalion passed through the division on the night of 13/14 July so as to conduct reconnaissance during the morning of 14 July in the direction of Gorki, Mühlenkamp's lead company encountered strong enemy forces in the woods east of Dischki. The enemy was in the process of attempting to ambush and eliminate an army artillery battalion that had encamped in the woods. Mühlenkamp attacked right into the enemy with his lead company. He was able to scatter the foe and also capture several artillery pieces. By acting on his own initiative, Mühlenkamp was able to save the artillery battalion from certain destruction. One of Mühlenkamp's officers, *SS-Obersturmführer* Fritz Vogt, particularly distinguished himself during this engagement. Vogt had already been awarded the Knight's Cross to the Iron Cross at the age of 22 at the end of the French campaign.

The penetration of the Dessna Positions near Jelnja and the subsequent defensive fighting in the Jelnja Bend saw all of the men of the division in hard fighting. At the time, Hausser summed up the situation in these words: "Division scattered across a large area—enemy everywhere!"

On 30 July, Mühlenkamp's soldiers assisted the men of *Infanterie-Regiment (mot.) "Großdeutschland"* in defending against a Russian attack. On 8 August 1941, Hausser was awarded the Knight's Cross to the Iron Cross for his performance thus far in the campaign. He later stated he wore it for every man of his division.[4]

The hard fighting continued through the late summer and into the fall. On 9 October, Johannes Mühlenkamp celebrated his 31st birthday among his comrades in the mud and the cold. At the time, the battalion was surrounded by marshland and woods. As the regiments of the division assumed the blocking positions near Istra and the patrols bogged down in the pathless marshes, "Hannes" Mühlenkamp would move forward to the most advanced outposts so as to gain a better appreciation for what was happening. During one of these "visits," the position was hit by a barrage from a Soviet rocket-launcher unit. Mühlenkamp was taken back to the rear by his adjutant, badly wounded.

He was evacuated to Berlin, where he subsequently received the German Cross in Gold in the hospital. While he was still convalescing in the hospital, he received orders entrusting him with the formation of the tank battalion

---

4. Author's Note: Hausser received the Oak Leaves to the Knight's Cross of the Iron Cross on 28 July 1943 as the 261st member of the German Armed Forces so honored. He was awarded the Swords to the Oak Leaves on 26 August 1944, the 90th recipient.

for *SS-Division "Wiking."* He grew familiar with the command and control of 59 fighting vehicles at the training areas in Wildflecken and Senne. In June 1942, his battalion was dispatched to join the division. He was greeted enthusiastically when he arrived at the division's location along the Mius. His tank battalion increased the combat power of the division considerably, and his tanks would prove themselves again and again in the coming weeks and months. It was time for Mühlenkamp the "tanker" to come to the fore.

✠

On 16 July 1942, the division was relieved-in-place from its positions along the Mius. Starting on 18 July, the division was moved to the area northwest of Taganrog. Its goal was the same as the other divisions attached to the *LVII. Panzer-Korps* of *General der Panzertruppen* Kirchner: the Caucasus and its oil. *SS-Panzer-Abteilung 5 "Wiking"* rolled forward as part of *Kampfgruppe Dieckmann*. It was this *Kampfgruppe* that propelled the German forces ahead in the advance on Rostow.

Although he had not completely healed from his wounds, Mühlenkamp led his battalion from the front. In the space of a few weeks of combat, he had succeeded in forming it into a cohesive whole. His division commander, *SS-Gruppenführer* Steiner, knew what an asset he had in this man and in this battalion. He employed the battalion wherever the enemy pressure was expected to be the greatest.

On 21 July 1942, Mühlenkamp received orders to attack across the tank ditch running from Ssultan-Saly and Krim. Just as he was rolling down into a

A T-34 engulfed in flames after a direct hit.

T-shaped *balka* with his first tanks, dogs started running towards his vehicles. *SS-Untersturmführer* Nikolussi-Leck, a platoon leader at the time, was the first to realize what was happening: The dogs had mines strapped to their backs that had detonating rods extending upwards. He radioed a warning to his other tankers. The men had no choice but to fire into the attacking dogs, setting off the explosions. The men later learned that the dogs had been trained to run under tanks, which would have then set off the powerful explosive devices.[5]

A tank then ran over a mine and was immobilized, its hull torn open. The first tank ditch had not even been reached yet. The attack bogged down and *gepanzerte Gruppe "Wiking"* encamped on the open steppes for the night.

The attack was continued the next day. "Hannes" Mühlenkamp realized that the division's right flank was exposed, a fact that *SS-Gruppenführer* Steiner had hammered home during the orders conference the previous evening. That morning, Mühlenkamp identified heavily reinforced concrete structures with gun embrasures. It was intended to eliminate these difficult targets with artillery fire and *Luftwaffe* support.

As Mühlenkamp wrote the following after the war:

> The terrain was broad, typically rolling tank country with obstacles consisting of ditches and wire. We had sappers with us to act as demolition parties; it was intended for them to breach these obstacles. It was also intended for Schlamelcher's artillery battalion to support us.
>
> The *Stukas* arrived very early—the division order for the attack had not even reached us yet!—and dropped their bombs on the heavily fortified positions.

Mühlenkamp then saw his opportunity. He issued his own attack order: "*Adler* (Eagle) to all stations: Prepare to attack!"

The battalion advanced in a column. In the lead was the 1st Company under *SS-Hauptsturmführer* Schnabel. It was followed by the 2nd Company of *SS-Obersturmführer* Flügel. Elements of the 3rd Company, the heavy company, brought up the rear. They reached the tank ditch, where they received fire and replied to it. Under their covering fire, the combat engineers went to work. *SS-Oberscharführer* Holzinger moved up between the tanks to the ditch with his sappers. They jumped into the ditch, emplaced their charges and then set them off. The walls of the ditch collapsed, making it trafficable for the tanks.

---

5. The insidious "mine-dog" device was not a success, however. Unfortunately, the dogs had been trained using Russian tanks and tended to run under them, rather than German ones—with predicable results. As a consequence, both Russian and German soldiers killed any dogs roaming the battlefield.

By then, the 1st Battalion of *SS-Panzergrenadier-Regiment 9 "Germania"* of *SS-Sturmbannführer* Dieckmann had also moved forward with its lead company. It crossed the ditch on foot. The first tanks were already rolling through the breach. They were closely followed by the remaining vehicles.

✠

The fighting on 23 July was tough and filled with casualties. The high-ground positions of the enemy could not be taken. At this point, *SS-Sturmbannführer* Dieckmann's communications personnel received an aerial reconnaissance report that indicated that the enemy had not occupied prepared positions farther to the south at Tschaltyr.

Mühlenkamp detached some of his tanks to help his comrade Dieckmann exploit the situation. With the assistance of these tanks, Dieckmann was able to capture a wooden bridge over a creek intact and thus clear the way at Tschaltyr Krym for the entire division to continue its further advance.

Around 1400 hours, the division's tanks reached the railway line north of the airfield along with Dieckmann's grenadiers. From this location, additional combat reconnaissance was conducted. The tanks then stormed on towards the Rostow airfield. In the course of the continued advance, *SS-Hauptsturmführer* Schnabel was wounded, but the tank battalion was on the southwestern outskirts of the city an hour later.

Blocking their path was another tank ditch that first had to be breached. Once this was done, *SS-Sturmbannführer* Mühlenkamp advanced to a road obstacle and observed the terrain. He saw that the railway bridge had already been blown up. Dieckmann's grenadiers penetrated into the city, effectively supported by fire from Mühlenkamp's tanks.

When the enemy pulled back to the south on 23 July over the mouth of the Don, Mühlenkamp pursued along the northern arm of the Don to the northwest and interdicted these withdrawal movements at Kalinin. As a result of this armored attack, he created a 15-kilometer-wide jump-off point for the next phase of the operation.

Mühlenkamp received the Knight's Cross to the Iron Cross for his actions at Rostow, particularly for the last advance he conducted, which was done entirely on his own initiative. He received the award on 3 September 1942. While leading his battalion, he had taken actions that resulted in the breaching of three tank ditches and created the prerequisites for the crossing of the Don by two divisions.

✠

The attack was continued from Rostow with 34 tanks. The battalion also had six self-propelled guns attached to it. Bataisk was soon reached and taken. The advance continued in giant leaps across the wide steppes. The Kuban River was reached and had to be crossed.

Mühlenkamp's tanks were instrumental in establishing the second bridgehead across the river. The battalion's tanks raced through Krapotkin with mounted infantry on their rear decks. Their objective was the bridge there. Just before reaching the bridge, however, it flew into the air at 1120 hours on 6 August. Despite this setback, the division's combat engineers had built a temporary bridge capable of supporting tanks by the morning of 7 August. The tanks rolled across the following night; Maikop was the next objective.

Kampfgruppe Gille, consisting of the tank battalion and Dieckmann's battalion, moved though forested terrain in the direction of this oil region. The enemy was pulling back. When this occurred, the commanding general of the *XXXXIV. Gebirgs-Armee-Korps, General der Gebirgstruppen* Konrad, recommended to the commander-in-chief of *Heeresgruppe A, Generalfeldmarschall* von List, on 10 August that *SS-Division "Wiking"* pursue the enemy through the mountains towards Tuapse. But things turned out differently.

On 12 August, *SS-Division "Wiking"* formed two assault groups and advanced in the Pschisch Valley towards Chadyshenskaja and in the Pschecha Valley towards Abscherowskaja. In the attack on Lineinaja, the tanks were employed. Mühlenkamp wrote about this after the war:

> After a march, there was suddenly a large open area in the middle of a forest. Lineinaja was on the western edge of the clearing. My tanks moved out in battle order and then took off for the city. Between the tanks were the Finnish volunteers.[6] The Finns took part in the tank attack by double timing. Our attack broke over Lineinaja like a storm. The Finns could no longer be controlled. They frequently lunged at the enemy soldiers, swinging their typical Finnish knives.

Lineinaja was taken, thus signaling an end to the offensive operations of the division in this sector. On 19 September 1942, the division was relieved and marched in combat groups via Maikop to the area of Prochladnaja in the eastern Caucasus. It was intended for the division to eject the enemy ensconced at Malgobek, which was on the demarcation line between Europe and Asia. The division was attached to the *LII. Armee-Korps*.

---

6. Translator's Note: The *"Wiking"* division was known for its component of Nordic volunteers, including an entire battalion of Finns, which was designated as the *finnisches Freiwilligen-Bataillon der Waffen-SS*.

The division marched through the Kurp Valley towards Ssagopschin. On 24 September, all of the division's senior commanders conducted a leaders' reconnaissance of the attack sector together with the division commander, *SS-Gruppenführer* Steiner. *SS-Obersturmbannführer* Reichel, the new operations officer of the division, briefed the attack plan. Mühlenkamp discovered that his tanks were to be part of the main effort along with *SS-Panzergrenadier-Regiment 10 "Westland"* in advancing along the valley in the direction of Ssagopschin.

The attack started at 0500 hours on 26 September. The grenadiers, who had been earmarked to eliminate threats to the flanks, suffered heavy casualties. At 0700 hours, the tank battalion and *"Westland"* moved out to attack. The tank ditch at Nishne Krup was reached at 0930 hours, and sappers breached the obstacle by flattening the walls.

SS-Hauptsturmführer Schnabel, the commander of the 1st Company, got his birthday wish and was allowed to be the first tank to move through the obstacle. The platoon leader of the 2nd Platoon, *SS-Untersturmführer* Kollotzschy, received a direct hit while negotiating the obstacle and was knocked out, blocking the passage point. The combat engineers blew a new breach but not before *SS-Obersturmführer* Flügel and his 2nd Company had to wait for four hours under withering Soviet artillery fire. Soviet close-air-support aircraft also attempted to knock out the tanks.

By 1600 hours, five tanks of the 1st Company reached the halfway point to Ssagopschin. At this point, they were cut off and had to establish an all-round defense. Flügel attempted to close the gap with his company. He was followed closely by the tank destroyers of the 3rd Company of *SS-Panzerjäger-Abteilung 5 "Wiking."*

Flügel and his men continued to advance, firing to both sides of the *balka* as they moved through it. Extremely heavy artillery fire began to fall on the company from the southern slopes. Mühlenkamp, who had moved towards the front as rapidly as he could, issued orders to Flügel to attack to the south in order to get into the dead zone of the artillery.

Flügel and his company then proceeded to attack into the Soviet artillery positions, where they were temporarily cut off.

Mühlenkamp then closed up to the five cut-off tanks of Schnabel's company. He employed one platoon of the 2nd Company against an enemy antitank-gun position, which was destroyed in the course of the night. When it dawned on 27 September, the division was stuck. Mühlenkamp's tanks were shelled by Russian artillery the entire day. When Mühlenkamp received his attack orders for 28 September, he protested that they could not be executed and succeeded in getting the attack moved up so that he could take advantage of the morning fog.

The *Panzer III's* and *IV's* moved out very early the following morning. The bulk of the tanks were in the middle of the Russian defensive positions between Ssagopschin and Kessem. Flügel and his company were still off to the south. Strong artillery fire recommenced from the Malgobek Heights. The main body of the battalion moved to the north to try to get under the fire of the guns.

The Soviets then attacked with large armored forces. Eighty tanks, among them T-34's, charged against the 40 tanks of *SS-Division "Wiking."* A bitterly contested engagement ensued. "Hannes" Mühlenkamp wrote about it after the war:

The sun broke through earlier than expected. The fog was suddenly gone. We were in the middle of the Russian field positions and between trenches and defensive clusters, all of which were well manned. I looked at the trenches we were overrunning from out of my turret and through the vision ports. They were firing machine guns and submachine guns against our hatches and vision ports; they were tossing hand grenades. Approximately 800 meters away, off to the right and arrayed along a broad front, were numerous T-34's. The tank duels started immediately, with heavy artillery fire mixed in amongst it. The first hit landed right behind my turret; the engine started burning. The turret had been lifted somewhat; the backrest to my seat had been shot off. I had been tossed forward and was lying on the main gun. I shouted: "Bail out!"

Then there was another hit; right against the front and one of the hatches! My driver, Fritz Kröbsch, collapsed; his head was covered in blood.

The third round struck the turret from the right rear. The hatch, which weighed approximately 200 pounds, fell into the forward fighting compartment and sliced off the right arm of my radio operator, Heinze, who was manning the hull machine gun. Everything happened in seconds. I pulled the driver and the radio operator out through the emergency hatch and dragged them several meters away from the tank. Then came my gunner. In the commander's tank, this was always the signals officer, in this case, *SS-Untersturmführer* Köntrop. (My normal command tank had been knocked out the previous day.)

Shortly before I was knocked out, I had observed a nearby Russian position from the turret. I thought to myself: "Get there and wait until the replacement tank pulls up."

With pistol in hand, I jumped towards the Russian trench. I needed some breathing space. We would then pull the wounded in after us. I observed how the Russians had bypassed us and had some elements between the tank battalion and *Westland* [*SS-Panzergrenadier-Regiment 10 "Westland"*]. This Russian formation was led magnificently.

Behind us, about 100 meters, a T-34 suddenly appeared and directed his machine guns against us. Köntrop cried out. A machine-gun salvo had taken off his right leg. I picked up Köntrop and dragged him into the Russian trench in front of us. I brought the badly wounded tank driver, Kröbsch, and the radio operator, Heinze, into the empty trench. The loader, who had not been wounded, retrieved the hull machine gun on my orders and then provided security for the wounded comrades. I wanted to run back to get help. At that point, Köntrop held on to me firmly. He was dead moments later.

I reached my replacement tank. The wounded as well as the dead were evacuated.

Obersturmführer Flügel, who had passed us on the left, was slugging it out with some Russian tanks behind Ssagopschin. To my right, the 1st Company [*1./SS-Panzer-Abteilung 5 "Wiking"*] had come to a standstill. *SS-Hauptsturmführer* Schnabel of the 1st Company and *SS-Hauptsturmführer* Darges of the 3rd Company had also been knocked out.

"Hannes" Mühlenkamp restored command and control to the battalion. He rolled on in his replacement tank. Just as he had gotten things back under control, his replacement tank was hit and he had to take over another vehicle. This tank was also hit, and Mühlenkamp had to change tanks for the third time on this 28 September 1942.

When the day drew to a close, the breakthrough still had not been achieved. While the attack proved unsuccessful, the tank battalion also succeeded in thwarting the Soviet plans to eliminate the division, when they launched their immediate counterattacks.

On 3 October 1942, *SS-Panzergrenadier-Regiment 9 "Germania"* returned to the division, after having been detached for operations in another sector. It was intended for this regiment to take Malgobek on 5 October with the support of the tank battalion. During this attack, *SS-Hauptsturmführer* Schnabel was killed. *SS-Untersturmführer* Nikolussi-Leck assumed acting command of the 1st Company in his place.

Despite the appearance of another regiment on the battlefield, the German attack in the Malgobek area ultimately bogged down, even though the town itself was captured.

The winter in the mountains set in. The soldiers of *SS-Panzergrenadier-Division "Wiking"*—redesignated as such on 9 November 1942—remained in defensive positions along the Malgobek sector until 11 November 1942, when they were pulled out of the line to be committed along the Terek, where a crisis situation had developed in the sector of the *III. Panzer-Korps* of *General der Kavallerie* von Mackensen.

On 16 November 1942, the tank battalion reached the area around Alagir and was immediately committed to combat. The battalion was attached to the *23. Panzer-Division* of *Generalmajor Freiherr* von Boineburg-Lengsfeld. The operation revolved around coming to the assistance of the *13. Panzer-Division* of *Generalmajor* von der Chevallerie, which had advanced as far as Ordshonikidse, where it was encircled and fighting.

The *13. Panzer-Division* was rescued over the course of the next month. On 14 December, the commanding general of the corps was transferred to another assignment and *SS-Gruppenführer* Steiner assumed acting command of the *III. Panzer-Korps. SS-Brigadeführer* Gille, the division artillery commander, took over the division.

On 22 December, the order to withdraw arrived. *SS-Panzer-Grenadier-Division "Wiking"* covered the withdrawal. Again and again, it was the tanks of "Hannes" Mühlenkamp that cleared the path for the division when it was in danger of being cut off.

The *III. Panzer-Korps* was pulled back to Piatigorsk, where it entrained and then detrained at Ssalsk on 1 January 1943. This armored corps was then placed under the overall leadership of *Generaloberst* Hoth for the relief effort on Stalingrad. The corps was able to advance to within 60 kilometers of the city.

When that effort ultimately failed, the division was again involved with covering the general withdrawal from the Caucasus. The BBC broadcast the following concerning the division on 14 February 1943:

> If the German divisions succeed in pulling out of the Caucasus in an orderly fashion, then this is ultimately due to the efforts of the *Waffen-SS Division "Wiking."*

The general direction of the retreat was Rostow, and Mühlenkamp has written the following about this phase of the war:

> The following applied at the time: Fight in all directions during the day and march towards Rostow at night. Usually, this was off to the side of the main road in horrific cold and with difficulty in orienting.

Recently, it got to -42° Celsius [-43.6° Fahrenheit]. Before we started the vehicles we had to heat up the final drives with 2-liter petroleum lamps. The engines were started with inertia cranks that were turned by hand. To do that on the 450-horsepower engine required two men. We often moved by compass, just like seafarers.

Enemy formations that attempted to attack the flanks of the division were destroyed by rapid attacks of the tanks. On 4 February, the tank battalion seemed to be involved everywhere along the division sector. Once again, Mühlenkamp:

We were moving back along the oil pipeline to Bataisk. Our dead comrades, whom we could no longer bury, were taken along with us.

✠

The year 1943 saw the division in retreat to the Donez and involved in the defensive fighting around Kharkov and Isjum. The defensive fighting along the Dnjepr and the Tscherkassy Pocket were milestones in the history of the division that was decimated more than all the rest. It was thanks to the efforts of the division commander that at least 800 men were able to escape the Tscherkassy Pocket. These men helped form the cadre for the reconstitution of the division.

When the decision was made to expand the tank battalion to a regiment, Mühlenkamp was chosen to lead it. Let us now continue the story where it first left off in the fighting around Kowel

✠

After Nikolussi-Leck had succeeded in breaking through to Kowel, Mühlenkamp then made every effort to get the rest of the regiment and the entire divisional *Kampfgruppe* to the beleaguered city. Late in March 1944, the 7th Company of the tank regiment arrived at the Maciejow rail station and detrained. It received orders to immediately go into combat against a Russian attack. The new *Panther* tanks of *SS-Obersturmführer* Schneider were able to stop the Soviets.

Attack followed counterattack. On 2 April 1944, Mühlenkamp directed his reconnaissance platoon leader, *SS-Untersturmführer* Manfred Renz, to conduct a reconnaissance-in-force with his *Panthers*.

The *Panthers* moved out over the broad snow-covered plains in biting cold. By the end of his patrol, Renz was only moving with one tank so as to dampen the noise of the armored vehicles as much as possible. His efforts met with success when he discovered a serious threat to the division's flanks from antitank guns at a certain location. He turned in a detailed spot report, which was also monitored by *SS-Obersturmbannführer* Otto Paetsch, the commander of the regiment's 2nd Battalion.

On 3 April, Mühlenkamp prepared to assault Kowel with everything he had. At 2300 hours, he called both Paetsch and Schneider and issued them the attack order. But the attack had to be postponed on the morning of 4 April, because the *4. Panzer-Division*, which was also supposed to participate in the attack and to which Mühlenkamp's *Kampfgruppe* was attached, was not yet ready. Mühlenkamp coordinated with *Generalleutnant* Dietrich von Saucken, the commander of the *4. Panzer-Division*, and von Saucken ordered the attack to start on 5 April. All of the operational tanks were rearmed and refueled on the night of 4/5 April. Later on, Mühlenkamp would write: "The actual recapture of Kowel would not have been conceivable without bringing in the *4. Panzer-Division* under *General* von Saucken and the *5. Panzer-Division* under [*Generalmajor*] Decker."

At 0315 hours on 5 April, Mühlenkamp's command tank rolled past the positions of the 1st Battalion of *SS-Panzergrenadier-Regiment 9 "Germania."* The regimental commander had issued orders to advance to the northwest edge of Kowel. One hour later, the city outskirts were reached without there being any enemy contact. While the grenadiers dug in, Mühlenkamp and his liaison officer, *SS-Obersturmführer* Sepp Martin, who was in a second tank, moved towards the Russian-occupied portion of the city. Suddenly, there was a loud explosion under the track of the commander's tank, which had run over a mine. Mühlenkamp jumped onto the other tank.

When it became light, Mühlenkamp had two more companies brought forward. *SS-Hauptsturmführer* Reicher came forward with his 6th Company, as did *SS-Obersturmführer* Schneider with his 7th Company. The companies knocked out enemy artillery pieces and overran obstacles. Then Schneider's tankers opened the hole that led into the encircled German forces. In the process, his tank was hit three times.

Using Schneider's company as his battering ram, Mühlenkamp had his elements move out again at 1510 hours. The tanks broke through stubborn resistance and reached the center of the city at 1700 hours. *SS-Gruppenführer* Gille immediately issued orders for the breakthrough to be expanded.

Despite this success, the enemy did not give up. Tough, seesaw fighting continued for another week. Wherever the enemy attacked, however, he found Mühlenkamp's tanks. Once again, "Hannes" Mühlenkamp demonstrated his prowess as an armor commander. He was not only personally brave, but also tactically adroit. He had a keen sense of the battlefield and was usually able to find the weak spots of the enemy. He led his tankers with circumspection born of experience and maintained his tanks at their peak level of performance. He led his forces with both heart and head.

✠

The situation at Kowel stabilized. It was not until 12 April that Russian forces again launched a major effort, this time against Hill 179. Mühlenkamp sent *SS-Obersturmführer* Jessen's 6th Company to deal with the problem. It was during this action that *SS-Untersturmführer* Grossrock, a platoon leader, excelled. He knocked out a number of T-34's with the six *Panthers* that were reporting to him. Grossrock was later submitted for the Knight's Cross to the Iron Cross for the operations of this day, which he received on 12 August 1944. Grossrock's days were numbered, however. He was killed in action on 4 April 1945.

A few days later, the tank regiment moved out to clear the western portion of Kowel. At the same time, the division employed *Kampfgruppe Dorr* against nearby Hill 189.5. Hans Dorr not only captured the objective, he continued well beyond it. The *SS-Sturmbannführer,* who was already a recipient of the Oak Leaves to the Knight's Cross of the Iron Cross, was presented with the Swords to the award on 9 July 1944. He was the 77th member of the German Armed Forces to receive the high decoration. Like Grossrock, he would also not survive the war.

On 20 April 1944, *SS-Gruppenführer* Gille became the 12th member of the German Armed Forces to receive the Diamonds to the Oak Leaves and Swords to the Knight's Cross of the Iron Cross. At the same time, Mühlenkamp was promoted to *SS-Standartenführer.*

The fighting continued in this sector, however. Again and again, it was Mühlenkamp's tanks that were called forward to straighten out lines, take back high ground and knock out enemy armor. By the beginning of May, the enemy had had enough and stopped his offensive efforts. On 8 May 1944, the tank regiment was withdrawn from Kowel to be designated as the operational reserve of the *LVI. Panzer-Korps* of *General der Infanterie* Hossbach. The "Vikings" had become the fire brigade for an army corps.

This phase of the war left a deep impression on Mühlenkamp, as he fought under *General der Infanterie* Hossbach and worked closely with both the *4. Panzer-Division* and the *5. Panzer-Division.* He later recalled that all of the senior commanders and operations officers he met during this phase of the war were superior officers and soldiers.

✠

On 22 June 1944, the Soviet Operation Bagration was launched, which
sent all of *Heeresgruppe Mitte* reeling. It remained quiet in the area around
Kowel at first. Up until 6 July, there was only skirmishing. Then all hell
broke out in this sector as well. The tankers of *SS-Panzer-Regiment 5 "Wiking"*
participated in a round of fighting that they would never forget for the rest
of their lives.

SS-Standartenführer Mühlenkamp was responsible for providing the
rearguard for the division out of Kowel. Russian aircraft attacked the German
positions, and then *SS-Hauptsturmführer* Reicher, the new commander of
the tank regiment's 2nd Battalion, discovered that 17 Russian tanks and
escorting infantry were moving out of the woods northeast of Nowe Koscary.
These forces were not engaged, however, because Mühlenkamp received
orders from the *LVI. Panzer-Korps* to move his regiment immediately to the
threatened area around Smydin. All of this Russian activity on 5 July 1944
gave the impression that a major Russian attack was about to be launched. In
"Hannes" Mühlenkamp's mind, it could only have one objective: Cholm and
the Bug River. Mühlenkamp shared his opinion with the corps commander,
when the latter came to visit the forces up front.

Mühlenkamp starting making preparations to counter this expected
offensive. He pulled his tanks back to a reverse-slope position in the area of
Maciejow. This appeared to be the only course of action available to stop the
enemy armored attack.

At 1215 hours on the next day, large enemy aerial elements attacked the
German main line of resistance. The area where Mühlenkamp's tanks had
been located the previous day was plastered with heavy bombs. This could
only mean one thing: the Russian attack.

The Russians then attacked the formerly held positions of the Germans.
This was followed by a huge onslaught of Soviet armor—some 400 armored
vehicles of all types and sizes—that rolled north of Maciejow. They were
headed west and rolled right past the ambush positions of Mühlenkamp's
tanks.

"Hannes" Mühlenkamp radioed the Finnish *SS-Obersturmführer* Olaf Olin,
who was in a specially selected position with his four *Panthers*. The commander
ordered the Finn to allow the first 10 tanks to pass before opening fire on the
last one and knocking out the first one.

The Finn succeeded in knocking out these 10 vehicles in accordance with
his regimental commander's instructions. Because this firing then focused
the Soviets' attention on that portion of the sector, Mühlenkamp then issued
orders to his remaining tanks to open fire.

The *Panthers* fired from their good hull-down positions. After the first volley of fire, the battlefield looked like a giant junkyard. Dozens of enemy tanks were ablaze, their ammunition detonating from the heat. The second salvo hammered out. When the smoke had cleared, more than 50 wrecked vehicles littered the open terrain.

The firefight lasted 30 minutes in all. Most of the Soviets tried to escape for those 30 minutes; some attempted to engage and destroy the *Panthers.* By the time it was all over, there were 103 knocked-out tanks in front of the *SS* tankers. Some of them were brand-new heavy tanks. At least another 150 vehicles had received some sort of battle damage; they limped back into the relative security of the woods from whence they had come.

The regimental commander of one of the Soviet tank regiments that had been employed was found in his shot-up vehicle a short while later by a patrol. His map had a thick arrow marked on it: It pointed towards the Bug and Cholm.

Because the corps had a hard time believing that this single regiment had been so successful on the battlefield that day against such an overwhelmingly numerically superior foe, it dispatched an officer to count the knocked-out vehicles. *Oberstleutnant i.G.* Peter Sauerbach reported back to the corps: "103 knocked-out and burnt-out tanks!"

There had never been anything quite like this. *General der Infanterie* Hossbach submitted Mühlenkamp for the Oak Leaves to the Knight's Cross of the Iron Cross. The German Armed Forces Daily Report of 11 July 1944 reported this impressive defensive achievement and mentioned the division and Mühlenkamp by name.

In a radio interview after the fighting, Mühlenkamp spelled out the recipe for his success:

> In addition to the quality of the tanks that we have, it comes down to the bravery and determination of their crews. All of them are men who have accompanied me for many years and who cannot be praised enough for their military professionalism. These wonderful tankers deserve my special thanks.

✠

The fighting continued. On 21 September 1944, Johannes Mühlenkamp was awarded the Oak Leaves to the Knight's Cross of the Iron Cross. He was the 596th member of the German Armed Forces to receive this coveted award. When *SS-Gruppenführer* Gille was entrusted with the formation of the *IV. SS-Panzer-Korps* on 12 August, he turned the division over to the capable hands of Mühlenkamp. Mühlenkamp commanded the division during the fighting around Warsaw.

On 9 October, Mühlenkamp had to leave the division, however. The senior leadership wanted to use his knowledge and capabilities to continue to build up and expand the armored formations of the *Waffen-SS*. He was designated as the inspector General of the armored forces of the *Waffen-SS*. *Generaloberst* Guderian was the one who lobbied for Mühlenkamp filling this position. He knew he had a good man in the *SS* tanker.

Mühlenkamp occupied this position until the end of the war, where he worked tirelessly to get the necessary fighting vehicles into the hands of the *Waffen-SS* soldiers at the front.

✠

Johannes Mühlenkamp passed away in Langelsheim (vicinity of Goslar) on 23 September 1986.

Massed *Panzer* forces cross the seemingly endless Russian steppes.

General der Panzertruppen Walther K. Nehring, a successful armor commander at both division and corps levels.

CHAPTER 14

General der Panzertruppe Walther K. Nehring

FROM THEORETICIAN TO COMMANDER OF AN ARMORED FIELD ARMY

At 0315 hours on 22 June 1941, 50 German batteries of differing calibers in the sector of the *18. Panzer-Division* opened fire on the Soviet field fortifications and bunkers on the far side of the Bug.

"Take a look at that, *Herr General!*" one of the liaison officers said, pointing to the muzzle flashes of a heavy battery that constantly lit up the sky.

"Impressive, but useless! The Russians have evacuated their positions along the frontier, with the exception of the border guards. I hope our wading tanks make it across the river. Let's go to the Bug!"

Walther Nehring, the division commander, took off. He had assumed command some eight months previously and transformed a number of disparate elements—former infantry battalions, horse-drawn artillery and three tank battalions, which had originally been formed for the invasion of Great Britain—into a modern armored division.

Since the tanks that had been earmarked for the cross-channel invasion had been set up to be submergible, they were selected to cross the Bug under water. It was 0445 hours when *Feldwebel* Wierschin entered the waters of the Bug with his specially modified tank.[1] Soldiers not familiar with the modified tanks watched slack-jawed as other tanks also entered the water and the waters slowly disappeared above the turret. Soon, the entire battalion had disappeared. Up front with his men was the battalion commander, *Major* Manfred *Graf* Strachwitz. Soon the tanks started exiting the waters on the far side.

There were dull thuds, as the rubber gaskets and seals were taken off the vehicles and tossed to the ground for later recovery. Eighty tanks of the division moved rapidly forward to establish a bridgehead for the entire division to cross. *Panzer-Regiment 18* advanced through Widomla to Pruzana, with *General* Nehring moving forward next to the battalion commander. It

---

1. Editor's Note: The converted tanks were both *Panzer III* and *Panzer IV*.

was at Pruzana that the first anti-armor engagement took place, when enemy armored cars were spotted.

After eliminating the enemy's reconnaissance elements, the division continued to stream forward. Minsk was taken. Nehring, who had been Guderian's right-hand man for a long time—first as an operations officer and then as his chief-of-staff—was transforming theory into practice. He was following Guderian's famous dictum—*Nicht kleckern, sondern klotzen!*—to the letter.

✠

Nehring always seemed to be up front with his adjutant, *Major* von Reinhard. On the night of 26/27 June, an incident occurred that many had feared all along might happen. The commander was looking for the headquarters of the tank regiment, since he had lost contact with it in the darkness. Dimly, the outlines of a palace could be seen. Nehring directed his driver to head for the palace. They headed towards the medieval structure and the bridge they needed to cross to get to it. Suddenly, they saw a shadow in front of them.

"A *Panzer III, Herr General!*"

"Stop!"

The lightly armored command *SPW* of the commander stopped about 50 meters in front of the tank. Nehring stood up and called out to the tank. All of a sudden, there was the sound of tank tracks behind their vehicle. Nehring turned around to see the machine-gun barrels on two Soviet T-26's.

"Take off to the right!" the general officer yelled to his driver, in a lightning-fast reaction. The driver stepped on it and out of the beaten zone of the machine-gun fire. The *Panzer III*, which had been posted at the bridge as security, came to life, and its turret started to traverse. A pyrotechnic was fired into the air, quickly fired by two quick rounds fired in succession from the *Panzer III's* 5-centimeter main gun.

Both of the Soviet vehicles were set alight before they could engage the German tank.

"That was close," the general said. "Let's get out of here right now!"

The next day, the headquarters of Guderian's *Panzergruppe 2* moved into the palace. Guderian did not realize that the two burned-out Soviet tanks outside the entrance had come within a hair's breadth of eliminating one of his division commanders and his battle staff.

✠

On the evening of 29 June, Nehring received orders to advance past Minsk and, moving on the Moscow highway, to initially take Borissow. It was intended for the division to take the important crossings over the Beresina there, which would allow Guderian's forces to continue their advance.

Later on, the general said that the entire operation seemed something akin to a suicide mission. Early in the morning, the division moved out for its advance of more than 100 kilometers through the enemy lines. When the division encountered the first of many Soviet echeloned defensive lines, it deployed to conduct an attack from a movement to contact. For the Soviets, the mission General Jeremenko had issued was simple: "Hold or die!"

It was important for Nehring to take immediate action, and that's what he did. While elements of the division fixed the Soviets from the front, *Schützen-Regiment 101* moved out to flank the position. At the same time, Nehring summoned *Major* Teege, the commander of the 2nd Battalion of *Panzer-Regiment 18*. Teege was to lead the division's advance guard, which was to move out as soon as the Soviet resistance weakened. Augmenting Teege's tanks were motorcycle infantry from *Kradschützen-Bataillon 88*, reconnaissance elements from *Aufklärungs-Abteilung 88 (mot.)* and a battalion of the divisional artillery (*Major* Teichert).

By noon, Teege's men had reached the outskirts of Borissow. The bridge over the Beresina was bravely defended by cadets and cadre from the armor school in the city. Since the element of surprise was lacking, Teege's force was too weak to take the bridge.

Generalmajor Nehring soon arrived, after having had a narrow escape from an encounter with a Soviet armored train. Fortunately for the general and his battle staff, the Soviets mistook the staff car for a Soviet one, since no Germans were expected to be in the area. Once the main body of the division had closed on the outskirts of the city, Nehring started committing it. He had *Schützen-Regiment 52* assault the Soviet bridgehead on the west bank of the river.

Tanks and artillery supported the assault. Cleverly led, the riflemen eliminated the enemy's machine-gun positions. *Unteroffizier* Bukatschek's platoon was the first to reach the bridge. Although wounded in the shoulder, he ran across and prevented it from being blown up. He later became the first soldier of the division to receive the Knight's Cross to the Iron Cross for his actions.

Just as Nehring had reached the edge of the woods in the vicinity of the highway and was discussing the situation with his commanders, approximately 20 light Soviet tanks launched an attack and headed straight for the commander's vehicle in rows of two. "Take cover, Heintze!" Nehring yelled out, and both of them jumped behind the command *SPW* at the same time. A few seconds later, the *SPW* was rammed by one of the Soviet tanks, which damaged its running gear. German forces soon came to the rescue and dispatched the Soviet force.

The tanks of the advance guard then crossed the bridge, followed closely by the motorcycle infantry battalion and Laube's *Flak* battalion, which had been given the mission of screening the bridge with its powerful 8.8-centimeter *Flak*. An immediate Soviet counterattack was turned back.

By the end of the day, the Beresina had been forced and the way was clear for the rest of *Panzergruppe Guderian* to move on to Orscha and Smolensk. Nehring's division received orders to move on in the direction of Orscha.

Two days later, at Lipki, 10 kilometers east of Borissow, there was an engagement with General Krejser's 1st Motorized Rifle Division. It was the first Soviet force encountered in the center sector of the Eastern Front that had the T-34 and KV-II. These attacked in addition to the light T-26's. The fighting seemed to be going against the Germans, whose 3.7-, 5- and 7.5-centimeter main-gun rounds were incapable of penetrating the armor of the enemy's steel monsters. The situation was turning critical. In the end, the only way to counter the new threat for the German tanks was to move under the enemy's fires and approach as closely as possible. At close range, it was possible to immobilize the tanks through hits to the running gear or jam their turrets through hits to the turret ring. It was only then that the Germans could approach weak spots on the enemy armor to provide the *coup de grace*.

According to Nehring later on: "It was there that German arms did not prevail. Instead, it was the German soldier with his bravery, his discipline, his gunnery training and his terrific means of command and control, the radio, that prevailed." The Germans were also helped by a decisive mistake on the part of the Soviets: They had employed their new and dangerous tanks individually, making it easier to isolate them and subject them to concentrated fires from several other tanks.

The advance from the Borissow bridgehead took the division as far as Tolotschino by 7 July. Once again, there was another round of tank-on-tank fighting. Guderian met with Nehring later that day and extended to him his praise for the division.

Passing around Orscha to the south, the division crossed the Dnjepr on 12 July at Kopys. It then advanced on Krassny-Gusino, fighting hard every step of the way. With the taking of Smolensk on 16 July, the first phase of the campaign in the Soviet Union was over for the *18. Panzer-Division.*

On 31 July, Guderian personally presented Nehring with the Knight's Cross to the Iron Cross (the award date was actually 24 July) for the operations involved in the taking of Borissow. For Nehring, it meant recognition for his entire division.

From 25 August to 22 September, the division was involved in localized operations on both sides of the Desna. The division was relieved by the *1. Kavallerie-Division* and sent to the Nowgorod-Ssewersk area to prepare for the fall offensive.

The attack for the *XXXXVII. Armee-Korps (mot.)* started on 30 September. It advanced on Tschamlysch, crossing the Ssew at Ssewsk. An intense armored engagement flared up at Tschamlysch on 2 October. Karatschew was taken on 5 October. Advancing at speed, four rivers were crossed. On the day of the fighting for Karatschew, *Leutnant* Heintze sent no fewer than 126 radio messages for the general in an effort to coordinate the efforts of the division.

The first snow fell on 6 October, followed by a thaw and the onset of a period of mud. There was hard fighting north of Karatschew until 10 October, before the enemy pulled back, defeated. Seven days later, the division received orders to advance through Orel and on to Kursk to relieve the *XXXXVIII. Armee-Korps (mot.)*, which had been encircled in the Fatesh area, stuck in the mud and without fuel. Due to the seriousness of the situation, Guderian personally issued the orders to Nehring.

On 20 October, the *18. Panzer-Division* took Fatesh in a tough fight, successfully executing the difficult mission it had been given.

On 13 November, the division moved out from Orel through Mzensk and in the direction of Jefremov, covering the east flank of Guderian's forces in their drive through Tula and on to Moscow. Extreme temperatures and snowfall severely hindered the forces. Despite that, Nehring was able to accomplish his mission, taking Jefremov on 20 November, after advancing 200 kilometers and engaging in heavy fighting.

In a continued advance, the forces of *Major* Seidlitz's *Panzer-Aufklärungs-Abteilung 88* took the village of Skopin, which turned out to be the eastern-most point reached by German forces in 1941. The planned assault on Moscow was called off, and the *18. Panzer-Division* went over to the defensive in the area between Turdej and Don.

Based on the overall situation, Nehring's forces also started a withdrawal on 14 December. On 25 December, a new line along the southern bank of the Susha, east of Mzensk, was reached. It was directed that it be held.

At the beginning of 1942, the division was given another difficult mission. It was directed to hack out the *216. Infanterie-Division*, which had been encircled in the Suchinitschi area for three weeks. That operation—moving more than 100 kilometers through the enemy in bitter cold and high snow—demanded the utmost from every soldier. Again, the division succeeded. On 24 January, the relief force linked up with the beleaguered division.

In a special decree by Hitler dated 28 January 1942, Nehring was singled out for praise because he had proven "that German soldiers could also fight in the winter." On 1 February, Nehring was promoted to *Generalleutnant*. At the same time, he was summoned to the *Führer* Headquarters. Hitler personally briefed Nehring on his upcoming assignment to the North African theater of operations. He was to assume command of the *Deutsches Afrika-Korps* in a decisive phase of the fighting there.

✠

Nehring came from an old West Prussian family, which had had its origins in the Netherlands. Following the reformation, it emigrated through Wesel to Brandenburg. His ancestors were farmers and estate owners. The family name of Nehring was mentioned for the first time in 1430 in the city of Danzig's citizenry register.

He was born on 15 August 1892 on the Stretzin estate in the district of Schlochau. He attended school in Zoppot and Danzig. He received his college preparatory degree from the St. Johann Gymnasium in the spring of 1911.

While attending school in Danzig, he developed a special fondness for the city. During his holidays, he often traveled to Groß Bendomin in the Berent district, which was the site of his mother's family's estate. It was there that he developed an interest in nature, hunting and agriculture. In 1913, he obtained his first hunting license.[2]

Nehring entered military service as an officer candidate in 1911, being assigned to the *Deutsches-Ordens-Infanterie-Regiment 152* in Marienburg. In 1913, he was commissioned, with his rank backdated to 1911. Along with millions of his countrymen, the young *Leutnant* went to war on 8 August 1914. He fought in the Battle of Tannenberg. At the Masurian Lakes he was wounded for the first time on 11 September 1914. In the assault on the Beynuhnen palace in northeastern Prussia, he was hit in the throat and head by a rifle bullet. His bravery was rewarded with the presentation of the Iron Cross, Second Class.

On 2 November 1914, just released from the hospital, Nehring was assigned to *Mobiles Ersatz-Bataillon 148*,[3] where he became the adjutant. The replacement battalion served a hastily assembled division that was entrusted with the security of the borders of eastern Prussia. He participated in fighting in the Kutno area, in Lithuania and Kurland. On 6 June 1915, he was promoted to *Oberleutnant*.

---

2. Translator's Note: The obtaining of a hunting license was never an easy process in Germany, unlike the United States. It usually required the taking of courses and the passing of an extensive examination.

3. Translator's Note: 148th Mobile Replacement Battalion.

Two days after his promotion, he was reassigned to *Armeeflugpark 8*[4] in Schaulen. He wanted to become an aviator, but on 21 June he was on board an aircraft as an observer when it crashed. Badly wounded, he spent the next few months in a hospital.

After he had convalesced, Nehring was reassigned to the western theater of war. He took command of a machine-gun company in *Infanterie-Regiment 22.* He fought with the company at Artois, in Flanders and the Siegfried Position. He was eventually awarded the Iron Cross, First Class.

During the spring offensive of 1918, Nehring was given acting command of the regiment's 3rd Battalion for several weeks. On 1 July 1918, he was shot in the stomach while fighting on Kemmel Mountain. That signaled the end of his front-line service in the First World War.

At the end of November 1918, Nehring was assigned as the adjutant to the senior officer for machine-gun forces in the *XX. Armee-Korps* in Allenstein. He was retained in the postwar army and, after 12 years of active-duty service, promoted to *Hauptmann* on 1 March 1923.

That was followed by three years of intensive training as a General Staff officer candidate in Military District I and then attendance at the General Staff officer course sponsored by the Ministry of Defense. He was accepted into the General Staff on 1 October 1926, where he performed duties in the operations directorate. It was there that he began to appreciate the terrific advantage of mobile, fast-moving forces which, because they were motorized, had to be armored and heavily armed. As part of his periodic troop duty, he was assigned to *Kraftfahr-Abteilung 6* in Münster on 1 March 1929. It was there that he received the mission of transforming a motorized company into the first motorized *combat* force of the German Army.

It was an experiment that worked and provided valuable lessons for the future motorization of the army. Nehring retained his interest in motorized forces and thus began his future close association with the *Panzertruppe.*

On 1 January 1932, he was transferred back to the Ministry of Defense, where he was assigned as the operations officer for the Directorate of Motorized Forces, whose chief-of-staff was *Oberstleutnant i.G.* Guderian. One month later, Nehring was promoted to *Major i.G.* That was followed by promotion to *Oberstleutnant i.G.* in September 1934. On 1 October, he became the operations officer for the Motorization Command in Berlin. Once again, Guderian was the chief-of-staff and, later, *Oberst i.G.* Paulus of Stalingrad fame.

In 1936 and 1937, as part of his continuing education and training as a General Staff officer, Nehring was detailed to numerous army formations, as well as to the *Luftwaffe* and the *Kriegsmarine.* On 1 October 1937, he assumed

---

4. Translator's Note: 8th Army Airfield.

command of *Panzer-Regiment 5* in Wünsdorf (Berlin), after having been
promoted to *Oberst i.G.* the previous March. It was his chance to transform
many of the tactical principles he had espoused and written about in the years
from 1934 to 1937 into practice.

By then, Guderian had become the head of mobile forces. In that
capacity, he saw to it that Nehring was transferred to Vienna on 1 July 1939 to
become the chief-of-staff of the newly forming *XIX. Armee-Korps (mot.)*, which
Guderian was earmarked to command. It was in that capacity that Nehring
participated in the campaign in Poland. During that campaign, he received
clasps to his First World War Iron Crosses, indicating he had been awarded
the same decorations in the current conflict as well.

During the campaign in the West, Nehring's job was to transform the
decisions of his commanding general far out in front into corresponding corps
orders. Following the first phase of the campaign, Guderian was directed to
form a *Panzergruppe*, a formation larger than a corps but smaller than a field
army. Nehring stayed on to be the chief-of-staff, while the operations officer
was *Major* Fritz Bayerlein. Both men would work closely together in various
headquarters for the remainder of the war.[5]

On 1 August 1940, Nehring was promoted to *Generalmajor*. Guderian had
recommended him for the Knight's Cross for his performance in France, but
the recommendation was turned down, since the Knight's Cross was not yet
awarded for superior performance in headquarters activities.

On 28 October 1940, he assumed command of the *18. Panzer-Division*,
which was in the process of being formed in Chemnitz. In later years, he
always thanked his operations officer at the time, Fritz Ester, for his assistance
in transforming the many disparate elements into a combat-ready formation
in such a short period of time.

✠

At the beginning of March 1942, he arrived in North Africa. *General*
Crüwell, who was the acting commander of the German forces in Africa at
the time, transferred command of the *Deutsches Afrika-Korps*, which was part of
Panzer-Armee Afrika, to him.

Panzer-Armee Afrika had just finished taking back all of the terrain it
had had to relinquish the previous year. The campaign, which started on
22 January 1942 from the area around Marsa el Brega, took 17 days. The

---

5. Author's Note: Bayerlein eventually rose to the rank of *Generalleutnant* and was the
   commanding general of an armored corps. On 20 July 1944, he became the 81st
   member of the German Armed Forces to receive the Swords to the Oak Leaves to
   the Knight's Cross of the Iron Cross.

Germans were then in the process of planning an attack on Tobruk to finally take the fortress and harbor, which had always been a thorn in the side of the Axis forces. The conventional wisdom held that if it fell, then the door to Egypt would swing wide open.

On the morning of 27 May, the *DAK* swung north after going around the southern wing of the Gazala Line at Bir Hachheim in a night march. The plan was to encircle the garrison at Bir Hachheim and cut it off from Tobruk.

The ultimate goal of the initial operations was the coast between Tobruk and the Gazala Line. Nehring had two armored divisions at his disposal. He employed the *21. Panzer-Division* on the left and the *15. Panzer-Division* on the right. Nehring positioned himself in the middle between the two divisions. The *21. Panzer-Division* succeeded in fighting its way forward to Akroma. The broad band of the coastal highway, the *Via Balbia*, was palpably near.

That afternoon, however, the enemy attacked at 1600 hours with 60 new tanks into the unprotected deep flank of the *15. Panzer-Division*. The division's tanks were far forward and a catastrophe appeared to be in the making.

Nehring was conducting reconnaissance with *Oberst* Wolz, the commander of a *Flak* regiment, when they were suddenly swarmed with trains elements. They then ran into the withdrawing corps headquarters. Soon, Nehring, Wolz and their immediate battle staffs were alone in the desert.

They intercepted a withdrawing *Flak* battery in a cloud of dust. Rommel appeared at the same time. In his typical manner, he brusquely asked Wolz: "Why aren't you firing?" He continued: "The *Flak* is responsible for everything, because it is not firing."

Wolz halted the battery. There were three guns. They were soon joined by three *Flak* that had been assigned to protect the *DAK* headquarters. They had barely emplaced when the enemy armored armada approached. About 40 tanks were counted.

The *Flak* started to engage, and the first enemy tanks were knocked out. At that critical moment, as the enemy tanks hesitated, Nehring had a idea: "A *Flak* barrier, Wolz! Your guns fire farther than the tanks. Establish a front with all available *Flak*!"

Rommel and Nehring set out to find the scattered *Flak* elements so as to form them into a defensive front. Soon there was a wall of guns stretching 3 kilometers. The enemy had taken too long to regroup. When they advanced to within 2,000 meters, 16 8.8-centimeter *Flak* opened fire. The enemy called off his attack. As it turned dark, 24 burning torches could be counted on the battlefield in front of the German guns. The innovation had worked to deadly effect.

Nehring set up his command post a few kilometers behind the *Flak* positions. The *DAK* was stuck between two strong foes: the reinforced Gazala

Position to its rear and strong armored forces to the east. During a situation conference with Rommel on the morning of 29 May, Nehring, along with the three General Staff officers—Bayerlein, Westphal and Gause—recommended the force attempt to escape the envelopment by punching its way to freedom to the west. The recommendation took on additional weight, when it shortages began to surface, especially in fuel and water. It was impossible to evacuate the wounded because of British patrols. With a heavy heart, Rommel agreed to the recommendation of his commanders and staff.

As with most things in warfare, the actual conduct of affairs turned out differently than planned. While looking for a way to punch through to the west, Nehring and Bayerlein ran into the British desert fort of Got el Ualeb, which was defended by the 150th Brigade. In order to get through, the fort had to be eliminated as a threat. During the fighting to eliminate the strongpoint, the headquarters of the *DAK* was attacked by fighter-bombers. Miraculously, Nehring escaped injury, even though shrapnel splattered his command vehicle.

Eventually, the 3rd Battalion of *Grenadier-Regiment 104* was able to take out the fort. The battalion commander, *Major* Ehle, was wounded next to Nehring during the fight. A few days later, the *15. Panzer-Division* succeeded in scattering the Indian 5th Infantry Division. One of the Indian division's brigades was encircled. *Hauptmann* Riepold's company from *Panzer-Regiment 5* closed the pocket from the north. Nehring was moving with the tank company when that occurred. One of the prisoners netted was Brigadier Desmond Young, the brigade commander, who was later to write the famous biography of Rommel.

On the morning of 11 June, Bir Hachheim fell to the south. Nehring then led his *15. Panzer-Division* forward so as to encircle the northern strongpoints. The enemy armored forces were gradually being reduced as well. During the morning of 15 June, the *15. Panzer-Division* reached the Mediterranean. That meant that the way to Tobruk was open. Five days later, the actual battle for the fortress started. The harbor city fell on 21 June, after having successfully resisted for 28 weeks the previous year.

Nehring and his staff had performed masterfully during the decisive, rapid attack. He seemed to be everywhere at once. He rallied his forces and led them forward. On Rommel's recommendation, he was promoted to *General der Panzertruppen.*

The advance continued east, with the combat power of Rommel's forces dwindling rapidly due to the overextended supply lines and the Allies successful interdiction of most of the logistical effort directed towards North Africa. The *DAK* was soon down to 65 operational tanks. As a result, the attack ordered by Rommel against the British field fortifications around El Alamein early on the morning of 1 July did not succeed.

In the weeks that followed, the British took the initiative and attempted to eliminate the German forces. There were days of intense armored engagements with seesaw fighting and mixed results. During an attack during the night of 21/21 June, the British lost 90 tanks, and the *DAK* held firm.

The fighting around El Alamein started to die down. Both sides were weak and had to wait for replacements and supplies, with the British having better chances of success in that regard. For the Axis forces, there were three courses of action, which Nehring later summarized thusly:

> Rommel could have waited, which was not in his nature and which was not his mission, or he could attempt to act before the enemy did.
>
> There was a third course of action: pull back to the west to better positions.
>
> Rommel decided—pressured by the Armed Forces High Command and Hitler—to attack!

On 30 August, *Panzer-Armee Afrika* moved out to attack again. The two armored divisions of the *DAK* attacked the southern portion of the Alamein Position at 2000 hours. The *15. Panzer-Division* had 70 *Panzer III's* and *IV's* at its disposal; the *21. Panzer-Division* had 120.

Nehring accompanied the attack of the *21. Panzer-Division* in his command *SPW*. With him were his chief-of-staff, Bayerlein, and his liaison officer, *Oberleutnant* von Burgsdorff. The attacking force moved through a minefield. The first tanks were immobilized when they rolled over mines. Machine-gun fire passed over the general's *SPW*. The first radio messages arrived, and they were not encouraging: *Generalmajor* von Bismarck, the commander of the *21. Panzer-Division*, had been killed. *Generalmajor* Kleemann, the commander of the *90. (leichte) Division*, another division under Nehring's command, had been wounded. Despite the leadership losses, the attack was pressed forward.

The morning of 31 August dawned; bombs hurled earthward. Fighter-bombers dove on the German tanks. One of them took up the general's *SPW* in its sights. The fighting elements fired with everything they had, but the pilot was persistent. It dropped a bomb, which landed near the front axle of the armored personnel carrier. Nehring was thrown against the superstructure's walls when it exploded. Shrapnel penetrated the thin armor. Nehring felt a hard blow to his arm, followed by throbbing pain in his head. Blood streamed down his face and dripped from his right sleeve. Despite the wounds, he remained standing.

Bayerlein and the radio operators were unscathed; they had been protected by the radio sets. Burgsdorff, who had just exited the vehicle prior to the attack, had been hit and mortally wounded. The corps quartermaster, *Oberleutnant* Schmitt, who had been standing next to him was also killed. *Unteroffizier* Voller, the general's *Kübelwagen* driver, came racing forward. Nehring was lifted into the staff car and immediately taken to the main clearing station. The war was over for him in that part of Africa. He was evacuated from the field hospital in Mersa Matruh on 10 September and flown back to Germany by way of Crete and then Athens.

After the Allied landings in Northwest Africa in Casablanca, Oran and Algiers, Nehring was returned to that theater of war on 15 November and designated as the commander-in-chief of ground forces in Tunisia. It sounded more impressive than it was, since there were virtually no German forces in Tunisia at the time. Part of his responsibilities was overseeing the introduction of forces into that country and the establishment of a defensive front.

The first element he received was *Fallschirmjäger-Regiment 5*[6] under *Oberstleutnant* Koch. It was followed by a fighter squadron and some Italian forces. Nehring was designated as the commanding general of the newly formed *XC. Armee-Korps*. His chief-of-staff was *Oberst i.G.* Pomtow. With him from the old "crew" was only his aide-de-camp, Sell, and *Major i.G.* Moll. The "Poor Man's War" had started.

Nehring had to constantly improvise until about half of the *10. Panzer-Division* finally showed up at the end of November in Bizerta and Tunis. On 1 December, Nehring had his weak corps attack the forward Allied forces in the vicinity of Tebourba. The fighting lasted four days. When it was over, there were 134 knocked-out enemy tanks on the battlefield. Nehring's success delayed the Allied plans for Tunisia for three months. As the Americans later said: "The race for Tunis had been won by the Axis."

On 9 December, Nehring was relieved of command and summoned away from Africa. He had always portrayed the situation in a professional manner and emphasized that Tunisia could not be held for the long term, an observation that was, of course, to be proven correct. That, of course, was not what his superior, *Generalfeldmarschall* Kesselring, wanted to hear, let alone Hitler. Replacing Nehring in Tunisia was *Generaloberst* von Arnim, who was simultaneously given command of the *5. Panzer-Armee*, a formation that had yet to be constituted.

Nehring was sent to the Eastern Front, where he assumed command of the *XXIV. Panzer-Korps* on 10 February 1943 in Krementschug in the southern sector. The corps was employed along a number of hot spots,

6. Translator's Note: 5th Airborne Regiment. More details can be found in *Jump into Hell* by the same author and also published by Stackpole.

including Taganrog, Kharkov, Isjum and then east of Stalino. On 2 August 1943, Nehring was wounded for the fifth time after a successful attack along the Mius. He was personally presented with the Gold Wound Badge by his superior, *Generaloberst* Hollidt.

In the middle of August, the general scored another defensive success, before his corps crossed the Dnjepr at Kanew, south of Kiev. At the time, there was a 100-kilometer gap in the front between the *8. Armee* and the *4. Panzer-Armee.* The situation offered the Soviet command a good opportunity to exploit. It was hoping to be able to permanently separate the two field armies through rapid action. As Nehring later wrote:

> Based on all those considerations and facts, the Soviet leadership decided to employ its airborne forces for the first time and only time in the Pekari-Shandra-Dudari area, that is, along the bend of the Dnjepr.

The airborne assault was bloodily countered by Nehring's corps. The airborne forces, which jumped into four areas in the corps sector, suffered bloody losses.

After that failure, the Soviets successfully shifted their main effort to the area around Kiev. On 24 December, they broke through the forces of the *XXXXII. Armee-Korps* in the area around Kasatin. In that extraordinarily difficult situation, *Generaloberst* Raus, the commander-in-chief of the *4. Panzer-Armee,* took extraordinary measures. He had Nehring and his aide-de-camp, *Oberleutnant* Lach, flown from the Dnjepr area, which had turned quiet, to the hot spot of the fighting. He told Nehring to stabilize the front. He had full command authority over the forces there, but he could not expect any reinforcements. Nehring was able to achieve the near impossible, and the front stabilized. On 8 February 1944, Nehring received the Oak Leaves to the Knight's Cross to the Iron Cross for his exceptional achievement. He was the 383rd member of the German armed forces to be so honored.

In the spring of 1944, Nehring's forces were part of *Generaloberst* Hube's *1. Panzer-Armee,* which found itself encircled by the Soviets from 24 March to 8 April. Despite all of the difficulties, Hube was eventually able to break out of the encirclement to the west; Nehring's corps successfully covered the northern area of the "wandering pocket" against Soviet forces advancing from the east.

July was spent with Nehring serving as the acting commander-in-chief of the *4. Panzer-Armee* as it pulled back as part of *Heeresgruppe Mitte* behind the Vistula south of Warsaw. The situation was so tense that he could not attend the wedding of his daughter. At the time, he could not know that he would be faced with one of the most difficult decisions of his military career in the Baranow area six months later.

After recovering from a lung infection in August and September, Nehring resumed his former command of the *XXIV. Panzer-Korps*. It was fighting in the Beskiden Mountains at the Dukla Pass in support of infantry divisions. Two weeks later, Nehring's headquarters was given the mission of commanding the field army group's operational reserve in the Kielce area. As such, his corps consisted of the *16. Panzer-Division*, the *17. Panzer-Division* and the *20. Panzergrenadier-Division*.

On 12 January 1945, the Soviets launched their large-scale offensive with the ultimate objective of Berlin from the Baranow bridgehead. In its first attack, it effectively destroyed the infantry divisions. Unfortunately, Nehring's divisions were placed too close to the front as a direct result of meddling by Hitler and despite the objections of all of the intermediate commands. As a result, the divisions were immediately involved in the fighting before there was a chance to consider their deliberate employment as complete formations.

Soviet armored forces poured through a 60-kilometer gap in the front towards Kielce. Nehring was ordered to remain in place and hold Kielce as a defensive bulwark. The only force fighting off to his left was the *XXXXII. Armee-Korps* under its new commanding general, *General der Infanterie* Recknagel. During the night of 14/15 January, radio traffic was received from the *9. Armee* which directed a general withdrawal. Nehring was faced with a difficult decision. He later wrote:

> Despite that [the directive to pull back], a new mission emerged for me and my corps, one founded in comradeship, that we would continue to fight in the Kielce area until the divisions of the *XXXXII. Armee-Korps*, which were echeloned as far forward as the Vistula, were passed back through [my] corps so as to then pull back in a consolidated fashion.
>
> That decision, which was made without second thought on my part, meant that the three divisions of my corps had to hold out in hard fighting until the evening of 16 January. During the night of 16/17 January, the withdrawal to the north was finally initiated and continued during the gray, snow-filled nights of 17/18 and 18/19 January; surrounded by the enemy and attacked on all sides; especially exposed to bomber and fighter-bomber attacks against the easily recognizable march columns and rest areas.

The "wandering pocket" then fought its way south of Lodz and across the Warthe. Remnants of the *XXXXII. Armee-Korps* and the *LVI. Panzer-Korps* moved back with Nehring's men. The commanding generals of the two shattered corps—Recknagel and Block—had been killed in the fighting.

After 11 days of desperate struggle, the corps succeeded in breaking through the last of the Soviet encircling forces on 22 January south of Lask. After a march of 250 kilometers, they were able to link up with *Panzer-Korps "Großdeutschland"* south of Sieradz.

That same 22 January, Nehring was honored for his accomplishment with the award of the Swords to the Oak Leaves to the Knight's Cross of the Iron Cross. He was the 124th member of the German Armed Forces to be so honored. Once again, upon receipt of the award, the general officer emphasized that he was wearing it on behalf of all of the soldiers he commanded.

Nehring's successes in the field proved that he was not only a far-seeing theoretician and author of numerous memorable tracts on the "army of tomorrow," but that he was also a decisive officer and goal-oriented troop leader who knew how to turn theory into practice. Although his theoretical writings ranked with those of Fuller, De Gaulle, Hart, Guderian, Moretta and Alléhaud, his troop leading in the field was only matched by Guderian.

When he arrived on the Oder at the end of January, he established a defensive front with his corps. The fighting withdrawal as far as the Lausitzer Neiße in a line running Forst–Cottbus–mouth of the Neiße demanded the utmost of Nehring, both as a man and as an officer. He could see the

Flak put an end to this British Lend-Lease "Matilda" outside of Krutoj-Log.

suffering of the German populace; he was worried about the fate of his wife and children, who were living in their house in Wünsdorf, not far from the new front lines. He had no time to visit, since the war allowed no respite.

At the end of February, he was given the mission of freeing the encircled city of Lauban and opening the important rail line through Silesia. The last large-scale attack of the German Army in the East took place from 1 to 8 March. It was conducted under the command of the newly formed *Panzergruppe Nehring*.

Nehring and his corps were then moved to the Sudeten area and reported to the *1. Panzer-Armee*. Shortly thereafter, on 21 March, Nehring was given command of the field army, which was involved in intense defensive fighting in Upper Silesia and Moravia. The defense of his sector and the subsequent withdrawal of the front once again demanded the utmost of the general and his forces, which consisted of some 24 divisions and around 350,000 personnel.

On 1 May 1945, the field army's front extended from Brünn to the north as far as the area around Bohemian Trübau. The friendly force on his right was the *8. Armee* of *General der Gebirgstruppen* Kreysing. On his left was the *17. Armee* of *General der Infanterie* Hasse.

When Nehring was asked after the war why he continued to hold out, he replied:

> Above all, it was just the natural obligation to save the hundreds of thousands of Silesian and Sudeten German refugees from the Soviets as they were being pushed to the West.

At the time, the overall military-political situation was unclear in that sector of the front. It was not until around noon on 8 May that an aircraft arrived from the field-army group with orders passed on from the Armed Forces High Command to unconditionally capitulate. On 9 May, Nehring attempted to surrender to the 26th Infantry Division of the U.S. Army, which had advanced through the Bavarian Woods. Despite surrender to the Americans, most of the fighting forces of the field army were later turned over to the Soviets in accordance with the terms of agreements that had been reached between the Soviets and the Western Allies.

Nehring was held by the U.S. forces until 20 September 1947. Following his release, he turned to writing military history. He was active in veterans' groups and in groups interested in returning lost German lands to Germany.

Walther K. Nehring passed away in Düsseldorf on 20 April 1983.

One of the thousands of T-34s that fell to German *Panzers* and *Flak*.

Feldwebel Ludwig Neigl, a highly successful *Nashorn* commander.

CHAPTER 15

Feldwebel Ludwig Neigl

HORNETS WITH DEADLY STINGERS

Another branch of the service that fought in armored engagements that was part of the *Panzertruppe* was the *Panzerjäger*—the tank destroyers. Initially limbered antitank guns, these forces were increasingly equipped with self-propelled gun carriages in the later war years. As the war progressed and Germany was increasingly placed on the defensive, the role of tank destroyers became more and more important. Although they were relatively poorly protected and the fighting compartments were not even usually enclosed, the tank destroyer was still a highly effective weapon when fighting in a defensive role and operating out of hide or ambush positions. In some cases, the *Panzerjäger* were equipped with vehicles that mounted the deadly 8.8-centimeter antitank gun, which brought success out of all proportion to their number.

This is the story of one of the most successful soldiers of the *Panzerjäger* force, *Feldwebel* Ludwig Neigl.

✠

Elements of the 14th Company of *Infanterie-Regiment 481 (256. Infanterie-Division)*, the antitank company of the regiment, were spending the night of 19/20 January 1942 in a barn near Nasserowo in the central sector of the Eastern Front. The gunners had left their antitank guns in position in the woods. Guards had been posted to sound the alert at the first indication of the approach of enemy forces. The guards were relieved every hour, due to the cold. Once back inside the comparative warmth of the barn, they had to immediately rub their noses, ears and fingers to prevent frostbite.

The thermometer sank to -39° Celsius (-38° Fahrenheit) in the gun positions that night. Ludwig Neigl, a *Gefreiter* and loader on a 3.7-centimeter antitank gun, rubbed his fingers together in the thick fur mittens. He observed his acting company commander look through binoculars off to his left. He was searching the open area for signs of the enemy. *Oberleutnant* Rumpel stopped short for a second.

"Alert!" he called out, half loudly. The wires were pulled that were connected to the empty shell casings that were hanging outside of each of the dugouts. Men hurried out into the open; still drunk with sleep, they ran to their trenches and fighting positions. The cannons were manned. Ludwig Neigl loaded high-explosive rounds. Suddenly, he also saw the attackers as they jumped up and ran at the position. They had been able to approach unnoticed to within 100 meters in their white camouflage snowsuits.

"Fire!"

Rounds landed among the attackers in the pale early-morning light and threw them into the snow. Neigl loaded the rounds feverishly. That went on for 10 minutes before enemy tanks appeared.

"Load AT!"

A T-26 approached Neigl's position rapidly. Neigl could see the mounted Soviet infantry as he loaded the next round. *Unteroffizier* Rüschkamp, the gunner, took aim and fired. The trajectory in the round was easy to follow due to the tracer element. It approached the turret of the T-26, sank somewhat and smashed into the weak rear of the vehicle. Figures fell off into the churned-up snow. Machine guns began to sweep the terrain to the front.

More Soviet tanks followed. The antitank guns of the company fired at a rapid pace. The Soviet attack against the positions of the division outside of Nasserowo was stopped.

"The 1st Platoon will conduct an immediate counterattack to get a couple of prisoners," *Oberleutnant* Rumpel directed. He went with the men. They ran

Neigl behind a 3.7-centimeter antitank gun before switching to the mechanized *Panzerjäger* force.

out onto the open field, while Neigl obtained more ammunition. Suddenly, Russian artillery opened fire. Stalin organs joined in as well, smashing into the patch of woods and turning the German lines into a sea of flames.

The platoon returned, bring prisoners with it. But the *Oberleutnant* was missing. No one knew where he was. One of the soldiers said he had seen him some 250 meters in front of the lines in a crater near the birch trees. Then he suddenly disappeared.

"We have to go out and look for him!"

"Anyone who goes out there is a goner!"

Impacting rounds tore up the area in front of the main lines. Because of the solidly frozen ground, they were unable to penetrate deeply. Instead, they churned up great fountains of snow.

"I'll get him!" Ludwig Neigl said.

No one said a word. Everyone stared at the athletic young man, who had often demonstrated both strength and endurance in the past. The 20-year-old with the laughing eyes and the square face took the submachine gun the platoon leader offered him. Then he disappeared in the roar of the impacting rounds.

Ludwig Neigl ran approximately 250 meters forward. As he made his way forward, Russian snipers fired at him without hitting him. He found the *Oberleutnant.*

"Here, Neigl!" Rumpel coughed out. He pointed to his bleeding upper thigh, which he had field dressed himself.

The field dressings Neigl had brought with him also helped staunch the blood flow. Ludwig Neigl then loaded his commander on his back and ran back to the German lines. He had to take cover again and again. On numerous occasions he sank into holes that had been filled with snow. He was at the end of his strength when he reached the main line of resistance. *Oberleutnant* Rumpel was taken to the dressing station.

Rumpel promised him the Iron Cross, First Class, before he was taken away.

But for Neigl, the spoken thanks and the proffered hand were more than enough sufficient gratitude. By this point, Neigl had already received the Iron Class, Second Class, the Wound Badge in Black and the Infantry Assault Badge.

Over the next few days, the Soviets attacked repeatedly, but they were always driven back. When they launched a heavy artillery preparation during the early-morning hours of 24 January 1942, the barn the men were in was torn apart by an impacting round. Neigl was wounded in the head. In spite of this, he remained at his post during the subsequent Russian attack until two bullet wounds to his legs made him combat ineffective.

After being admitted to the main aid station at Rshew, he was further evacuated to a military hospital in Krakow. A few weeks later, after he was capable of being moved again, he went on a hospital train to Reutlingen. His head wound proved to be quite serious. It affected him so much that by the time he left the hospital, he only weighed 97 pounds. For his convalescence, Neigl was transferred to the military reserve hospital at Urach in Wurttemberg.

✠

Ludwig Neigl was born in Augsburg on 5 August 1921. He was the 15th child born into the family of Georg Neigl. As a youth, Ludwig distinguished himself in sporting competitions at his school. He enjoyed sprinting, gymnastics and handball. Because he was also intelligent, his parents sent him to a vocational school for business after he finished grade school. He was successful there and, after a short period of time, became a salesman in a car dealership in Augsburg. He devoted his free time to sports. He was one of the main players of the semi-professional handball team in Augsburg.

On 1 August 1940, Ludwig Neigl entered the *Reichsarbeitsdienst,* the *Reich* Labor Service. He initially served at Penzberg in Bavaria after his basic training and was then transferred to coastal duty at the airfield at Kerkeville in the vicinity of Cherbourg. He served as a member of the ground crews and refueled and rearmed the *Bf 109's* of the *Richthofen* fighter wing. While there, he saw *Kommodore* Wick, the wing commander, decorated with the Oak Leaves to the Knight's Cross of the Iron Cross on 25 October 1940. Wick was only the fourth member of the German armed forces to be so honored at that point. The anxious hours of 28 November 1940, when the wing commander did not return from a mission, were a painful memory to Ludwig Neigl for the rest of his life.

On 28 January 1941, Neigl was released from his service in the *RAD* at Kirchseeon (near Rosenheim in southern Bavaria). When he returned home later that day to his parent's home in Augsburg, his mother handed him his draft notice for the military, which was already waiting for him. This was a heavy blow for Ludwig's mother. Her husband had died in 1939 and three of her sons had already been called up. Neigl was assigned to *Infanterie-Regiment 40* and was trained as a *Panzerjäger.*

✠

In September 1941, Neigl was transferred to the *256. Infanterie-Division,* which was employed in the central portion of the Eastern Front and needed replacement personnel. He saw combat for the first time behind the gun shield of his 3.7-centimeter antitank gun at Stariza. He then saw action at Mologino and Rshew. Neigl proved himself and was awarded the Iron Cross, Second Class, after his gun knocked out its fifth tank. He also froze through the terrible first winter in Russia. He was out of the line for a short time due to a wound he received. This was followed by the operations at Nasserowo, where he received the previously described three wounds on one day. These took him out of action for eight months.

✠

In September 1942, Ludwig Neigl was sent back to a replacement unit at Borna (near Leipzig), even though he still had not fully recovered. At the end of September, he was sent back to the Eastern Front. He was assigned to *Heeres-Panzerjäger-Abteilung 519*, a battalion equipped with the *Hornisse* ("Hornet") tank destroyer. The battalion commander was *Major* Wolf-Horst Hoppe, an officer who knew how to instill trust and confidence in his men.

Obergefreiter Neigl was initially assigned to the Headquarters Company. He observed how the Hornets were employed and how they racked up their initial successes. He grew familiar with the deadly weapon—a lengthened *Panzer IV* chassis with a lightly armored superstructure housing the deadly 8.8-centimeter *Pak* as its main gun. In his new unit, Neigl had jumped to the head of the class, going from the puny 3.7-centimeter antitank gun— derisively referred to as the army's doorbell, because it only served to notify the enemy that he was being fired at—to one of the most powerful and effective antitank guns of the war.

From an armament perspective, the Hornet was in a class by itself. It could defeat any known enemy tank at the time. Neigl was to find that out for himself shortly. The tank destroyer could hammer apart any tank out to 2,000 meters. This helped offset the light armor protection afforded the crew, since enemy tank main guns at the time had little penetrating power at such ranges.

Major Wolf-Horst Hoppe, Neigl's battalion commander.

Ludwig Neigl was promoted to *Unteroffizier* in February 1943. Shortly after his promotion, he was summoned to the Headquarters Company commander, *Hauptmann* Strehler.

"Neigl, what would you say if you could be the gun commander of a *Hornisse?*"

"That would be great, *Herr Hauptmann!* I would like that a lot!"

That was the start of Neigl's career as a Hornet commander. He took over a crew that was already experienced with the vehicle. His platoon leader, *Leutnant* Kombiki, watched the new gun commander carefully after he first arrived, but he soon saw that Neigl did not need a lot of supervision.

✠

Neigl and his crew knocked out their first T-34's at Ossiniki and Sumy (both the town and its cemetery). At Lake Slobotka, his Hornet took on four Russian tanks all by itself and eliminated them. At the beginning of December, he was wounded on his gun, when a shell casing exploded and he was hit by fragments. The wound at the back of his head was not life threatening, however. He was kept at the battalion aid station by *Major* Hoppe. The battalion commander was fearful that if he were evacuated, he might never see Neigl again. Thanks to the treatment of the battalion surgeon, *Oberstabsarzt Dr.* Brunz, his wound healed completely.

Neigl had barely returned to the battalion when *Leutnant* Kombiki was so badly wounded that he died a short while later. *Hauptmann* Strehler summoned Neigl and informed him that he was to serve as the platoon leader. Neigl then had two additional guns to be responsible for.

Serving as the local fire brigade in the Vitebsk area, Neigl's guns knocked out tank after tank. Neigl was one of the first soldiers of the battalion to receive the Tank Assault Badge. By the time he received the award, he had already knocked out 10 tanks.

On 10 June 1944, he was summoned to the battalion commander. *Major* Hoppe extended his hand to Neigl after the latter reported. Both men had come to know and respect each other as a result of the many operations that *Major* Hoppe almost always personally participated in.

"*Unteroffizier* Neigl, I have to tell you something!" *Major* Hoppe continued after a short pause. "It comes as no news to you that your twin brothers Karl and Anton were killed along the southern banks of the Dnjepr and that your brother Joseph has been missing since Stalingrad. It is my sad duty to inform you that your brother Alois and his two children were killed in a bombing attack in Röthenbach."

After another pause to allow Neigl to absorb the bad news, the *Major* continued: "Based on a *Führer* directive, your mother has submitted a request that you, as her youngest soon, be released from frontline duty and employed in the homeland. The request was approved. You are being transferred back home."

It was not until the afternoon of 23 June that Neigl had to give up his platoon. The rear area for the battalion was the village of Kokuwiatschino in the vicinity of Vitebsk. Only Neigl's platoon had been pulled back there; all the other combat elements of the battalion were engaged.

Neigl was ready to depart at 1600 hours when all hell broke loose in Vitebsk. Indirect and aimed fire commenced all at once. A few minutes later, orders came down to employ Neigl's three tank destroyers. The Soviets had broken into the municipal area of Vitebsk with tanks in two places and were attempting to eliminate those German forces still fighting in the city.

"Come along with us one more time, Ludwig!" his comrades implored him as they received orders to move out. But the adjutant of the Headquarters Company had received his orders: "You are supposed to go back to the trains in Oserki tonight, Neigl. You are to depart from there to Germany. Strict orders from the old man!

Ludwig Neigl took leave of his comrades. He reached the command post of the Headquarters Company in a wooden building in the woods near Oserki an hour before midnight. He received his release papers from *Hauptmann* Strehler. It was intended for him to depart for home the following morning. Because the night was mild, he settled in some 50 meters from the command post to get some sleep. He was awakened an hour later by loud yelling. He heard his name again and again. He pulled himself together, and the motorcycle dispatch rider told him he was to report to *Hauptmann* Strehler immediately.

Once at the command post, the company commander filled Neigl in: "The Russians have broken through at Vitebsk in two places. They have encircled a large number of our forces, including your old platoon. There is a danger that the Russians will push through this gap and break through as far as Beschenkowitschi. If they do that, they will have everything that is still in the Vitebsk area."

"The bridge, *Herr Hauptmann!*" Neigl exclaimed involuntarily.

"You're exactly right . . . the bridge. The Russians will want to take the bridge there . . . maybe blow it. By doing that they'll be able to prevent anyone from getting out of the area."

"What can I do, *Herr Hauptmann?*"

"Three new tank destroyers have arrived, Neigl. In addition, there are some replacements from Germany. You are not required to participate in any combat operations any more, but . . . "

"*Herr Hauptmann*, please let me have the three guns!"

"That's what I was hoping, Neigl! The *3. Panzer-Armee* had ordered that an AT platoon be sent out immediately. It's to screen in the area of the horseshoe bend of the Düna, particularly at the bridge at Beschenkowitschi, and knock out any approaching Russian tanks."

One and one-half hours later, the tank destroyers appeared at the trains area. But the crews that Neigl had to work with were not trained on these weapons; only the drivers had experience.

Early in the morning, *Unteroffizier* Neigl headed to the command post of the *3. Panzer-Armee* with his three guns. *Feldwebel* Müller was the gun commander of *034*; *Unteroffizier* Stemm was in charge on *034*. Neigl assumed command of *035*. On their way to the field-army command post, Neigl got acquainted with his crew members and familiarized them as much as he could with the tank destroyer.

Once in Beschenkowitschi, Neigl reported to an *Oberst* Schmidt, the senior tank destroyer officer on the field-army staff. Schmidt repeated the order to move into the area north of Beschenkowitschi along the horseshoe bend of the Düna. He was to prevent the Russians from taking the bridge at Beschenkowitschi at all costs. The bridge could not be blown either, since that would block the route out for any German forces within the horseshoe bend.

Neigl continued on immediately. At 0600 hours, he had two of his tank destroyers positioned in the vicinity of Bondarewo and the third one south of the Düna on the edge of the same village.

When three T-34's attempted to breakthrough around noon, they were knocked out. Enemy aircraft flew over the tank destroyers, but they did not see the vehicles, because they had been well camouflaged.

Around 1800 hours, a dispatch rider appeared. Enemy tanks had broken through the main line of resistance at Osetki. Neigl headed in this direction with his three vehicles. Neigl discovered a few T-34's there that were attempting to head east.

"33 and 34, this is 35: Engage at will!"

The first round from the *Hornisse* of *Feldwebel* Müller hit one of the enemy tanks. The tank stopped and smoke started to pour out of it. The remaining tanks then turned towards Neigl and his vehicles.

"Distance . . . 400 . . . 12 o'clock . . . fire when ready!"

The main gun thundered, and the tank destroyer swayed backwards from the concussion. The spent shell casing clattered as it was ejected from the breech. A flame jumped out of the enemy tank that had been hit; then it exploded.

"Pivot right!"

The tank destroyer jerked around. *Obergefreiter* Berke, the driver, knew what he was doing. The second T-34 soon came into sight. It was also dispatched with the first round from the powerful main gun.

Standing to the left rear of the open fighting compartment, Neigl observed to the front. The four remaining T-34's were racing towards his vehicle. The tanks suddenly stopped to take a firing halt. Their rounds screamed over the tank destroyer, which had taken advantage of good cover in a depression.

"Fire!"

The turret of the lead T-34 was ripped out of its race, skidded along the back deck and then landed on the ground. Even before the remaining tanks could return fire, another round went screaming from the *Hornisse* and smashed into one of the middle tanks. It was set aflame.

The remaining two tanks turned around to flee. The next round took out one of them as well. The following round immobilized the final T-34, when it tore off one of its right rear roadwheels. The turret turned around so as to engage the Germans, but it received a second round from a distance of 250 meters and was destroyed.

Within a few minutes Neigl's *ad hoc* platoon had knocked out a total of seven enemy tanks; Neigl's crew had accounted for six of them.

The tank destroyers then received strong artillery fire. Neigl ordered his guns to return to a reverse-slope position south of Juzuki.

They reached those positions without encountering the enemy. Neigl began to observe the terrain in the direction of the enemy with his binoculars and saw Soviet infantry attempting to cross the Düna north of the town.

"Engage the Ivans with HE!"

All three of the guns hammered the Soviet crossing effort. The rounds landed in the Soviet castoff point. Trees were torn down. Two Soviets boats were hit just after they had cast off and sank. As suddenly as it had begun, it was over. The enemy gave up on his attempt to cross the river at this location.

New orders arrived via a messenger. Two of the tank destroyers were to move to the northern outskirts of Mamoiki and one to Bondarewo to support the *56. Infanterie-Division.*

The night passed relatively quietly. Neigl had barely slept the previous two nights. The two tank destroyers at Mamoiki pulled out at around 0200 hours on the morning of 25 June to occupy new positions. In the process, *Hornisse 033* under *Feldwebel* Müller had problems with its gun and had to return to the Headquarters Company. Once at the new position, Neigl received a report that enemy tanks had broken through the German lines near Juzuki.

He immediately headed in this direction with his two guns. At the western outskirts of Mamoiki, the *Hornisse* of *Unteroffizier* Stemm encountered a KV-II and a T-34. The loader was injured when the first round was fired. He was standing too close to the gun, and the breech hit him and threw him to the floor of the fighting compartment.

In the meantime, *Unteroffizier* Stemm had directed the second tank—the T-34—be engaged. The inexperienced gun commander got his thumb caught in the breechblock as it closed, and it tore off his thumb. The round hit its intended target and knocked it out, but when the gunner, Zimmermann, saw the torn-off thumb on the floor of the fighting compartment, he became hysterical and could not be calmed down. As a result of this series of calamities, the gun only had a radio operator and a driver left who were capable of doing anything. The radio operator gave Neigl a running commentary on what had happened; the *Unteroffizier* remained calm. Neigl ordered the driver to pull back to a position some 800 meters to the rear.

He breathed a sigh of relief when he saw the Hornet disappear to comparative safety behind the reverse slope. At this point, he was all alone. He was then informed by a patrol that a large number of enemy tanks had concentrated in a patch of woods north of Mamoiki. Despite his situation, Neigl knew what he had to do.

He moved as close to the patch of woods as he dared to without the enemy hearing or seeing him. He left the vehicle and climbed up a tree. He was able to observe eight enemy tanks through his binoculars. It looked like they were preparing to move out for an attack. Like greased lightning, Neigl climbed back down the tree and raced to his gun.

"Men, eight tanks are preparing to attack. We're attacking them first!"

He looked into blanched faces.

"Move to the reverse slope on the road, Berke!" The tank destroyer moved out.

"Pretty shitty, *Herr Unteroffizier!*" *Obergefreiter* Schwarz, the gunner, said to Neigl. "The field of fire's only 80 meters, if the Ivans appear up there."

"What are you bitching about . . . even you should be able to hit at that range!" Neigl said in an effort to reduce the tension. That said, even he was a little uneasy about the short distance and the ability to stop all of the enemy tanks in time. But he had little choice; there was no other place at the moment where he could establish a firing position. To the left and the right of the hilltop over which the enemy would have to come were buildings. These would serve to help constrict the enemy's avenue of approach.

Twenty minutes passed before the first T-34 could be seen on the hilltop. The gun was aiming at this exact spot, and the gunner was able to fire immediately.

The turret of the T-34 was lifted clean off the hull with an ear-deafening crash when the round hit the tank. When the second tank appeared up top, two of the young crewmembers left the *Hornisse* in sudden panic. *Unteroffizier* Neigl jumped into the gunner's seat; an *Obergefreiter* assumed duties as loader. The second round roared as the firing mechanism was depressed; the second tank disappeared in flames. A third T-34 appeared at that same moment. Apparently, he could not make out the location of the tank destroyer due to the smoke from the two burning tanks, however. Neigl took aim again. Another one of the steel giants was dispatched with a single round.

"None of the tanks can get through now, Lümbke, the road is blocked!" Neigl said to his replacement loader, who had remained with him.

How many tanks were still on the other side of the hill, however? Would they attack again? These thoughts raced through Neigl's mind. At this point, two more tanks broke out to the right of the road from behind the buildings. The tank destroyer shifted in its position somewhat. Neigl fired again. He needed two rounds this time to eliminate the lead tank. The second one was eliminated after a second round. Neither one of the two new tanks had been able to get off a single round because they could not identify the German tank destroyer.

The smoke thickened more and more. The *Obergefreiter* grunted in horror when two more tanks emerged. They passed their burning comrades and fired blindly towards the perceived German position. The muzzle flashes of the main guns of the two T-34's could be seen through the thick gunpowder smoke and the black, oily clouds of petroleum fires.

"Take it easy, Lümbke! They can't see us."

The *Obergefreiter* loaded the next round. By this time, the next tank had closed to within 35 meters. Neigl took up a sight picture; at this range, the round penetrated cleanly though the entire tank and set off its main-gun ammunition. The men in the open fighting compartment of the Hornet heard the howling of the shrapnel as it exploded outwardly. The seventh tank approached rapidly. The loader got all tangled up. Neigl was about to load the round himself, when the round was slammed home into the breechblock in the nick of time. At that range, there was no missing the T-34. The tank filled the sight picture! The armor-piercing round destroyed the enemy barely 10 meters in front of the *Hornisse.*

Neigl wanted to breath a sigh of relief, when a main gun fired from the hilltop on the other side. The round from the eighth T-34 hit the tank destroyer and penetrated the front armor. The hard blow sent Neigl to the floor of the fighting compartment. The driver, Berke, was killed instantly. The loader disappeared. Soviet troops advanced rapidly.

Summoning up all of his strength, Ludwig Neigl crawled a few meters off to the side and then ran through a tall field of grain back to the position where he had ordered the remaining *Hornisse* with its shaken-up crew. Later on, Neigl never could remember exactly what transpired after his tank destroyer had been knocked out. His comrades had to fill him in.

The driver and the radio operator of *034* were still with the vehicle. The two wounded had gone back with the gunner.

"We have to continue to attack!" Neigl called out to the driver.

"But you'll be all alone topside, *Herr Unteroffizier!*"

"Hey, you . . . come here!" Neigl ordered an infantry *Obergefreiter* who happened to be nearby. The infantryman had seen the intense fighting that had just occurred. "You're my loader . . . All you have to do is ram a round in here . . . Understood?"

"Understood!" the infantryman replied and jumped up into the fighting compartment.

"Let's go, Heinemann! Head for the bridge at Beschenkowitschi!"

The *Nashorn* (Rhinoceros), later known as the *Hornisse* (Hornet). Lightly armored but powerfully armed with the 8.8-cm L/71 *Pak 43/1*.

The last operational tank destroyer moved out. Neigl positioned it just in front of the large bridge over the Düna.

✠

Two hours later, the T-34 that had knocked out Neigl's gun earlier attempted to take the bridge in a *coup de main* with a handful of mounted Russian combat engineers. The first round from the *Hornisse* blew up the T-34. That signaled the end of the immediate armored threat to the area.

At that point, Neigl blacked out. Several days later, Neigl discovered that a combat engineer, *Unteroffizier* Xaver Räck, had picked him up and taken him to the rear.

On 1 July, *Major* Hoppe visited Neigl in his ward. He brought him a pair of *Feldwebel* shoulder straps and told him he had been promoted for bravery in the face of the enemy. The *Major* then presented him with the Iron Cross, First Class.

His commander informed him that Neigl's *ad hoc* platoon had thwarted the efforts of the Soviets to break through and thus enabled all of the German forces still in the horseshoe bend of the Düna to pull back along the main supply route in the direction of Lepel.

The battalion commander had also submitted Neigl for the award of the Knight's Cross to the Iron Cross for his decisive actions.

On 27 July 1944, Ludwig Neigl received the Knight's Cross while still assigned to the Headquarters Company of *schwere Heeres-Panzerjäger-Abteilung 519*. The transfer home had been forgotten about. In all, Neigl and his platoon had accounted for 63 enemy tanks since he had become a platoon leader. Neigl was especially proud of the fact that the commander-in-chief of *Heeresgruppe Mitte* at the time, *Generalfeldmarschall* Walter Model, had sent him a personal letter of congratulations.

After he had recovered in November 1944, *Feldwebel* Neigl received a supply job in his battalion in order to keep him from the front lines. Although he did not return to Germany for home-front duties, he was out of direct harm's way in the battalion trains. His commander, *Major* Hoppe, received the Knight's Cross on 15 July 1944.

✠

When the battalion was moved to the Western Front and was employed in the Ardennes offensive, *Feldwebel* Neigl was used as a liaison officer between *Generalfeldmarschall* Model and the *General der Panzertruppen West*. He continued on in this assignment after the offensive.

On 25 March 1945, he was hit by a fighter-bomber attack in the vicinity of Höchst while performing his duties. Neigl's driver, Rolf, was sitting on the vehicle's fender as an air guard; Neigl himself was actually driving. In the vehicle were two wounded soldiers and a young boy. When Neigl asked about the status of the aircraft, Rolf shook his head.

Suddenly, however, two Mosquitoes rushed towards them. The first salvo went through the roof of the staff car and over the head of *Feldwebel* Neigl. Neigl stopped. The two fighter-bombers were turning around. When Neigl looked around, he saw that the two wounded soldiers had been hit in the stomach and wounded again. Rolf had been hit in the upper thigh and Neigl himself received face wounds. Both of his eardrums had been damaged.

That wound brought a final end to Neigl's service in the military. He was released from the service after a short stay in a military hospital and sent home. He was picked up by the Americans and spent a few days in a POW camp at Fürstenfeldbruck, before he was released. In September 1945, he started to work for the city of Augsburg, where he continued to work until his retirement.

Ludwig Neigl passed away in his hometown of Augsburg on 23 September 2003.

Unfortunately of poor quality, this photograph purports to show Neigl in front of his tank destroyer.

Generalmajor Adalbert Schulz, one of only 27 members of the German Armed Forces to be honored with the Diamonds to the Oak Leaves with Swords to the Knight's Cross of the Iron Cross.

CHAPTER 16

Generalmajor Adalbert Schulz

WITH THE "GHOST" DIVISION IN THE EAST AND WEST

Generalmajor Rommel, the commander of the *7. Panzer-Division,* issued his orders on the evening of 6 June 1940:

> Gentlemen, the division will attack in two groups, deeply echeloned, at 1000 hours on 7 June. Whenever the terrain permits it, it will deploy. The right attack group consists of *Oberst* Bismarck's men, supported by the 1st Company, *Panzer-Regiment 7* advances on the left, reinforced by a light artillery battalion, a light *Flak* and a heavy *Flak* battery and the antitank forces. The reconnaissance battalion and the motorcycle infantry follow the left attack group. Behind them is *Schützen-Regiment 6* with light and heavy *Flak* and the heavy divisional artillery. *Schützen-Regiment 6* is responsible for guarding the open right flank of the division.

That day, the forces of Hoth's corps had advanced 25 kilometers deep into the enemy lines. The *4. Armee* then issued orders for Rommel's division to exploit the penetration and advance along the Dieppe-Paris road.

✠

"Panzer . . . marsch!"

Hauptmann Schulz was standing in the commander's cupola of his tank, a battered tanker's cap on his practically bald head. Following him was the platoon leader's vehicle and the command vehicle of *Oberst* von Bismarck.

It was 7 June 1940. The tanks had started to move out and were going around a village. Their route took them through a field of grain. On the far side of the field, in a depression, French motorcycle infantry were in the process of mounting up. They were completely surprised by the German assault. A few of them attempted to get away, but a few machine-gun rounds from the tanks convinced them to stop. The remaining French soldiers surrendered.

"Keep going, Schulz!"

The rapidly advancing tanks and men of von Bismarck's *Kampfgruppe* surprised the hapless French at a number of other locations as well. The men were taking great amounts of spoils of war, but they continued to move on. What mattered most to them was taking the day's objective. The tanks ran into a heavy artillery battalion and captured it intact. At 1300 hours, the town of Fenquiéres appeared in the binoculars of Schulz. He also observed the wooded terrain west of Saumont. As the tanks started to approach the wooded tract, they were greeted by antitank-gun fire and artillery. Schulz did not spare any words: "Get the guns! Comb the woods!"

The tank hatches slammed shut and the gunner's started searching for the antitank guns in their sights. Schulz's gunner, Melchers, fired at the muzzle flashes he saw. After four rounds, there were no more muzzle flashes from that position.

The tanks reached the edge of the woods and entered. Trees and vegetation were overrun, tree trunks cracking and shattering under the pressure of the steel. The French artillery was in a large clearing. There was a short, sharp firefight, and the tanks emerged the victors. The French surrendered and, as the tanks continued to advance through the woods north of Saumont, British forces were also captured.

✠

Schulz had already proven himself during the campaign when he advanced on Hersin-Barlin (south of Béthune) on 23 May. He turned back a large French armor force that was attacking from Noeux-Mines against the positions of *Schützen-Regiment 7*. On 6 June, he had distinguished himself again when his *Panzer-Regiment 25* assaulted south. In his history of the 7. *Panzer-Division,* Hasso von Manteuffel described the fighting of that day:

> The division fought and took its objective of the day—the high ground at Hescamps, just south of Thieulloy-la-Ville—despite the immediate counterattacks of enemy armored units and mechanized battle groups against its front and flanks and despite the tough and occasionally bitter resistance from the woods, hedgerows and outskirts of villages.

✠

For his decisive operations on 7 June, von Bismarck submitted Schulz for the Knight's Cross to the Iron Cross. He was later presented with the award, along with von Bismarck, on 29 September 1940. It was the first of many high awards for the gifted armor commander.

✠

Adalbert Schulz was born in Berlin. He first saw the light of day on 20 December 1903. Following college preparatory and trade school—Schulz originally want to go into banking—he made a surprise decision and joined the police. He underwent the necessary training and rose rapidly in the ranks, becoming a lieutenant in 1934. One year later, he was absorbed into the army, like a great many of his comrades. He participated in the march into Austria and the Sudetenland as an *Oberleutnant* in an armored division. At the start of the campaign in the West, he was the company commander of the 1st Company of *Panzer-Regiment 25*.

At the start of the campaign against the Soviet Union, he was a battalion commander in the regiment. On the first day of the offensive, he rolled with his regiment in the direction of Olita. The city was reached around 1245 hours. Schulz's battalion was able to take intact one of the two bridges over the Njemen. Forces from the regiment took the other.

When the tanks reached the high ground on the far side of the river, they were engaged by numerous tanks, some of which had been dug in. The Soviets then attacked in an effort to reduce or eliminate the two bridgeheads. The fighting lasted until late in the evening. Schulz crew was credited with six "kills." In all, 82 enemy armored vehicles were destroyed or knocked out. *Oberst* Rothenburg, the regimental commander, later recalled: "The tank-versus-tank engagement at Olita was the most difficult one of my life."

By the late evening of 23 June, German tanks were already east of Wilna. Both Rothenburg and *Major* von Steinkeller, the commander of *Kradschützen-Bataillon 7*, the divisional motorcycle infantry battalion, were mentioned by name in the Armed Forces Daily report on 8 July for their role in those successes.

During the evening of 26 June, the division reached the Minsk-Moscow Highway at Sloboda. The following day, Rothenburg was badly wounded in the area between Minsk and Borissow. A captured armored train had caught fire, and shrapnel from one of the exploding artillery rounds struck the regimental commander. Since the regiment was also cut off from the division at the time, he could not be evacuated immediately. The division commander, *Generalmajor Freiherr* von Funck, offered to fly him out. He also offered to provide an 8-wheeled armored car to escort him to the rear. Rothenburg declined both offers, stating it would weaken the fighting forces. Instead, he chose to be evacuated in a staff car. He paid for that decision with his life.

On the morning of 28 June, as he was moving through terrain that had not yet been completely cleared, he was ambushed by a Soviet unit and killed. *Oberstleutnant* Thomale, the commander of the 3rd Battalion, assumed acting command of the regiment.

On the lake narrows 20 kilometers southeast of Demidow, the Soviets offered significant resistance to Schulz's battalion on 14 July. Skillfully deploying his forces, Schulz was able to take the deeply echeloned field positions. Boldly attacking, breaking any and all resistance, Schulz's battalion continued the advance that evening, closely followed by the riflemen of *Oberst Freiherr* von Boineburg's *Schützen-Brigade 7*. By 2030 hours, Jarzewo was reached. The intense fighting in that area lasted for three weeks. For his skillful command of the division, von Funck was awarded the Knight's Cross to the Iron Cross on 15 July.

Following the pocket battles of the summer, the division enjoyed a brief rest period. With the resumption of offensive operations on 16 November, Schulz's battalion was employed against strong Soviet defensive positions at Jegorjewskoje. By 20 November, the regiment reached the major road at Spass Saulok. By doing so, it created the prerequisites for the attack on Jamuga-Klin.

For the first time, Schulz's men were faced with the T-34 and special tactics had to be created to combat the dreaded Soviet tank, since the main guns of most of the German vehicles were incapable of penetrating the Soviet armor, even at very close range. Despite the challenge posed, Schulz's battalion entered Klin three days later. On 28 November, the division forced the Moscow-Volga Canal at Jachroma.

The regiment then received instructions to screen *Kampfgruppe von Manteuffel* in the Oljgowo-Shukowo-Stepanowo area. It was a difficult time for the tankers. Strong Soviet forces forced the division back across the canal. The tremendous cold affected the mechanical reliability of the tanks, which had not been prepared for the severe Soviet winters, and turret races and gun recoil mechanisms jammed and gun optics fogged up internally.

Schulz had to defend against Soviet forces feeling their way forward against Stepanowo on 2 December. Their probes were turned back, but they repeated their efforts on 3 December. When one of the tanks ran out of ammunition while engaging infantry, the tank commander had his radio operator run into the village to get some belted ammunition. *Obergefreiter* Frey entered the headquarters of the battalion, only to find Schulz sitting next to an oven and reading a book.

"*Herr Major,*" Frey sputtered, "we don't have any machine-gun ammo, and the Ivans . . . "

"Grab hold of yourself and have Eichmann give you a few belts of ammo," the recently promoted officer responded in his clipped Berlin accent.

When Frey returned to his tank, he told his commander what had happened, adding that "it can't be all that bad . . . the 'Old Man' hasn't even climbed aboard his crate."

On the morning of 4 December, however, all hell broke loose in Stepanowo, when German bombers accidently bombed the village. As if the whole thing had been arranged, the Soviets then attacked right afterwards, prepping the village with artillery and mortar fire. The Soviets entered the locality. This time, Schulz was in his "crate."

He ordered the broken down tanks to button up and had the operational tanks maneuver to provide cover. The tankers used machine guns to sweep the Soviet infantry from the tanks they were riding on. Despite those efforts, the Soviets continued attacking, even as it turned twilight.

Schulz had his tankers fire onto the slope with high-explosive rounds. Even though the enemy forces could not be directly seen any more, that was their only possible avenue of attack. The hillside was soon lit up by tracer rounds and explosions. Occasionally, one of the motorcycle infantry, who were with Schulz's battalion, fired a pyrotechnic into the air.

The commander was to be found with the 4th Company, which was in the thick of things. When it started to turn light on 5 December, Schulz could see the horrific effect the ricocheting high-explosive rounds had had exploding on the hard-frozen ground. Despite the local success, orders arrived the next day to pull back. The danger of being cut off was too great.

Schulz ordered the tanks that could no longer be moved to be blown up. Within the 4th Company, only one *Panzer IV* could be saved. After moving 20 kilometers, however, its final drive broke, and it also had to be blown up. In temperatures of -40 degrees (-40 Fahrenheit), the tankers of the 4th had to march by foot back to Klin, a distance of 180 kilometers. They were frequently attacked from the side and the rear by the Soviets. By Christmas, the *Kampfgruppe* reached its designated winter positions without leaving a single man behind. Schulz—although frequently attacked and cut off—had made the impossible possible.

On 31 December, Schulz was awarded the Oak Leaves to the Knight's Cross of the Iron Cross for his achievements and personal bravery. He was the 47th member of the German Armed forces to be so recognized. On 27 January 1942, the tank regiment reported it had only five tanks operational—4 *Panzer 38(t)'s* and 1 *Panzer IV*. In the middle of March, the division was pulled out of the front lines. It was intended to reconstitute the division in France. Schulz, who had just been promoted to *Oberstleutnant*, was designated as the regimental commander.

Initially, the division was dispatched the south coast of France as a result of the Allied landings in Northwest Africa. It remained there until 24 November 1942. On 27 November, four *Kampfgruppen* occupied the French naval port of Toulon. When the Italians took over responsibility for the coastal defense in December, the division was free for other commitments. It was issued winter clothing and sent east by rail.

The second deployment to the Soviet Union for the division started in Schachty. The division had been allocated to *Armeegruppe Hollidt.* One operation followed the next. In the space of two days, the regiment was credited with knocking out 41 enemy tanks.

The division was earmarked for participation in Operation "Citadel" and was staged in the Dorogobush area on 3 and 4 July 1943. The infantry elements crossed the Donez at 0225 hours on 5 July and blasted a path through the Soviet field fortifications. The tanks were not able to cross the river until around 1800 hours. The tanks immediately went forward and clashed with a concentration of Soviet armor around Rasumoje. An officer from *Panzergrenadier-Regiment 6* later wrote about the tank attack:

> We still had some time before our faithful helpers, the tanks, appeared and took over the attack spearhead. We were up front by ourselves for an hour when a mighty rumbling could be heard behind us. We jumped up and saw a magnificent sight. The steel colossus rolled towards us in a long column. Leading his regiment in his command vehicle was *Panzer-Schulz.* There was no limit to our enthusiasm. Any signs of being tired had vanished.
>
> Arriving at our location, the tanks stopped. *Oberstleutnant* Schulz apologized for not having been able to lend a hand earlier; he had had to wait for the bridge to be erected and he praised us for the aggressively conducted attack. Then the tanks rolled forward.

Schulz and his men cut a broad swath for the grenadiers. During the advance on Generalowka on 6 July, there was another round of hard fighting. *Hauptmann* Fortun was killed after he had helped thwart a Soviet immediate counterattack. Schulz recommended him for the Knight's Cross to the Iron Cross, the posthumous award being presented on 7 August 1943.

On 7 July, Schulz's regiment formed the basis for the formation of *Kampfgruppe Schulz.* By 14 July, the battle group had crossed the Ssewernyi-Donez at two points and formed bridgeheads. On 14 July, the enemy launched strong counterattacks, in the course of which elements of the *SPW* company of *Panzergrenadier-Regiment 6* were encircled.

✠

"*Herr Oberstleutnant*, wake up!"

A hand shook the commander's shoulder. Schulz recognized his adjutant, *Oberleutnant* Rothe.

"What's going on?"

Schulz looked at his watch; it showed 0219 hours. Schulz had gotten three hours of sleep after two days without any.

"The Soviets have encircled the mechanized infantry in the river fork at Kirikowka. The enemy is attacking from the northeast with 100 tanks and is also on the near bank of the Worsskla, to the south of the grenadiers, with additional tanks."

"Have the regiment prepare to move out. Get the command tank ready!"

Schulz pulled on his black *Panzer* tunic, threw his cap on his head and stumbled out into the darkness. The command tanks and the two vehicles for the messengers were standing by.

"Well, let's do it! . . . *Panzer marsch!*"

The three vehicles rolled out to the pre-designated staging area. One of Schulz's radio operators was already calling the battalion commanders. Twelve tanks were operational in all. They linked up with Schulz's *R 01* in short order. On orders from the commander, they dispersed to form an inverted wedge, leaving the road and crossing a meadow. Standing in the commander's hatch, Schulz attempted to make things out in the darkness. In the shadows of a peasant's hut near the edge of a wood line, tanks started moving.

The word went out to be prepared to make contact.

A few minutes later, Schulz ordered his small force to attack, and the tanks rumbled in the direction of the hut. A low fence appeared in front of the tanks and was quickly overrun. The reports of the firing from the main guns of the tanks echoed through the night. The hut started to catch fire, with the result that the silhouettes of other T-34's could be seen. Looking through the hardened glass of his vision ports, Schulz could see two turrets traversing in his direction.

He directed two tanks to fire at the immediate threat. The main guns erupted in the early morning twilight. Both of the enemy tanks were struck and black smoke started billowing skyward. Cutting off to the right, the tanks then followed the river line. They encountered another concentration of Soviet armor. In a short, sharp firefight, the enemy was defeated and whatever had not been knocked out fled the battlefield. All of a sudden, waving figures could be seen in front of the tanks. Schulz flung open his hatch. He heard the grenadiers yelling from foxhole to foxhole: "Schulz is here!"

Schulz had his tanks pursue the fleeing Soviets so as to give the grenadiers a little more breathing room. The tanks then formed a protective ring around the infantry positions. Once the last grenadier was back across the river, they moved back to their lines.

On 15 July, orders were received from higher headquarters to call off the attack all along the front. Six days later, the division moved through Bjelgorod to the Borissowka-Graiworon area, where it became the operational reserve of the field-army group.

For his role in the fighting during Operation "Citadel," Schulz was later awarded the Swords to the Oak Leaves to the Knight's Cross of the Iron Cross. He was the 33rd member of the German Armed Forces so honored (6 August 1943).

On 15 August, *Generalmajor Freiherr* von Funck left the division. *Generalmajor* Hasso von Manteuffel became the new commander. Five days after assuming command, von Manteuffel was wounded in the shoulder and back by a Soviet rocket attack. The general had his wounds dressed and then mounted his command vehicle and continued operations.

During the fighting around Paraschonowka, 40 enemy tanks were knocked out or destroyed. Schulz's command tank was hit; it was the ninth time for Schulz. After an hour, the damage to the running gear was repaired and Schulz also continued operations.

On 7 October, the Red Army resumed its offensive from Vitebsk towards the Taman Peninsula. The *7. Panzer-Division* conducted a delaying action. Brusilow had to be abandoned. Fastow then fell and, finally, Shitomir was also taken by strong Soviet armored formations. The division pulled back to Berditschew. It appeared there was no end to the Soviet advance; a catastrophe was looming and something had to be done to stop the assault. Von Manteuffel decided to retake Shitomir.

When the division attempted in vain to enter the city on 18 November, the division commander received a radio message from Schulz an hour before darkness was to fall. Schulz requested von Manteuffel come to his location. The general officer was there in 10 minutes, since he knew Schulz would not make such a request without there being something important behind it.

Schulz reported that his men had overrun an antitank gun that was manned by a drunken crew on the outskirts to the city. The Soviets had apparently begun to celebrate too early. Von Manteuffel reacted immediately, ordering his formations to move out again and resume the attack. They were directed to follow *Kampfgruppe Schulz*.

Just before the attack started, von Manteuffel sent out another radio message: "Our Christmas presents are in Shitomir!"

Schulz moved out with six tanks, including three from an attached *Tiger* element, the general's *SPW* and a hundred mechanized infantrymen. They advanced towards the city, with Schulz in the lead. A large fire on the city's outskirts lit up the night. The edge of the city was reached, and the group started receiving fire from an antitank gun. The six tanks responded, and soon the threat was eliminated. The infantry squads advanced behind the individual tanks.

Schulz recommended to the division commander that they both dismount and continue on foot. They left their vehicles, and hurried forward to the lead infantry, helping direct the attack. The men worked their way methodically through the city and, by 0300 hours, it was in their hands. The commanders were overwhelmed by what their men had achieved. On 20 November, the Armed Forces Daily Report concentrated on the daring feat of arms, and von Manteuffel wrote the following in an order of the day:

> . . . my thanks is extended to the tank regiment under the command of its battle-proven commander, *Oberstleutnant* Schulz, the mechanized infantrymen, who fought in an incomparable fashion, the armored artillery and the *Flak* forces, who provided support everywhere, the tank destroyer personnel, the combat engineers and the armored signals soldiers.

A short time later, Schulz was promoted to *Oberst* ahead of his peers. In addition, von Manteuffel recommended him for the next higher level of the Knight's Cross. On 23 November, the division commander became the 332nd member of the German Armed Forces to be honored with the award of the Oak Leaves to the Knight's Cross of the Iron Cross. He was summoned to the *Führer* Headquarters to be presented with the award. While he was there, he was asked whether he had any desires. Von Manteuffel replied that he only desired to see *Oberst* Schulz receive the Diamonds to the Oak Leaves.

On 14 December 1943, Schulz became the 9th member of the German Armed Forces to receive the Diamonds to the Oak Leaves. It was a tribute to him and his death-defying devotion to duty, but also to the bravery and performance of his regiment. *Generalfeldmarschall* von Manstein sent Schulz a long congratulatory telegram. Schulz celebrated the award with a close circle of comrades from the regiment and the division. In addition to the bottle of cognac, there was Schulz's inevitable cigar.

While he served in the Soviet Union, Schulz was wounded several times, without ever having left his troops. When he went forward the next day to visit the mechanized infantry attached to him, one of the grenadiers held up a piece of cardboard from a box on which was written: "Hearty congratulations to our honorary grenadier, *Oberst* Schulz!"

Schulz ordered his driver to stop. None of those present would ever forget the officer. Standing there in his filthy *Panzer* uniform, a threadbare cap on his head, wrinkles around his eyes and two deep folds of skin between his nostrils and the corners of his mouth, Schulz proceeded to toss packs of cigarettes to the grenadiers on the ground, cigarettes that he had brought up front just for them.

On 24 January 1944, von Manteuffel was reassigned from the division. He transferred the reins of command to Schulz, who had been promoted to *Generalmajor* that same month. Early on the morning of 28 January, the 8-wheeled armored car, which was outfitted as a communications center and which constantly accompanied the division commander, stopped in front of Schulz's command post. There were already a few *SPW's* and armored cars there. The radio vehicle moved to the head of the column. It was still dark, and a light snowfall made visibility even worse. The new commander wanted to make his first division-wide tour that morning.

Schulz soon came out of the command post, a medium-sized figure wearing a specially made camouflage jacket. He greeted his crew and adroitly mounted the vehicle. It was something he had done 178 times before, if only the attacks were counted.

"Well, then, let's go . . . *Panzer marsch!*"

The senior signaler, *Funkunteroffizier* Hinzpeter, checked his communications and reported that contact had been established. As always, Schulz preferred to be in the turret. As the vehicle moved through the darkness, he alerted the driver to any unexpected obstacles in the way. The movement to the forward command post took several hours. The corduroy roads did not allow fast movement, and the muddy stretches were even worse. They finally made it to the forward command post, a house with landline connections. The liaison officers for the regiments were waiting. Schulz discovered that the Soviets had entered Schepetowka and ejected the regiment that had been defending there.

Schulz did not have to consider matters for long: "We're taking the old positions back!"

The division received orders to form up to attack. When reports of strong enemy resistance filtered in, Schulz could not contain himself. He personally headed out in the most direct route to Schepetowka with an attack group consisting of a few tanks, *SPW's* and self-propelled 2-centimeter *Flak*. The small battle group soon reached the headquarters of *Panzergrenadier-Regiment* 7. After conversing with the commander in the command post, Schulz came back out to his command vehicle, where Hinzpeter handed him a message: "Attack group has reached the outskirts of the locality. Six enemy tanks and assault guns destroyed."

Schulz confidently predicted his men would be back in their old positions by evening. He mounted up and moved on towards Schepetowka.

The new commander of the tank regiment reported that 10 enemy tanks had been eliminated. He finished his report by saying that three enemy tanks had fled, but that they were being pursued.

Schulz ordered his crew to move on towards the train station.

The general had his vehicle stop next to a knocked-out vehicle. He dismounted and went over to the men. Two of the crew were wounded.

"Did you get hit bad? . . . Here, have a cigarette!"

He watched the medical orderly tend to the men. A salvo of rockets from a Stalin organ howled overhead.

"Ivan's looking for us," Schulz said grimly. He issued orders for the envelopment of the remaining enemy forces in the town. By 1000 hours, they had been wiped out.

A new report came in: "Schepetowka taken; 13 tanks destroyed!"

Schulz ordered his vehicle to move to the front.

The commander of the northern attack force reported to Schulz that his forces were making good progress. The attack to the south was having a harder time, however.

The general moved though the town towards the south. His vehicle was only able to move slowly. A glance at his watch told him it was already 1130 hours. Since he had not heard any messages from the southern group for some time, he had a message sent inquiring whether it had reached its objective.

Hinzpeter began to send the Morse code, the general standing next to him.

"The message has gone through, *Herr General.* Told to wait three minutes."

"Let's continue on."

They soon reached the lead elements of the southern group, whose few tanks, *SPW's* and *Flak* vehicles were widely dispersed. The enemy was peppering the terrain with mortar fire. Mortar shells impacted close to the general's vehicle.

"Damned mortars!" Schulz growled. He had made the acquaintance of some of their shrapnel several times previously. He raised his binoculars to his eyes and observed the terrain. "Up there . . . about 1,500 meters away. A couple of larger houses in front of the woods. Something there doesn't look quite right. Let's go over to the *Flak* and have them spray the area."

The command vehicle moved out. As it advanced, Schulz was able to identify another gun. When they reached the *Flak*, Schulz called out: "To the left . . . in front of the houses . . . next to the hedge . . . antitank gun!"

"Identified, *Herr General!*"

A burst of fire emanated from the *Flak*. A series of hits caused the enemy's ammunition stockpile to go up.

"Hinzpeter: Send another message. Ask them where their answer from 1130 hours is? It's already 1135 hours."

Hinzpeter tapped out another message.

"*Herr General,* the response: Wait another minute."

But Adalbert Schulz would never hear that answer.

Mortar fire started to come in from out of the woods behind the houses. It impacted right behind the command vehicle. The ground was churned up all around for a distance of 300 meters.

Oberleutnant Rothe, the general's aide-de-camp, called out to the general: "Close the hatch!" Suddenly, there was another loud crash next to the vehicle. Blood streamed down into the fighting compartment. Without waiting for orders, the driver put the vehicle in gear and took off towards the rear as quickly as he could. Rothe and the rest of the crew tried to dress the gaping head wound of their division commander, which was oozing blood. The hole in his forehead and the other one at the back of his head gave them little hope, however.

The aide-de-camp tried to talk to his commander, but the only response was some moaning and gurgling.

The vehicle headed straight for the closest clearing station. The command vehicle stopped in front of a battalion command post and the battalion surgeon appeared almost immediately. The young face blanched: "Get to the main clearing station immediately. You must be quick, very quick!"

The division logistics officer raced ahead and cleared the road for the vehicle with the general. The senior surgeon was already waiting for the general when he arrived. The general was taken to the operating room and placed on a table.

✠

At 1300 hours on the same day, the telephone rang at the division command post. *Oberstleutnant i.G.* Bleicken, the division operations officer, answered. When he hung up, his face was chalk white. He said only four words: "The general is dead!"

✠

The tank with the casket in the rear deck slowly approached the open gravesite. The men stood in a large circle in the snow: tankers and grenadiers closely packed together. Six officers carried the casket. As it was lowered into the grave, they took their leave of their general.

To each of them, it was as if they had lost their father. They had certainly lost a mentor, teacher and shining example. Everything that makes the measure of a great man and human being had been incorporated in that soldier. In the hearts of his men, he remained unforgotten: their honorary grenadier Schulz.

Schulz next to the division commander of the *7. Panzer-Division, Generalleutnant* Hasso von Manteuffel, in the vicinity of Shitomir.

Hauptmann Wolfgang Wahl in the desert shortly after being awarded the Knight's Cross to the Iron Cross. He wears an Italian version of the tropical desert battle dress.

CHAPTER 17

Hauptmann Wolfgang Wahl

WITH *PANZER-REGIMENT 8* IN AFRICA

Evening descended on 17 November 1941 over the desert of North Africa at Gambut. The main body of *Panzer-Regiment 8* had taken up encampment in tents and dugouts. The regiment, the armored heart of the *15. Panzer-Division* and led by *Oberst* Cramer, was supposed to be one of the lead attack elements of the *Deutsches Afrika-Korps* for a new advance. *Oberst* Cramer was a gifted armor leader, who had been awarded the Knight's Cross on 27 June 1941 after the fighting at Sollum.

General der Panzertruppen Rommel had issued his orders on 26 October. The time for the attack was only set imprecisely: " . . . between 15 and 20 November." It was Erwin Rommel's intent to break through the defensive positions on the eastern side of Tobruk with the newly formed *90. leichte Division* and the *15. Panzer-Division*. At the same time, the Italian XXI Army Corps was to hold the remainder of the siege ring around the city. The *21. Panzer-Division*—the new name for the *5. leichte Division* after its re-designation—was being held as a reserve force to the east of Gambut.

In order to be able to effectively engage Tobruk with the artillery forces under his command, Rommel had *Artilleriekommando 104*, an artillery command and control headquarters. The artillery forces under its command seemed to continue to grow on a daily basis. Since the beginning of November, they numbered 9 21-centimeter howitzers, 38 15-centimeter howitzers and 12 10.5-centimeter cannon. As a result, Rommel had a quite respectable artillery force by North African standards.

The tankers of *Panzer-Regiment 8* saw their most senior commander again and again during the preparatory phase for the upcoming offensive. Rommel was constantly inspecting his forces. One time, Rommel found *Feldwebel* Kruschinski of the 1st Company of *Panzer-Regiment 8* lying in a foxhole with a fez on his head. When he summoned *Hauptmann* Kümmel, the company commander, to address the situation, Rommel saw that Kümmel could not hide a grin on his face.

"What a goat screw!" Rommel said and moved on to the 2nd Battalion of *Panzer-Regiment 8* under the acting command of *Hauptmann* Wahl. Fortunately, everything was in order when the commander-in-chief arrived. It was not because those companies were especially well disciplined, however. It seemed that the "early-warning system" worked quite well within the regiment.

Finally, the day of the attack was established. It was intended to move out on 23 November. On this particular 17 November, the tankers of *Panzer-Regiment 8* and the motorized infantry of *Schützen-Regiment 115* of the division were ready. They were just north of the Trigh Capuzzo, the road in the desert that led from Capuzzo through Sidi Azeiz—"Sidi Nowhere" was the name given to the forgotten outpost in the language of the African campaigners—through Sidi Rezegh and on to Tobruk.

Hauptmann Wolfgang Wahl was at his 5th Company's location discussing matters with its commander, *Oberleutnant* Körner, when he felt a raindrop.

"Rain, *Herr Hauptmann!*" *Oberleutnant* Heß, the battalion adjutant, cried out with enthusiasm. "Real rain!"

"It's probably just mosquito piss!" *Oberleutnant* Körner interjected, somewhat rudely.

But seconds later it became clear that this was not just mosquito piss, it was a rain shower of epic proportions. It appeared to be coming down in buckets from the African skies. The tankers and the tank mechanics crawled out of their holes and enjoyed the shower. It had not rained in this particular area in more than 60 years.

When it was over, they returned to their tents and dried off. Wolfgang Wahl went to his command post in order to review everything that his division commander, *Generalmajor* Walter Neumann-Silkow, had stressed to his commanders.[1]

A new surprise was about to greet the men, however. The water started rushing down from the Halfaya Plateau along its gullies. It then flowed into the dried-out *wadis* and carried everything along that was in them.

"Get in your tanks!" *Hauptmann* Wahl shouted, as it started to become threatening. They mounted their vehicles and slammed the hatches shout. They could be assured of being safe from the raging waters there.

The radio operators among the various staffs continued to transmit to all stations within range: "Flooding!—Flooding!"

Ironically, this was the same codeword that had been chosen by the senior signals officers for an alert. When the word was chosen, no one thought it could ever be confused with anything else. But it had rained and the men manning the radio sets were not sure what to make of it, until the constant repetition impressed upon them the seriousness of the situation.

When it finally became light again after the floodgates had opened, the men of the 2nd Battalion of *Panzer-Regiment 8*, along with everyone else in

---

1. Author's Note: *Generalmajor* Neumann-Silkow had received the Knight's Cross as an *Oberst* and commander of the *8. Schützen-Brigade* on 5 August 1940.

the area, had to shovel out their vehicles from the mud. At the same time that everyone on the German side was busy with an entrenching tool on the morning of 18 November, the British offensive—Operation "Crusader"—was already moving out.

✠

The British had beaten the Germans to the punch. While the *Deutsches Afrika-Korps* (*DAK*) was planning its offensive under Rommel, the British had been planning their own offensive operation. The objective was twofold: eliminate the *DAK* and relieve the fortress of Tobruk, which had been under siege since May.

It was the Commonwealth XXX Army Corps that was advancing from the east over the border during this rainy night. The corps consisted of the British 7th Armoured Division, the South African 1st Motorized Infantry Division and the 2nd Guards Brigade. Given its composition, it was essentially the counterpart of the *DAK*.

The British XIII Army Corps was composed of infantry formations (a New Zealand and an Indian division) and was intended to fix the Germans.

The British 8th Army operational reserve was the 4th Armoured Brigade. This particular brigade had just been outfitted with Stuart light tanks that had just arrived from the United States.

The commanding general of the XXX Army Corps was General Norrie; General Godwin-Austen commanded the XIII Army Corps.

✠

"Gentlemen, I got you here because the enemy has launched an offensive," *Oberst* Cramer said to his assembled battalion and company commanders. They all looked at their regimental commander expectantly. He continued:

"Tommy has attacked *Ariete* [one of the Italian armored divisions] at Bir el Gobi with his 22nd Armoured Brigade. The 7th Armoured Brigade is advancing on Sidi Rezegh. Its lead elements were hit at Gabr Saleh. We have just received word that the newly arrived 4th Armoured Brigade has also advanced.

"The *21. Panzer-Division* has already moved out to launch an immediate counterattack. *Oberst* Stephan intends to hold up the 4th Armoured Brigade."

This was the start of the briefing of *Oberst* Cramer to his officers. They also discovered that *Generalleutnant* Crüwell, the commander of the *DAK*, had gone forward to *Kampfgruppe Stephan* with Rommel. Rommel intended to lead the attack personally.

During the afternoon of 18 November 1941, Wahl's battalion was also employed against the enemy. By evening of this day, it was fighting British tanks that had advanced as far as the combat-outpost lines of the regiment.

Hauptmann Wahl fanned his tanks out along a broad front. They were able to engage and turn back the enemy, who was also widely dispersed.

The next day, however, the enemy attacked the regiment's positions again along a more narrow front. *Major* Fenski, who had assumed acting command of the 1st Battalion from *Major* Crohn, employed *Hauptmann* Kümmel's 1st Company against the enemy tank forces that had advanced as far as the Trigh Capuzzo. Kümmel's eight tanks were able to turn the enemy out of his positions and push him back to Hill 106.7. Johannes Kümmel, who had been awarded the Knight's Cross on 9 July 1941, had his tanks consolidate on the objective and then pull back to their jump-off positions. Once there, Kümmel discovered that his division was to link up with the *21. Panzer-Division* the following morning.

✠

The next morning, *Panzer-Regiment 8* turned from the Trigh Capuzzo and headed west. It had been alerted that the 7th Armoured Division had reached Side Rezegh. Cramer ordered his regiment to attack the enemy tanks on the southeastern and eastern outskirts of Sidi Rezegh. The tank companies deployed for battle. Wahl led his battalion somewhat to the southwest into the desert, where he then turned back again. When he reached the attack area, the 1st Battalion was already committed. Once again, it was Kümmel from that battalion who was in the limelight. His company had been the first element to have to withstand the withering fire from an English antitank-gun position. Kümmel's vehicle was knocked out; he was not wounded, but he would have to sit out the fight temporarily.

While this was going on, the 2nd Battalion had reached the battlefield and was engaging the enemy. *Leutnant* Adam, the acting commander of the 6th Company, personally knocked out several vehicles with his crew. *Oberleutnant* Wuth, the acting commander of the 8th Company, was likewise successful.

The fighting continued in a seesaw fashion over the course of the next few days and Cramer led his tanks in a wild hunt for quarry through the area of operations. He was directed to encircle the 4th Armoured Brigade on the morning of 22 November. Both battalions gave pursuit and scored local successes.

Officers of *Panzer-Regiment 8* outside of Tobruk in may 1941. From left to right: *Oberstleutnant* Ramseur (commander of the *II./Panzer-Regiment 8*); *Oberstabsarzt* Dr. Becker (regimental surgeon); *Oberleutnant* Jahns (regimental adjutant); and *Major* Crohn (commander of the *I./Panzer-Regiment 8*).

Once darkness fell, however, contact was lost with the enemy. *Major* Fenski's battalion was directed to take the lead, while Wahl's battalion was held back for disposition by the division commander. Fenski and his men continued the hunt. That night, his battalion found a large tank assembly area of the enemy. He succeeded in surrounding it.

By the time Wahl's battalion and the rest of the regiment had arrived on the scene, Fenski was able to report that he had taken a brigadier general, 17 other officers and numerous enlisted personnel prisoner. In addition, he had captured 35 tanks and 15 armored vehicles.

"That means the Knight's Cross for you, Fenski!" *Oberst* Cramer said, beaming. It seems the only one they did not get was the brigade commander, Gatehouse, who had been summoned to report to General Gott an hour before Fenski and his tankers had arrived. The 4th Armoured Brigade had ceased to exist, but the gods of war did not smile on Fenski the following day. He was killed at the Battle of Sidi Rezegh on *Totensonntag*, the German Memorial Day, on 23 November.[2]

The fighting of *Totensonntag* will be followed in some detail, because it is here that Wahl and his battalion played a significant role.

---

2. Author's Note: Fenski was posthumously awarded the Knight's Cross on 31 December 1941.

✠

As the sun rose on *Totensonntag*, Cramer led his regiment from out of the area around Bir Sciaf Sciuf to the southwest. All of the companies had been told the division commander's intent: "The enemy must be beaten decisively today!"

The morning was spent with several successful engagements against enemy trains elements as well as securing the supporting documents necessary for the attack planned that afternoon. The day also started out as a costly one: Fenski was killed early in the morning. Another disaster could have befallen the regiment: *Oberst* Cramer accidentally ran into an enemy artillery position in his command tank and an accompanying vehicle. His tank received several hits. Despite this, he was able to fight his way back to the 1st Battalion, where the knowledge gained by his encounter with the enemy was put to good use.

Around noon, the regiment advanced to Bir el Gobi, where contact was established with the *Ariete* Armored Division. When it turned afternoon, little did anyone realize it would become one of the costliest days of the war for *Panzer-Regiment 8*.

At 1430 hours, the regiment was about nine kilometers southeast of the area around Side Rezegh, where it was oriented to the north in preparation for an attack. It was on the left and *Panzer-Regiment 5* of the *21. Panzer-Division*, which was attached to the division for this operation, was on the right. The latter had some 40 tanks operational. Both of the regiments were arrayed in two echelons. In the case of *Panzer-Regiment 8*, the first wave consisted of the 1st Battalion, which was followed by the regimental staff and elements of *Flak-Regiment 33*. The second wave consisted of the 2nd Battalion.

On order from the division, *Schützen-Regiment 115* was to follow the 2nd Battalion of *Panzer-Regiment 8* mounted on its trucks. The tank battalion was directed to support the motorized infantry and enable their penetration through the enemy lines. But as the attack was forming up, *Schützen-Regiment 115* was unable to link up with the tankers, because it had gotten stuck in the marshy terrain at Sidi Muftah and was also receiving artillery fire from both the north and the east.

Despite that, the division gave the order to move out at 1454 hours. The objective was to eliminate the South African division, which was in the area of Sghifit and Adeimat and heavily reinforced by armored elements. The enemy artillery fire increased as the division moved out, even though it had already shelled the division's assembly area with harassing fire. The German artillery was unable to conduct effective counterbattery fire, because the enemy artillery was in well-prepared field positions that were reinforced in the course of the day.

The artillery did fire preparatory fires for the armored attack, however, once it started moving. Shortly after the attack started, Cramer realized that his only chance for success was if his reinforced regiment were to remain true to the designated direction of attack into the middle of the enemy positions and he did not worry about threats to his flanks. He went to the head of his attack formations and personally led the regiment towards its objective. Any deviations from the line of march were speedily corrected by the regimental commander himself.

At 1530 hours, Kümmel's company broke into the enemy lines and eliminated a number of heavy weapons. This penetration seemed to cripple the enemy. Wherever Kümmel's tanks appeared, the enemy surrendered after a few well-placed rounds. The fire coming from the enemy's antitank guns and antiaircraft guns steadily slackened. The enemy's artillery continued its intensive firing into the ranks of the 2nd Battalion and the rearward elements, however. Wahl saw his battalion take its first casualties. At the same time, a radio message arrived from Kümmel, who was also the acting commander of the 1st Battalion: "Request the infantry be brought up. They are needed to comb the battlefield and pick up the prisoners."

Schützen-Regiment 115, which had finally made it forward, was led forward. It advanced as far as the point where the tanks of the 1st Battalion had penetrated. From this point on, it advanced only hesitantly.

Cramer had decided in the meantime to aggressively carry the attack forward without waiting for the motorized infantry to completely close up. In true tanker fashion, he believed that success was only possible with an aggressively mounted and rapid advance that crippled the enemy. Cramer radioed Wahl: "Listen up, Wahl! Turn a little bit to the northwest to give the infantry some breathing room. I also want you to attack those 20 odd tanks that are attempting to advance into the division's left flank!"

"What's going on with *Panzer-Regiment 5, Herr Oberst?*" Wahl wanted to find out what was happening on the east flank.

"By last report, that regiment has moved too far east as a result of the enemy's heavy defensive fires. Only a few of its tanks have gotten through to Kümmel's men."

At this point, it was clear to Wahl that he would have to do everything on his own. He could expect no help from the other tank formations on the battlefield: "Fifth on the left flank. Sixth on the right. Eighth behind it. Everybody follow me!"

Wahl led his vehicles against the enemy tank force. When the enemy was sighted, Wahl had his tanks pick up their speed, so as to move under the enemy's fire. A minute later, he told his companies to engage at will.

Two company commanders of the *II./Panzer-Regiment 8* just before the attack on the British 7th Armoured Division, the "Desert Rats": *Leutnant* Adam (6th Company) and *Oberleutnant* Körner (5th Company). Both officers were killed in the attack.

The flames spit out of the muzzles of the main guns. The first enemy tanks fell victims to Wahl's tankers' guns. About this time, the 8th Company had advanced enough to participate in the fighting. The gunners took up sight pictures in their optics and fired at the enemy. Without waiting, the loaders rammed home the next rounds. More and more enemy tanks were engaged and destroyed; evidently, they had not been expecting enemy armor to surface in this area. Nevertheless, more and more of Wahl's tanks also reported being hit. He ordered his forces to maneuver around the enemy who had stopped to put up a fight.

All of a sudden, the remaining enemy tanks turned around and disappeared out of sight into a shallow depression. Wahl reported the results of the engagement to his commander and then continued north in the ordered direction of attack.

The farther he advanced, the more he received enemy artillery and antitank-gun fire. Wahl's tanks could only advance meters at a time. They were soon in the enemy's lines. The tank commanders were reduced to tossing hand grenades from out of the turrets in order to combat the dug-in infantry on the ground. It was impossible to engage them otherwise. As soon as the tanks passed the dugouts, however, the surviving "Tommies" rose out of their holes and engaged them with all weapons at their disposal. Even Wahl's tank was hit more than once by a Molotov cocktail or a satchel charge of grenades. The resulting explosions from the satchel charges knocked his crew off of their seats.

Finally, after what seemed like an eternity, the German motorized infantry began to close up. They suffered heavy casualties on their trucks from the artillery fire and the antitank guns. Direct hits took out first three, then a total of four trucks carrying the infantry. Every one on board each of these trucks was either killed or wounded. Again and again, Wahl and his men had to take on and eliminate antitank guns before they could jump forward. One could follow the line of advance of the motorized infantry by the trail of burning and destroyed vehicles.

Cramer, who seemed to be everywhere on the battlefield at once, frequently came to Wahl's location and participated in the fighting. By 1620 hours, Cramer had the following situation on his hands:

His 1st Battalion had successfully broken through the enemy positions to the north and was in his rear area, looking for his artillery. The 2nd Battalion was in a refuse left formation and deep within the enemy's positions, where it was holding out for the motorized infantry to close up. Wahl's tanks had eliminated local resistance in their positions and had knocked out numerous enemy tanks.

Panzer-Regiment 5 had gone completely off to the right; its help in this fight could not longer be expected.

Hauptmann Wahl's crews were having a hard time dealing passively with the incessant artillery fire as they waited for the motorized infantry to finally close with them. In order to avoid losses to the artillery, the battalion was almost forced to keep moving forward. Consequently, the infantry fell farther and farther behind. At this point, Cramer appeared: "Wahl, you have to turn around and bring the infantry forward, no matter what it takes!"

By this time, the desert in this area had been covered by thick clouds of smoke and sand, making visibility practically nonexistent. In this situation, Wahl had to turn his companies around. Wolfgang Wahl accomplished this in textbook fashion, but he soon discovered the price he would have to pay in terms of losses to his officer corps. The first ominous message came from the 5th Company: *Oberleutnant* Körner, the acting commander, had been killed. Then *Leutnant* Adam, the acting commander of the 6th Company was killed. Following him were *Oberleutnant* Wuth, the acting commander of the 8th Company, *Leutnant* Liestmann and *Leutnant* Pirath. Many of Wahl's tanks were burning. In some instances, the crews were able to dismount. The 6th Company radioed: "*Oberfeldwebel* Schultz is commanding the last tank of the company."

Many brave noncommissioned officers and enlisted personnel also died in the desert at Sidi Rezegh along with their officers. Among them was

Oberfeldwebel Mehlig, who had once taught *Generalleutnant* Bayerlein how to drive a tank.

It was thanks to support from the 1st Battalion of *Flak-Regiment 33* of *Hauptmann* Fromm that the disengagement from the enemy worked. Fromm's gunners allowed Wahl's tankers to turn around, thanks to their deadly aimed fire. Wahl went to the location of the bogged-down infantry with his few remaining tanks and brought them several hundred meters forward. Then he was alone with his tanks again; the infantry was unable to advance in the murderous fire the enemy was offering.

Cramer then personally brought forward the last remaining regimental reserves in order to get the attack moving again. These were combat engineers on trucks and the tanks of the regimental headquarters. The regimental combat engineers fought with amazing élan. They tackled the enemy gun crews in the middle of the heaviest of fires and silenced the guns.

By 1625 hours, radio communications with the 1st Battalion had been lost. Antitank rounds had destroyed Kümmel's radio. Kümmel had to lead his battalion using signal flags while standing fully exposed in his commander's hatch. At 1655 hours, he had a messenger take the following to the regiment: "First Battalion has broken through to the airfield at Sidi Rezegh. Contact established with elements of the *21. Panzer-Division* attacking from the north."

As a result, Cramer's planned decision to have Kümmel's battalion turn around and send it to help Wahl was no longer necessary. When the enemy attempted to break out to the southeast and the south with tanks and trucks at 1700 hours, he was defeated by Wahl's battalion and the combat engineers.

The enemy resistance, which was being continuously beefed up by the introduction of reserves from the rear, had collapsed as a result of the rapid advance and breakthrough by Kümmel's men. The enemy's attempt to break out through Wahl's battalion also shattered on the iron-like defense it offered.

Generalmajor Neumann-Silkow, who was bringing up the remaining forces of the division right behind the tanks, proved to be the guarantor that the attack momentum never let up as a result of his calm and confident demeanor. Wahl likewise understood how to impart the same confidence to his men, despite the high casualties. The names of Kümmel, Wahl and Cramer are inseparably linked to this victory on *Totensonntag.*

A large amount of enemy tanks, artillery pieces, antitank guns and trucks remained behind on the battlefield. By the onset of darkness, more than 1,000 prisoners had been collected.

Cramer assembled his regiment at the Sidi Rezegh airfield. To get there, he had to pass though the area where Wahl and his men had been fighting.

He could see traces of the hard fighting that had taken place there. And if the mission of Kümmel's battalion as a battering ram had been difficult, the mission of the sister battalion was even more difficult. The daily logs of *Panzer-Regiment 8* recorded this as follows:

> More difficult was the mission of the 2nd Battalion. Because of this, the regimental commander personally accompanied it . . . Both battalions accomplished the missions that had been assigned to them in an exemplary fashion and brought about the decision in spite of heavy losses and without the motorized infantry being available.

The total losses of the regiment of 23 November 1941:
- 14 *Panzer II's*
- 30 *Panzer III's*
- 9 *Panzer IV's*
- 2 command and control tanks

Of those, the following were total losses:
- 6 *Panzer II's*
- 10 *Panzer III's*
- 3 *Panzer IV's*

The regiment had entered the battle on 18 November 1941 with
- 28 *Panzer II's*
- 76 *Panzer III's*
- 21 *Panzer IV's*
- 4 small command and control tanks
- 2 large command and control tanks

✠

Wolfgang Wahl was born in Döbeln on 15 July 1913, the son of *Hauptmann* Wahl, who was serving with the Saxon *Infanterie-Regiment 139*. After receiving his college-preparatory diploma, he entered the *Reichswehr* on 1 April 1933 and was assigned to *Kraftfahr-Abteilung 4* in Dresden. This decisively influenced his decision to become a tanker, since the soldiers for the fledgling *Panzertruppe* were taken from the ranks of the motorized battalions.

He received his commission as a *Leutnant* in *Panzer-Regiment 5* at Wünsdorf on 1 April 1935. On the day that *Panzer-Regiment 8* was formed, 1 October 1936, Wahl was assigned to it. On 1 August 1938, Wahl was promoted to *Oberleutnant*. He became the commander of the regiment's 6th Company and, serving in this capacity, he broke through the Weygand Line at Amiens in France on 6 June 1940, earning the Iron Cross, First Class. During the breakthrough, which saw his company involved in heavy fighting and taking heavy casualties, Wolfgang Wahl was badly wounded for the first time. Soldiers of the regiment carried him from the battlefield between the German and the French lines after his tank had been knocked out.

He later said the following about this operation: "There is nothing special to say about this. I did what a company commander has to do in that type of situation."

These words characterize the personality of Wahl, both as a soldier and as a human being. He was a circumspect leader to his subordinates. Every man of his company—and later, of his tank battalion—respected him highly.

When the *15. Panzer-Division* set off for Africa in the spring of 1941, *Panzer-Regiment 8* also belonged to it. Heretofore, it had been a part of the *10. Panzer-Division* in both the Polish and French campaigns. The regiment had been officially transferred to the newly forming division on 18 January 1941.

Oberstleutnant Cramer assumed command of the regiment from *Oberst* Elster in March 1941, when the regiment was still at its home base of Schwetzingen and preparing for its employment in Africa. It was transferred gradually from the Heidelberg area to the south, where it finally landed at Tripoli at the end of May 1941.

The division commander, *Generalmajor* von Prittwitz, who had preceded the division to Africa, had already been killed before his division arrived during a reconnaissance trip to Tobruk (10 April 1941).

One of the 160 German tanks that was unloaded from the ships and then rolled east was commanded by *Oberleutnant* Wahl, who was still in command of the 6th Company. The new division commander, *Generalmajor Freiherr* von Esebeck,[3] received his tanks at Tobruk. He then led them on to Bardia, where they received orders to attack Fort Capuzzo.

It was there that Wahl took part in his first tank engagement in Africa. His battalion commander at the time was *Oberstleutnant* Ramsauer; the 1st Battalion was commanded by *Major* Crohn. Fort Capuzzo was taken in a *coup de main*.

The next objective was the Halfaya Pass. It was there that the 2nd Battalion assisted appreciably in eliminating the fighting positions of the enemy. The battalion rolled into the pass and shot up everything it encountered. A short while later, the pass was in the hands of the *DAK*. It was due primarily to *Hauptmann* Wilhelm Bach, the acting commander of the 1st Battalion of *Schützen-Regiment 104*, that the enemy gave up in this sector. For this, he received the Knight's Cross on 9 July 1941.

---

3. Author's Note: *Freiherr* von Esebeck had received the Knight's Cross as an *Oberst* and the commander of the *6. Schützen-Brigade*.

When the English started their offensive with the telling name of "Battleaxe," *Panzer-Regiment 8* became involved in heavy fighting starting on 15 June 1941. *Oberstleutnant* Ramsauer was wounded on 16 June; even the regimental commander's tank was knocked out. Cramer had to be evacuated with wounds to his arm and head. Capuzzo, which had been lost, could not be regained for another 24 hours. At that point, the enemy started withdrawing.

After 72 hours of uninterrupted armor operations, the tankers could enjoy a few hours of rest and quiet. *Generalmajor* Neumann-Silkow, who had assumed command of the *15. Panzer-Division* in the meantime, submitted *Hauptmann* Kümmel for the Knight's Cross. Kümmel received the high award on 9 July 1941. For his role in that round of fighting, his soldiers dubbed him the "Lion of Capuzzo."

Winston Churchill wrote about this defeat of his forces:

Inconsolable, I wandered the halls [of his estate at Chartwell] for hours on end. Everything had fallen apart in the desert on 17 June 1941.[4]

✠

Wolfgang Wahl assumed acting command of the battalion. He was promoted to *Hauptmann* on 1 August 1941 and was eventually designated the official battalion commander. The battle for Sidi Rezegh, described in detail at the beginning of the section, saw him in the middle of a major offensive. It was to be a few days later when he would make a name for himself.

It was on 30 November 1941, when the *DAK* was given the mission of conducting another large-scale attack. It was Rommel's intent to attack Sidi Rezegh from the southwest with *Kampfgruppe Mickl*. *Oberst* Johann Mickl— Knight's Cross on 13 December 1941—led the group that consisted primarily of motorized infantry. At the same time, the *15. Panzer-Division* was to attack the town from the west, while the *21. Panzer-Division* approached from the east. There were only 28 medium and 11 light tanks left in all of the *15. Panzer-Division*. That was all that was left operational of the original 160. The *21. Panzer-Division* had exactly 21 operational tanks at its disposal.

When the enemy opened fire from several heavy and medium artillery batteries on the assembly areas of the *15. Panzer-Division*, Wahl attacked with his battalion. Heavy fighting developed in the vicinity of Bel Hamet. In a dramatic round of fighting, Wahl and most of his tankers were able to escape

---

4. Translator's Note: Source unknown. Reverse-translated from the German text into English without access to the original text.

the wrath of the enemy artillery fire while attacking the gun positions in a series of skillfully executed fire-and-movement maneuvers. Several enemy artillery batteries were overrun, and a large number of prisoners was taken.

Not only did *Hauptmann* Wahl orchestrate his forces skillfully, he also selflessly led from the front. In the course of the fighting, he received his third wound, this time to the head. His wounds were severe enough to require evacuation from the theater, and he eventually wound up at the naval hospital in Stralsund.

It was there on 18 January 1942 that he was presented the Knight's Cross by a *Kapitän zur See* in front of the assembled higher-ranking officers of the garrison. The recommendation for the award, which had been approved on 6 January, contains the following:

> *Hauptmann* Wahl—awarded the Iron Cross, Second Class, in Poland and the Iron Cross, First Class, in France—has distinguished himself through his bravery as an acting battalion commander in a tank regiment in all of his operations in Africa. Through skillful leadership, he has contributed decisively to the successes of his division. On 30 November 1941, he succeeded in eliminating several enemy batteries at Bel Hamet with his battalion and taking numerous prisoners. The overall success of his battalion is primarily due to his personal and brave devotion to duty.

✠

When *Panzer-Armee Afrika* set out on its last large-scale offensive to the east on 26 May 1942, *Hauptmann* Wahl was back with his battalion. At this point, *Oberstleutnant* Teege led the regiment. When the 1st Battalion encountered an antitank-gun belt and the completely new U.S.-supplied Grant medium tank[5] and was no longer able to advance on 27 May 1942, the 2nd Battalion rolled into battle. Wahl's men were able to advance completely by surprise into the enemy's flank, and they succeeded in weakening the enemy.

Generalmajor von Vaerst,[6] the new division commander, continued the advance. It was imperative to always "head where Rommel was."

When the *15. Panzer-Division* was attacked by surprise by 65 Grants outside of Acroma, it was *Generalleutnant* Walter K. Nehring, the commanding

5. Editor's Note: The rather ungainly looking Grant mounted a 37-mm gun in a turret and a 75-mm gun in a side sponson with limited traverse. Nevertheless, the Grant was an effective tank and the high-explosive rounds from the 75-mm could eliminate German anti-tank guns at long range.

6. Author's Note: Von Vaerst had received the Knight's Cross when he was an *Oberst* and commander of the *2. Schützen-Brigade.*

general of the *DAK*, who saved the division. He established a wall of *Flak* for the enemy to run into. The heavy 8.8-centimeter guns under *Oberst* Alwin Wolz, the commander of *Flak-Regiment 135*, knocked out more than half of the attacking tanks.

The *15. Panzer-Division* continued the attack and encountered the Indian 5th Infantry Division at Bir el Tamar. The division effectively eliminated the Indian 10th Brigade as a fighting force.

Then came 20 June 1942: the assault on Tobruk started. Wahl also participated in this with his battalion. It succeeded in breaking open several of the defensive rings that had been established around the city. It then had to cross the broad tank ditch. *Generaloberst* Rommel showed up at the battalion's location and encouraged the tankers to go as fast as they could. Fort Gabr Gasem was taken by the *15. Panzer-Division*. At this point, Tobruk fell into German hands.

The division then advanced through Mersa Matruh and towards El Alamein. On 15 July 1942, Wahl was seriously wounded (for the fifth time) during the fighting for the Ruweisat Ridge and taken prisoner by the British. He was evacuated to Egypt and then on to South Africa. A few weeks later, after he had recovered, he was sent to the United States. It was there in December 1943 that he received the news that he had been promoted to *Major*. He was released from captivity in 1946.

After the war he studied architecture and entered into that practice.

Wolfgang Wahl passed away at Schopfheim/Lörrach on 26 September 1985.

A British Grant tank of the famous "Desert Rats."

Leutnant Joachim Weissflog was awarded the Knight's Cross to the Iron Cross just before the war ended in March 1945.

CHAPTER 18

Oberleutnant Joachim Weissflog

TANK COMMANDER IN THE EAST AND IN THE WEST

The morning of 24 August 1943 had just dawned. The enemy was preparing to force a breakthrough through the positions of the *1. Panzer-Armee* in the area around Saporoschje. The *16. Panzergrenadier-Division*—the *Windhund* ("Greyhound") Division—had recently arrived in the sector, as had the *23. Panzer-Division*. These reinforcements had been sent by *Generalfeldmarschall* von Manstein to help halt the forces of two Soviet field armies.

The Soviets had been attacking this area since 17 July 1943. The *16. Panzergrenadier-Division* had arrived at the beginning of August. The morning of 24 August would prove to be a difficult test for a few soldiers of the greyhound division.

✠

"Do you hear something, Jochen?" *Hauptfeldwebel* Schröder radioed to his comrade to the right, *Leutnant* Joachim Weissflog.[1]

The platoon leader in *Panzer-Abteilung 116* was also listening to the front in the open commander's hatch of his *Panzer IV*. He also heard the rumbling in the distance. It consisted of the rattling of metal tracks and the ever-present sound of misfires among the engines of the approaching tanks.

"There they are, Schröder. They're coming!"

The two *Panzer IV's* were positioned on a rise to act as early warning for the tank battalion, which was incorporated into the division's blocking position farther to the rear.

Joachim Weissflog, who had been commissioned a *Leutnant* in his battalion on 1 June, raised the binoculars to his eyes to search the terrain in front of him. He saw a cloud of dust that rose in the distance and which was rapidly approaching his position. Suddenly, the contours of the first few tanks emerged from the cloud.

"Straight ahead . . . 1,200 meters . . . enemy tanks, Schröder!" he radioed over to his comrade.

---

1. Translator's Note: Other sources spell his name as Weißflog.

"Targets identified!" came the reply. Both tank commanders alerted their crews at the same time. They disappeared into the respective fighting compartments and viewed the rapidly approaching enemy through their optics. Weissflog counted 18 T-34's, which became easier and easier to pick out of the haze.

The loader reported that both the main gun and the coaxial machine gun were loaded and ready to fire. A few seconds later, *Hauptfeldwebel* Schröder opened fire in his tank against the approaching enemy vehicles.

The first round left the long barrel of the *Panzer IV.* The sound of the empty shell casing being ejected and striking the deflector reverberated through the tank. The casing then fell into the cloth collector bag. The loader rammed the next round into the chamber as the first round slammed into the targeted T-34. The hit caused it to burst into flames.

"Target, Schröder! Keep it up!" the *Leutnant* radioed over to his comrade. He waited a bit before he issued his fire command. The second round from Schröder's main gun also hit the enemy and, once again, another T-34 remained stationary on the battlefield. A garish lance of red flame sprang out of the tank commander's hatch. The ready ammunition on board went up in a thunderous explosion.

"Pull back to the depression behind us!" Weissflog radioed his comrade.

Both of the tanks rolled back a short distance and took cover in a shallow depression. In the meantime, the enemy artillery had commenced firing. It fired along a frontage of two kilometers against the German positions. In short order, four salvoes of rounds landed on the previously occupied position. The resulting clouds of smoke obscured the Germans' vision of the approaching enemy tanks. Joachim Weissflog had to think for a second. If he pulled back farther, then the enemy would succeed in his breakthrough attempt by being able to get around the battalion. There was no other choice—both of them had to roll forward again. They had to go back to the high ground if they hoped to hold up the enemy.

"We're moving forward!" Weissflog radioed his wingman. Schröder acknowledged the order immediately. Weissflog then called down to his driver: "Back to the old position!" The driver immediately engaged the clutch, and the tank took off. The tanks picked up speed as they advanced to the high ground. They advanced into the middle of the thick wall of smoke and dust. When the impenetrable wall of haze suddenly lifted, the Soviet T-34's appeared right in front of them, the lead tanks barely 50 meters away.

"Fire at will!"

Both tanks screeched to an immediate stop. The gunners took aim at the enemy, and the reports of the main guns could be heard almost simultaneously. A few seconds later, there was the sound of steel on target, followed by another near simultaneous discharge of main guns.

Four of the sixteen enemy tanks were in flames after these four rounds were fired. The enemy force was completely disoriented by this sudden attack by fire. Their visibility had also been obscured by the smoke and dust; they had likewise not seen anything. Further, they were not expecting to see anything. The two German tanks that appeared were a complete surprise for them.

"Move forward slowly . . . orient to the left!" Weissflog then instructed his gunner to search to the right.

The turrets of the two tanks turned in opposite directions. They then fired at the tanks as they encountered them in rolling through the middle of the enemy formation. The loaders and gunners worked feverishly. They were supported in their efforts by the drivers, who took short changes in course as new enemy targets appeared out of the haze.

The first rounds fired in return from the long-barreled T-34's started to land next to Weissflog's tank, which had taken a firing halt. Flames could be seen from inside the fighting compartment. The rank smell of cordite worked oppressively on the lungs of the five tankers, who were enclosed in this steel box and who had to fight if they wanted to survive.

Three . . . four . . . five minutes passed. The enemy tanks attempted to flee to the flanks. They were identified, engaged and destroyed. Exactly eight minutes after the first tank was spotted, 16 knocked-out enemy tanks littered the battlefield. The clouds of dense, oily smoke, the fires and the lances of flame emanating from the sympathetic explosions of detonating ammunition gave witness to the destruction of the enemy tank wedge.

As a result of their actions, the two tanks of *Panzer-Abteilung 116* had prevented the potential envelopment of their lines and given the *Panzergrenadiere* the opportunity to successfully fend off the subsequent attack by Soviet infantry. Of the 16 tanks, *Hauptfeldwebel* Schröder had knocked out 10; *Leutnant* Weissflog accounted for the other six.

✠

A few weeks later, on 14 September 1943, the Soviet divisions of the Woronesch Front broke through the northern wing of *Heeresgruppe Süd* and advanced to the southwest in the direction of the Dnjepr. As a result, the German front had to be pulled back behind the river.

In the area around Saporoshje, the city on the bend of the Dnjepr, a bridgehead remained on the eastern bank. The *16. Panzergrenadier-Division* was in this bridgehead and engaged in bitter fighting. *Leutnant* Weissflog made a name for himself there as well. In one round of fighting, he advanced with his four tanks into the enemy field fortifications and engaged the enemy antitank guns that were attempting to prevent his breaking through.

At this point, enemy tanks also advanced against his small force. The four German tanks replied to the enemy fire. They knocked out a number of T-34's and the local German attack was successful.

Over the course of the next few days, the tankers of *Hauptmann* Gerhard Tebbe—who was known to his soldiers as *Panzer-Tebbe*—were involved in what seemed like never-ending heavy fighting. On 14 October, Tebbe's battalion was able to block a deep armored penetration by the enemy at the Saporoshje reservoir. All of the tanks of the battalion were involved in the fighting. If the enemy had succeeded in reaching the reservoir embankment, he would have been able to close the trapdoor behind the division.

The same day, *General* Henrici, the field-army group commander, made the decision to blow up the reservoir dam at 1845 hours. When the field-army staff attempted to notify the *16. Panzergrenadier-Division*, however, no radio contact could be made. A liaison officer was dispatched from the field-army group to find the division's command post. He found it in a peasant's hut on the northern outskirts of the city and informed *Generalleutnant Graf* von Schwerin of the order.

During the next few hours, the soldiers of the division screened the double-decker bridge over the Dnjepr until the last soldier had crossed. *Leutnant* Weissflog and his platoon participated in this effort. At midnight, the bridge and the reservoir dam were finally blown.

The Armed Forces Daily Report of 27 October 1943 described the operation as follows:

> The *16. Panzergrenadier-Division,* a division from the Rhine/Westphalia area, under the command of *Generalleutnant Graf* von Schwerin, has earned special recognition for its exemplary performance of duty during the large-scale retrograde movements east of the Dnjepr and during the fighting for the bridgehead at Saporoshje.

On 4 November 1943, *Generalleutnant Graf* von Schwerin became the 41st member of the German Armed Forces to receive the Swords to the Diamonds of the Knight's Cross to the Iron Cross. Exactly one month earlier, *Leutnant* Weissflog had received the third level of the Tank Assault Badge, signifying participation in at least 50 separate armored engagements.

✠

Joachim Weissflog was born on 24 February 1923 at Lommatzsch. From October 1939 through May 1940, he performed voluntary war service for the city administration of Lommatzsch. He then volunteered for the *Panzertruppe*; he wanted to become a career soldier. On 18 May 1940, he was assigned to the 2nd Company of *Panzer-Ersatz-Abteilung 1* in Erfurt. After his basic training was completed, he was assigned in October to the 6th Company of *Panzer-Regiment* 1 in Zinten in East Prussia. His company commander at the time was *Oberleutnant* Darius. Weissflog would participate in the first stage of the Russian campaign with this commander. The division was employed in the north; the objective was Leningrad. Weissflog was a gunner for *Unteroffizier* Dormann.

Joachim Weissflog during some sort of organizational sporting event. Note the *"Windhund"* (Greyhound) badges on the caps of the personnel.

He participated in all of the fighting until as far as northeast of Kalinin. At this point, his place was taken in the crew by another soldier because of a wound he had suffered. As a result, he probably escaped death, since newly promoted *Feldwebel* Dormann took part in an operation the next day in which his tank was knocked out and he was killed.

When the 1st Battalion of *Panzer-Regiment 1* was reassigned to the *16. Infanterie-Division (mot.)* and redesignated as *Panzer-Abteilung 116*, Joachim Weissflog was with the battalion. He would remain with this division until the very end, participating in heavy fighting in both the east and the west.

On 13 May 1942, the battalion detrained at Kursk. He fought in the summer offensive of 1942 as part of the crew of *Oberfeldwebel* Gustel Lange. On 1 July 1942, he was promoted to *Unteroffizier*. His assignment to the officer-candidate school at Zossen (Berlin) interrupted his frontline service. By the time he arrived back at his old battalion, it was in the Rostow and Taganrog areas. As a *Fahnenjunker-Feldwebel*—an officer candidate with a rank of *Feldwebel*—Weissflog climbed back into his tank and was soon engaged without interruption in the fighting withdrawal. When the division eliminated the Soviet IV Guards Mechanized Corps in the Federenko Valley as part of the *XXXX. Panzer-Korps*, Joachim Weissflog demonstrated that he was a warrior who always saw a way out of hopeless situations.

In June 1943, the division was redesignated as the *16. Panzergrenadier-Division*. That same month—on 1 June 1943 to be exact—Joachim Weissflog was commissioned a *Leutnant*. The battalion commander had had his eye on the promising young officer for some time. This scrutiny intensified after the Soviet summer offensive was successfully beaten back in difficult fighting in August.

Leutnant Weissflog proved his mettle again in the armored fighting in September in the Isjum and Slawjansk areas. He and his platoon were in constant defensive fighting during the Soviet offensive at Stepanowka. It was men like Joachim Weissflog and Hans Bunzel who ensured the battalion of its success. In this round of fighting, *Panzer-Abteilung 116* was credited with knocking out some 86 tanks.

This was followed by the fighting at Saporoshje, which has already been described, and the battles at Ssaksagen, Dnjepropetrowsk, Kriwoi Rog and Nikopol. It was at Nikopol that *Leutnant* Weissflog again shone.

At Nikopol, the division was being used as a fire brigade again. On New Year's morning of 1944, *Leutnant* Weissflog and his section of tanks rolled off to the sounds of tanks that were echoing his way through the thick fog.

✠

"All elements: Stand by to engage!"

Leutnant Weissflog's orders were received by the individual tanks. The hatches slammed shut, and the loaders reported that the weapons were ready. The silhouettes of the first T-34's appeared through the thick haze. Through his optics, Weissflog occasionally saw bright flames shoot out of the exhausts of the tanks that were rolling right across his front.

"Off to the left . . . 100 meters . . . 10 o'clock!"

"Identified!" the gunner reported. He made his final adjustments and depressed the firing mechanism.

The tank rocked backward somewhat from the concussion of the firing of the main gun. The round raced through the fog and bored into the flank of a tank. It went up in flames. That was the opening chord to the symphony of death that was to follow. An armored engagement ensued against a fourfold superior enemy. Enemy tanks appeared from out of the fog again and again. Fire was received from the long-barreled Soviet main guns, the muzzle flashes piercing the fog, clouds of gunpowder smoke and the onset of snowfall.

Using fire and movement, Weissflog and his tanks advanced across the open area, which was covered with stands of vegetation. A T-34 suddenly surfaced in front of Weissflog. It fired and its round hammered obliquely against the turret walls of Weissflog's tank. The round ricocheted skyward with a terrible howl. Before the enemy could get off another round, Weissflog's gunner had him in his sights. The German round struck the enemy tank between the turret and the hull, dislodging the turret. The T-34's main gun pointed towards the ground. There was no chance for the hapless Russians to get off another round. The second German round sealed the T-34's fate.

"Move to the rally point!" *Leutnant* Weissflog ordered his crews. The tanks moved out. The reports of main gun firing could be heard again and again; more and more knocked-out enemy vehicles littered the snow-covered battlefield. They bore witness to the ferocity of the struggle, which also saw two of Weissflog's tanks hit and immobilized.

Despite the enemy's superiority, the small German force had surprise on its side. It was able to take on an advancing armored formation of the enemy and almost completely destroy it. After the last surviving enemy tanks had turned around and disappeared into the fog, 15 knocked-out tanks were counted on the battlefield.

Once again, the name of the thin, wiry *Leutnant* was on everyone's lips. Joachim Weissflog had virtually no equal in his skills as a tanker. *Hauptmann* Tebbe submitted the platoon leader for the German Cross in Gold.

Leutnant Weissflog was wounded again a short while later. He was evacuated to a field hospital and then to a rear-area hospital in Poland. From there he was transferred to the military hospital at Pützchen, near Bonn. At the end of April 1944, he was enjoying convalescent leave in his home town, where he was registered in the "Gold Book" of the town that was reserved for distinguished citizenry. He had been awarded the Wound Badge in Gold on 15 February 1944 and received the German Cross in Gold on 28 April 1944.

✠

When *Leutnant* Weissflog returned to his battalion, it was in the Grafenwöhr Training Area for reconstitution and reequipping with the *Panther* main battle tank. The rest of the division was in France for its reconstitution and conversion to an armored division. It was redesignated as the *116. Panzer-Division*. Weissflog's battalion was redesignated as the *I./Panzer-Regiment 16*. The battalion would not rejoin its parent division until November 1944, however.

When the Allies succeeded in breaking through on the invasion front, the battalion was transported in August 1944 in an expedited fashion to the area of Remiremont and Epinal in France, where it was attached to the newly formed *Panzer-Brigade 111* under *Generalmajor* Bronsart von Schellendorf.

It was with this formation that Joachim Weissflog entered combat for the first time with the *Panther*. There was heavy fighting around Lunèville and

Juvelice. The brigade commander was killed. Despite this heavy blow, the brigade was able to accomplish its assigned mission: The enemy advance via Straßburg to Freiburg was prevented. As a result, the *11. Panzer-Division* was able to pull back from Marseille.

The battalion was then attached to the *11. Panzer-Division*. Its commander, *Generalleutnant* Wend von Wietersheim, led these forces in the bitter fighting in the Parroy Woods, at Geradmer and at Hagenau. He soon learned to appreciate the asset he had attached to him and attempted to have it permanently assigned to him. These efforts floundered due to the resistance of the battalion's soldiers and *Major* Tebbe, who was still its commander. When the detachment orders came, the battalion had to turn over all of its tanks to *Panzer-Regiment 15* of the *11. Panzer-Division*. The battalion personnel returned to Grafenwöhr to be reissued new vehicles.

✠

After the battalion received its tanks, it rejoined its parent regiment on 16 November 1944. At the time, the regiment was located at Grevbroich and under the command of *Oberst* Bayer. The division participated in the Ardennes offensive, where it was part of *General der Panzertruppen* von Manteuffel's *5. Panzer-Armee*, and this signaled a new, dramatic episode in the career of Joachim Weissflog. It was during this operation that he faced his greatest challenges.

The offensive started on the morning of 16 December 1944. The division's objective was to take an important bridge over the Meuse south of Namur. *Kampfgruppe Bayer* advanced at the head of the division. Together with the *2. Panzer-Division*, it took Laroche by 20 December. The *116. Panzer-Division* then disengaged from the enemy and advanced through Laroche towards the northwest and the southern bank of the Ourthe River. These movements were done in conjunction with the *2. Panzer-Division*, which had advanced considerably farther.

The division's next immediate objective was Hotton. This important road hub had to be taken in order to be able to continue the advance on Marche and Ciney. *Kampfgruppe Bayer* advanced on Hotton. In an engagement waged against a few enemy tanks and antitank guns, the Germans lost five tanks, including one *Panther*. The attack bogged down. Because the town could not be taken quickly, the division rerouted its advance towards Marche-en-Famenne, moving via Hampteau, Verdenne and Marenne. *Kampfgruppe Bayer* was encircled during this movement. The *Kampfgruppe* suffered horribly at the hands of American artillery, which knocked out all of its heavy weapons

Leutnant Weissflog with his tank crew.

with the exception of its tanks. On 26 December, the situation appeared hopeless.

That evening, *Leutnant* Weissflog received the mission of advancing out of the woods one kilometer north of Verdenne with the last nine tanks of the regiment and opening the way through the stoutly held encirclement for the men of *Panzergrenadier-Regiment 60*. He was to force the way back to friendly forces.

There was no time to waste. The Germans had had to fend off five attacks in the last few hours. It was thanks to the formidable presence of *Oberst* Bayer, who seemed to have a sixth sense in knowing where there would be trouble, that the attacks were turned back. It was also *Oberst* Bayer who saw the need to break out and ordered it.

By this time, *Leutnant* Weissflog had recorded more than 150 separate tank engagements. He was one of the most experienced tankers in the regiment; he was the right man for this difficult assignment.

The tanks rolled out at 1830 hours. They were received by heavy fire from the well-manned defensive positions at Marenne. Weissflog radioed his men: "Move like a bat out of hell and get through!"

They overran the enemy field positions, crushed fences under their tracks and knocked over walls. They fired to all sides and enabled the *Kampfgruppe*, which then followed, to make it through Marenne without any casualties.

On the far side of Marenne, however, Weissflog started to receive fire again. The muzzle flashes of the antitank guns could be seen through the darkness. Weissflog radioed back to *Oberst* Bayer that he would not be able to get though this second defensive position. The *Oberst* informed Weissflog to bypass the enemy via Fasol and move through the woods south of it.

Joachim Weissflog was prepared for this eventuality. He knew that he then had to parallel the enemy's defensive positions for some 1.5 kilometers before he would be able to find his breakthrough opportunity south of Fasol.

The tanks swung to the south. They were received by rifle, machine-gun and antitank-gun fire. They fired to all sides and finally reached Fasol. The tanks encountered stiff resistance when they moved through the village. The lead tank received a direct hit and was knocked out. A few seconds later, a second tank was in flames. It appeared that tanks and antitank guns would eliminate Weissflog's small *Kampfgruppe*.

The narrow path through the village was blocked by the two burning tanks. The remaining tanks started receiving machine-gun fire from the right. Enemy forces that had reoccupied Marenne started firing from the rear. Weissflog needed to make a decision; there was no time to ask for orders. He directed his tanks forward.

"Turn right! Everyone follow me!"

Turning sharply to the right, they were able to get around the two knocked-out tanks. At this point, however, they were heading into the mined field positions of the Americans. Six enemy antitank guns opened fire.

"Overrun them!"

The tanks picked up speed and headed for the guns. Rounds raced past them; then they were on the guns, which they crushed beneath their tracks.

It appeared that success was imminent, but three Shermans turned up on the left flank.

"Knock them out!"

Although Weissflog's tank had been hit in the turret by an infantry hunter/killer team, he was able to knock out the three Shermans in a few minutes. There was no stopping at this point. Firing to the left and the right, the entire *Kampfgruppe* followed the tanks and reached the safety of the woods south of Fasol.

Taking all of their wounded with them, they were able to escape the enemy's encirclement. Not only had Weissflog knocked out tanks 45 to 47, he had also saved the *Kampfgruppe*.

On 5 January 1945, *Major* Tebbe submitted *Leutnant* Joachim Weissflog for the Knight's Cross to the Iron Cross. He wrote the following in the award recommendation:

> *Leutnant* Weissflog, who was wounded during the attack on Samreé
> on 20 December and was wounded again for the 11th time during
> the breakout effort at Fasol, is the picture of a hard, experienced,

self-confident and terrifically brave frontline officer, who takes no personal consideration for himself and who approaches his missions unflappably, even against vastly superior numbers.

As a result of his personal efforts and his electrifying aggressiveness, he played a decisive role in the success of the breakout of the *Kampfgruppe* and its evacuation of all wounded.

/signed/ Tebbe

Major and Battalion Commander

✠

On 5 March 1945, Joachim Weissflog received his richly deserved award. He had already been promoted to *Oberleutnant*, with an effective date of 1 January 1945.

After the regiment received a short reconstitution at Mönchengladbach, it was employed on the lower Rhine. Weissflog was wounded again at Sonsbeck and was transferred to the reserve military hospital at Königstein (near Frankfurt am Main). He voluntarily returned to his battalion and fought in the withdrawal actions from the lower Rhine to the Ruhr area. The fighting continued on to the Harz Mountains. Weissflog was captured by the Americans north of Magdeburg and was transferred to the Russians from the POW camp at Gardelegen. In the fall of 1945, he was released from Soviet control, probably because his wounds prevented him from being of use in Soviet forced-labor camps.

Joachim Weissflog passed away on 11 August 1995 in Herzogenrath (Aachen).

Late-model *Panzer IV Ausf. Hs* in 3-color camouflage schemes.

Oberfeldwebel Gustel Lange, an experienced tanker.

Major Gerhard Tebbe, also known among his men as *Panzer-Tebbe*.

Two successful German officers interviewed after an operation by a war correspondent.

The loader of a *Tiger* at work. The *Tiger I* had a basic load of 92 main-gun rounds, as well as the capacity to stow 3,920 rounds of machine-gun ammunition.

Rank Comparisons

U.S. ARMY	BRITISH ARMY	GERMAN ARMY
Enlisted Men		
Private	Private	*Schütze*
Private First Class	Private 1st Class	*Oberschütze*
Corporal	Lance Corporal	*Gefreiter*
Senior Corporal	Corporal	*Obergefreiter*
Staff Corporal		*Stabsgefreiter*
Noncommissioned Officers		
Sergeant	Sergeant	*Unteroffizier*
	Staff Sergeant	*Unterfeldwebel*
Staff Sergeant	Technical Sergeant	*Feldwebel*
Sergeant First Class	Master Sergeant	*Oberfeldwebel*
Master Sergeant	Sergeant Major	*Hauptfeldwebel*
Sergeant Major		*Stabsfeldwebel*
Officers		
Second Lieutenant	Second Lieutenant	*Leutnant*
First Lieutenant	First Lieutenant	*Oberleutnant*
Captain	Captain	*Hauptman*
Major	Major	*Major*
Lieutenant Colonel	Lieutenant Colonel	*Oberst Leutnant*
Colonel	Colonel	*Oberst*
Brigadier General	Brigadier General	*Generalmajor*
Major General	Major General	*Generalleutnant*
Lieutenant General	Lieutenant General	*General der Fallschirmjäger, etc.*
General	General	*Generaloberst*
General of the Army	Field Marshal	*Feldmarschall*

Select Bibliography

Primary Sources

Barkmann, Ernst. *Mit dem Panther im Westen und Osten* Unpublished manuscript: ?

Bergmann, S. *Mein Regimentskommandeur Adalbert Schulz.* Unpublished manuscript: ?

Bix, Hermann. *Brief an meinen General.* Unpublished manuscript: ?

——. *Kampfberichte.* Unpublished manuscript: ?

——. *Lebenslauf.* Unpublished manuscript: ?

Brehm, Werner. *Mein Kriegstagebuch, 1939–1945.* Unpublished manuscript: ?

Bunzel, Hans. *Kampfberichte.* Unpublished manuscript: ?

——. *Lebenslauf.* Unpublished manuscript: ?

Cossel, Hans-Detloff von. *Schwarze Husaren voran!* Unpublished manuscript: ?

Eberbach, Heinrich. *Dokumente.* Unpublished manuscript: ?

——. *Kampfberichte.* Unpublished manuscript: ?

——. *Lebenslauf.* Unpublished manuscript: ?

Edelsheim, Reichsfreiherr Maximilian von. *Radfahr-Abteilung 1 bei Brok.* Unpublished manuscript: ?

——. *Schützen-Regiment 26 im Vorstoß auf Woronesch.* Unpublished manuscript: ?

Eremenko, A.I. *Schörner, General und Feldmarschall.* Unpublished manuscript: ?

Fischer, Gerhard. *Gefechtsberichte.* Unpublished manuscript: ?

——. *Panzerkampf in der Puszta.* Unpublished manuscript: ?

Gradl, Hans. *Briansk im Handstreich genommen.* Unpublished manuscript: ?

Henne, Hans, and Heinz Thiel, *Drei grüne Leuchtkugeln.* Kottbus: ?, 1944.

Hoth, Hermann. *Fernsehgespräch Stalingrad.* Unpublished manuscript: ?

Hubatsch, Hillgruber, Schramm (editors). *Das Kriegstagebuch des OKW.* Frankfurt a.M.: ?, 1961/1963.

Jähde, Willy. *Schwere Panzer-Abteilung 502 im Osten.* Unpublished manuscript: ?

Kempf, Werner. *Briefe.* Unpublished manuscript: ?

——. *Dokumentarsicher Lebenslauf.* Unpublished manuscript: ?

Kurze, Max. *Als Panzerjäger in einer Infanterie-Division.* Unpublished manuscript: ?

Langkeit, Willy. *Gepanzerte Kampfgruppen in Rußland.* Unpublished manuscript: ?

Manteuffel, Hasso von. *Vor Moskau—Jachroma.* Unpublished manuscript: ?

Mühlenkamp, J. R. *Gefechtsberichte.* Unpublished manuscript: ?

———. *Kriegstagebücher.* Unpublished manuscript: ?

Neigl, Ludwig. *Mit meiner Hornisse im Osten.* Unpublished manuscript: ?

Wahl, Wolfgang. *Gefechtsbericht.* Unpublished manuscript: ?

———. *KTB-Aufzeichnungen.* Unpublished manuscript: ?

Weissflog, Joachim. *Gefechtsberichte.* Unpublished manuscript: ?

———. *Lebenslauf.* Unpublished manuscript: ?

Secondary Sources

Alman, Karl. *Sprung in die Hölle.* Rastatt (Germany): ?, 1964.

Andronokow, A. G., and V. D. Mostowenko, *Die roten Panzer.* Munich: ?, 1963.

Antonow, A. S. *Der Panzer.* Berlin: ?, 1959.

Bauer, Prof. Eddy. *Der Panzerkrieg.* Bonn: ?, 1965.

———. *Angriffsziel Festung Europa.* Balve (Germany): ?, 1960.

———. *Duell der Giganten.* Balve (Germany): ?, 1961.

Bernig, Heinrich. *Hölle Alamein.* Balve (Germany): ?, 1960.

Borchert, Hubert. *Panzerkampf im Westen.* Berlin: ?, 1940.

Buchner, Alex. *Der deutsche Griechenlandfeldzug.* Heidelberg: ?, 1958.

Busse, Theodor. *"Die letzte Schlacht der 9. Armee."* Unknown periodical: ?, 1955.

Carell, Paul. *Die Wüstenfüchse.* Hamburg: ?, 1961.

———. *Sie kommen.* Oldenburg: ?, 1960.

———. *Unternehmen Barbarossa.* Berlin: ?, 1963.

———. *"Verbrannte Erde."* Unknown periodical: ?, 1964–1965.

Carius, Otto. *Tiger im Schlamm.* Neckargemünd: ?, 1960.

Cassidy, Henry. *Moskau, 1941–1943.* Zurich: ?, 1944.

Cramer, Hans. *Die-Panzer-Lehr- und Versuchs-Abteilung, 1937–1940.* Minden: ?, 1961.

De Beaulieu, Charles. *Der Vorstoß der Panzergruppe 4 auf Leningrad, 1941.* Neckargemünd: ?, 1961.

Damns, Helmut G. *Geschichte des zweiten Weltkriegs.* Tübingen: ?, 1965.

Dörr, Hans. *Der Feldzug nach Stalingrad.* Darmstadt: ?, 1955.

Dotti, Stefano. *Reitirata in Russia, 1942–1943.* Bologna: ?, 1956.

Eremenko, A.I. *Tage der Bewährung.* East Berlin: ?, 1961.

Esebeck, Hanns-Gert von. *Afrikanische Schicksalsjahre.* Wiesbaden: ?, 1961.

Eimannsberger, L. von. *Der Kampfwagenkrieg.* Munich: ?, 1934.

Ettighoffer, P. C. *44 Tage und Nächte.* Stuttgart: ?, 1953.

Fey, Willi. *Panzer im Brennpunkt der Fronten.* Munich: ?, 1959.

Fretter-Pico, Maximilian. *Mißbrauchte Infanterie.* Frankfurt a.M.: ?, 1957.

Fuller, J. F. *Der zweiten Weltkrieg, 1939-1945.* Vienna: ?, 1952.

————. *Erinnerungen eines freimütigen Soldaten.* Berlin: ?, 1939.

Gackenholz, Hermann. *Zusammenbruch der Heeresgruppe Mitte, 1944.* Frankfurt a.M.: ?, 1957.

Görlitz, Walter. *Ich stehe hier auf Befehl.* Frankfurt a.M.: ?, 1960.

Grams, Wolf. *14. Panzer-Division.* Bad Nauheim: ?, 1957.

Guderian, Heinz. *Achtung Panzer!* Stuttgart: ?, 1936.

————. *Die Panzertruppe und ihr Zusammenwirken mit anderen Waffen.* Berlin: ?, 1943.

————. *Erinnerungen eines Soldaten.* Heidelberg: ?, 1951.

————. *Mit den Panzern in Ost und West.* Berlin: ?, 1942.

————. *Panzer—marsch!* Munich: ?, 1956.

Haupt, Werner. *Kiew—Die größte Kesselschlacht der Geschichte.* Bad Nauheim: ?, 1964.

————. *Baltikum, 1941.* Neckargemünd: ?, 1963.

————. *Berlin—Hitlers letzte Schlacht.* Rastatt: ?, 1964.

Halder, Franz. *Kriegstagebuch.* Stuttgart: ?, 1962–1964.

Hayn, Friedrich. *Die Invasion.* Heidelberg: ?, 1954.

Heidkämper, Otto. *Witebsk, Kampf und Untergang der 3. Panzer-Armee.* Heidelberg: ?, 1954.

Hermann, Dr. Carl-Hans. *"General Kempf—75 Jahre".* Unknown periodical: ?, ?.

————. *"General Kempf gestorben."* Unknown periodical: ?, ?.

Hoth, Hermann. *Panzer-Operationen.* Heidelberg: ?, 1956.

Hofmann, Rudolf. *Die Schlacht um Moskau.* Frankfurt a.M.: ?, 1960.

Jacobsen, Dr. H.A. *Der zweiten Weltkrieg in Chroniken und Dokumenten.* Darmstadt: ?, 1959.

————. *Dokumente zum Westfeldzug.* Göttingen: ?, 1960.

———— and Dr. J. Rohwer. *Entscheidungsschlachten des zweiten Weltkriegs.* Frankfurt a.M.: ?, 1960.

Janatscheck, Fred. *"Der General und die Division."* Unknown periodical: ?, ?.

Jungenfeldt, Ernst Freiherr von. *So kämpften Panzer.* Berlin: ?, 1941.

Kalmov, Kyrill. *Sowjetmarschälle haben das Wort.* Hamburg: ?, 1950.

Karov, D. *Die Partisanenbewegung in der Sowjetunion.* Munich: ?, 1954.

Keilig, Wolf. *Das deutsche Heer, 1939–1945.* Bad Nauheim: ?, 1955.

————. *Rangliste des deutschen Heeres.* Bad Nauheim: ?, 1955.

Kern, Erich. *Der große Rausch.* Göttingen: ?, 1961.

Kesselring, Albert. *Soldat bis zum letzten Tag.* Bonn: ?, 1953.

Kissel, Hans. *Die Panzerschlachten in der Puszta. Oktober 1944.* Neckargemünd: ?, 1960.

Kjellberg, Sven H. *Rußland im Krieg, 1920–1945.* Zurich: ?, 1945.

Knobelsdorff, Otto von. *Geschichte der 19. Panzer-Division.* Bad Nauheim: ?, 1958.

Koch, Herbert. *Ein Mann und eine Panzerkampfgruppe.* Unknown periodical: ?, ?.

Koch, Lutz. *Erwin Rommel.* ?: ?, 1950.

————. *"General der Panzertruppen von Knobelsdorff."* Rastatt: ?, 1961–1965.

————. *"General der Panzertruppen von Manteuffel."* Rastatt: ?, 1961–1965.

————. *"Generalfeldmarschall Model."* Rastatt: ?, 1961–1965.

————. *"Generalleutnant Bayerlein."* Rastatt: ?, 1961–1965.

————. *"Generalleutnant Unrein."* Rastatt: ?, 1961–1965.

————. *"Generalleutnant von Wietersheim."* Rastatt: ?, 1961–1965.

————. *"Generalmajor Niemack."* Rastatt: ?, 1961–1965.

————. *"Generalmajor von Oppeln-Bronikowski."* Rastatt: ?, 1961–1965.

Kollatz, Karl. *"Generalmajor Werner Marcks."* Rastatt: ?, 1961–1965.

————. *"Hauptmann Fritz Feßmann."* Rastatt: ?, 1961–1965.

————. *"Major Peter Frantz."* Rastatt: ?, 1961–1965.

————. *"Major Sepp Brandner."* Rastatt: ?, 1961–1965.

Konrad, Rudolf. *Kampf um den Kaukasus.* ?: ?, ?

————. *Der Kampf um Kreta.* Herford: ?, 1965.

————. *Die Abwehr- und Rückzugskämpfe auf Sizilien.* Neckargemünd: ?, 1966.

Kurowski, Franz. *Die Panzer-Lehr-Division.* Bad Nauheim: ?, 1964.

————. *Von den Ardennen zum Ruhrkessel.* Herford: ?, 1965.

———— and Gottfried Tornau. *Sturmartillerie—Fels in der Brandung.* Herford: ?, 1965.

Lemelsen, Joachim. *29. Division.* Bad Nauheim: ?, 1960.

Liddel-Hart, Basil. *The Rommel Papers.* London: ?, 1948.

————. *Jetzt dürfen sie reden.* Stuttgart: ?, 1950.

————. *Die Rote Armee.* Bonn: ?, ?

Liss, Ulrich. *Westfront.* Neckargemünd: ?, 1959.

Mackensen, Eberhard von. *"Das III. Panzer-Korps im Feldzug, 1941/1942."* Unknown periodical: ?, ?.

Manstein, Erich von. *Verlorene Siege.* Bonn: ?, 1955.

Manteuffel, Hasso von. *Die 7. Panzer-Division im zweiten Weltkrieg.* Ürdingen: ?, 1965.

————. *Die Schlacht in den Ardennen, 1944–1945.* Frankfurt a.M.: ?, 1960.

Mellinthin, F. W. von. *Panzerschlachten*. Neckargemünd: ?, 1963.

Middeldorf, Eike. *Taktik im Rußlandfeldzug*. Berlin: ?, 1956.

Montgomery, Field Marshal Bernard Law. *Memoirs*. London: ?, 1966.

Möller-Witten, Hanns. *Männer und Taten*. Munich: ?, 1959.

———. *Mit dem Eichenlaub zum Ritterkreuz*. Rastatt: ?, 1962.

Moorehead, Alan. *Afrikanische Trilogie*. Braunschweig: ?, 1948.

Munzel, Oskar. *Gepanzerte Truppen*. Herford: ?, 1965.

———. *Panzertaktik*. Neckargemünd: ?, 1959.

———. *"Das Ende der 1. Panzer-Armee."* Deutscher Soldatenkalender: ?, 1960–1963.

Nehring, Walter K. *Der wandernde Kessel*. Munich: ?, 1959.

———. *Die Geschichte der deutschen Panzerwaffe, 1916-1945*. Berlin: ?, 1969.

———. *"18. Panzer-Division, 1941."* Deutscher Soldatenkalender: ?, 1960–1963.

———. *"Russische Fallschirmspringer gegen das XIV. Panzer-Korps."* Deutscher Soldatenkalender: ?, 1960–1963.

———. *"Vor Tobruk, 1942."* Deutscher Soldatenkalender: ?, 1960–1963.

Philippi, Alfred. *"Generaloberst Hoth—80 Jahre"*. Unknown periodical: ?

——— and F. Heim. *Der Feldzug gegen Sowjetrußland*. Stuttgart: ?, 1962.

Ploetz, A.G. *Geschichte des zweiten Weltkriegs*. Wurzburg: ?, 1960.

Podzun, Hans-Hennig. *Das deutsche Heer, 1939*. Bad Nauheim: ?, 1953.

Polag, Dr. Hans. *"Panzerführer Generalmajor Eberbach."* Unknown periodical: ?

Rebentisch, Ernst. *Zum Kaukasus und zu den Tauern*. Esslingen: ?, 1963.

Rehm, W. *Jassy*. Neckargemünd: ?, 1959.

Reinhard, Hans. *"Der Vorstoß des XXXXI. Armee-Korps (mot.) im Sommer 1941."* Unknown periodical: ?

Rommel, Erwin. *Krieg ohne Hass*. Heidenheim: ?, 1950.

Samsonov, Aleksandr M. *Die große Schlacht vor Moskau, 1941–1942*. East Berlin: ?, 1959.

Scheibert, Horst. *Nach Stalingrad 48 Kilometer*. Neckargemünd: ?, 1958.

———. *Zwischen Don und Donez*. Neckargemünd: ?, 1961.

Schulz, Johannes. *Der Weg nach Tobruk*. Balve: ?, 1959.

———. *Die verlorene Armee*. Balve: ?, 1959.

———. *Endstation Kaukasus*. Wuppertal: ?, 1962.

———. *Unternehmen Overlord*. Balve: ?, 1960.

Senger und Etterlin, Frido von. *Krieg in Europa*. Cologne: ?, 1960.

Senger und Etterlin Jr., Dr. F. M. *Der Gegenschlag*. Neckargemünd: ?, 1959.

———. *Die deutschen Panzer, 1926–1945*. Munich: ?, 1965.

———. *24. Panzer-Division, vormals 1. Kavallerie-Division*. Neckargemünd: ?, 1962.

Seemen, Gerhard von. *Die Ritterkreuzträger 1939–1945*. Friedberg: Podzun-Pallas-Verlag, 1976.

Spaether, Helmut. *Geschichte des Panzer-Korps "Großdeutschland."* Duisburg-Ruhrort: ?, 1958–1959.

Stoves, Rolf O. *1. Panzer-Division, 1935–1945*. Bad Nauheim: ?, 1962.

Strutz, Dr. Georg. *Die Tankschlacht bei Cambrai*. Berlin: ?, 1929.

Testke, Hermann. *Bewegungskrieg*. Heidelberg: ?, 1955.

Thorwald, Jürgen. *Das Ende an der Elbe*. Stuttgart: ?, 1950.

———. *Es begann an der Weichsel*. Stuttgart: ?, 1949.

———. *Wen sie verderben wollen*. Stuttgart: ?, 1952.

Tippelskirch, Kurt von. *Geschichte des zweiten Weltkriegs*. Bonn: ?, 1951.

Toland, John. *Ardennenschlacht 1944*. Bern: ?, 1960.

U.S. Army, U.S. Military Academy. *The War in North Africa*. ?: ?, 1950.

Union War Histories. *Crisis in the Desert*. Pretoria: ?, 1952.

Vormann, Nikolaus von. *Tscherkassy*. Heidelberg: ?, 1954.

Wagener, Carl. *"Der Vorstoß des XXXX. Panzer-Korps von Charkow zum Kaukasus"*. Unknown periodical: ?

Wehren, Wolfgang. *Geschichte der 16. Panzer-Division*. Bad Nauheim: ?, 1958.

Westphal, Siegfried. *Heer in Fesseln*. Bonn: ?, 1950.

Wilmot, Chester. *Der Kampf um Europa*. Braunschweig: ?, 1949.

Young, Desmond. *Rommel*. Wiesbaden: ?, 1950.

Zimmermann, Hermann. *Der Griff ins Ungewisse*. Neckargemünd: ?, 1964.

Index

Stackpole Military History Series

Real battles. Real soldiers. Real stories.

Stackpole Military History Series

Real battles. Real soldiers. Real stories.

Stackpole Military History Series

NEW for Fall 2010

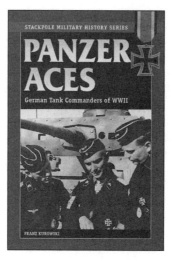

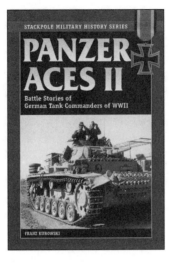

Stackpole Military History Series

TIGERS IN THE MUD
THE COMBAT CAREER OF GERMAN PANZER
COMMANDER OTTO CARIUS

Otto Carius,
translated by Robert J. Edwards

World War II began with a metallic roar as the
German Blitzkrieg raced across Europe, spearheaded
by the most dreadful weapon of the twentieth century:
the Panzer. Tank commander Otto Carius thrusts the
reader into the thick of battle, replete with the
blood, smoke, mud, and gunpowder so common
to the elite German fighting units.

$19.95 • Paperback • 6 x 9 • 368 pages
51 photos • 48 illustrations • 3 maps

 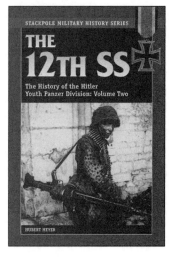

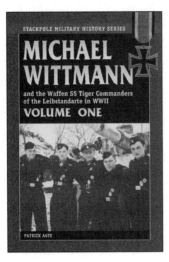 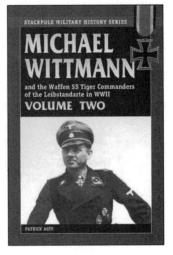

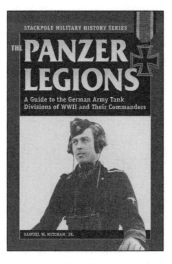

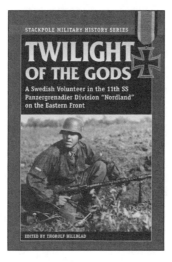

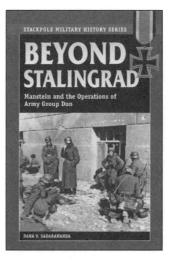

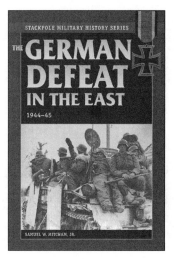